The Arts of Empire

The Arts of Empire

The Poetics of Colonialism
from Ralegh to Milton

Walter S. H. Lim

DELAWARE

Newark: University of Delaware Press
London: Associated University Presses

Associated University Presses
440 Forsgate Drive
Cranbury, NJ 08512

Associated University Presses
16 Barter Street
London WC1A 2AH, England

Associated University Presses
P.O. Box 338, Port Credit
Mississauga, Ontario
Canada L5G 4L8

The paper used in this publication meets the requirements of the American National Standard for Permanence of Paper for Printed Library Materials Z39.48-1984.

Library of Congress Cataloging-in-Publication Data

Lim, Walter S. H., 1959–
   The arts of empire : the poetics of colonialism from Ralegh to Milton / Walter S.H. Lim.
     p. cm.
   Includes bibliographical references (p.   ) and index.
   ISBN 0-87413-641-5 (alk. paper)
   1. English literature—Early modern, 1500–1700—History and criticism. 2. Imperialism in literature. 3. Ralegh, Walter, Sir, 1552?–1618. Discovery of the large, rich, and beautiful empire of Guiana. 4. Spenser, Edmund, 1552?–1599—Political and social views. 5. Milton, John, 1608–1674—Political and social views. 6. Donne, John, 1572–1631—Political and social views. 7. Politics and literature—Great Britain—History. 8. Shakespeare, William, 1564–1616. Othello. 9. Colonies in literature. 10. Race in literature. I. Title.
PR428.I54L56 1998
820.9′358—dc21
                                              97-39171
                                                CIP

PRINTED IN THE UNITED STATES OF AMERICA

For my wife,
Rebecca Joanne Paradise

Contents

Acknowledgments

I AM GRATEFUL TO HIRAM COLLEGE, OHIO, WHERE I USED TO TEACH, for offering me two summer faculty research awards to begin work on this book. Since then, I have benefited much from exchanges with colleagues as well as scholars working in the area. I wish to thank Nathan Godfried and Ismail Talib for drawing my attention to important materials; and to Paul Yachnin, Paul Stevens, Willy Maley, and David Edwards for sharing with me their work on the English Renaissance. I am also grateful to the following for taking time off from their very busy schedules to read draft chapters at short notice: Barnard Turner, Rajeev Patke, Terence Dawson, Susan Ang, Gilbert Adair, and Arthur Lindley. I owe a special debt to Gilbert Adair for his deep enthusiasm in this project throughout, and also for generously sharing with me many invaluable insights. I also owe a great intellectual debt to Richard Strier, who taught me how to read Spenser in relation to the politics of Ireland in the English Renaissance. Under his direction, the NEH Seminar held at the University of Chicago in the summer of 1991—"Renaissance and Reformation in Tudor-Stuart England"—provided a conducive and stimulating climate for thinking on the subject of Renaissance colonialism and imperialism. The head of my department, Ban Kah Choon, must be thanked for getting me study leave to spend more time in the libraries during the summers. The two anonymous readers for the University of Delaware Press must be thanked for offering comments and suggestions that enabled me to consider topics and literature not adequately accounted for. The staffs of the Regenstein Library of the University of Chicago, the John P. Robarts Research Library and Thomas Fisher Rare Book Library of the University of Toronto, the Kent State University Library, and the Central Library of the National University of Singapore have been unfailingly generous.

Important and invaluable support for all that I do come from my parents, Stephen and Helen, and my sister, Loretta: to them I owe more than I can express. My parents-in-law, Dr. Joseph and Mary Ann Paradise, have generously made their home available

to me whenever I visit and do my research in the States. Last but
not least, I wish to thank my wife, Rebecca Paradise, for giving
much-needed emotional support and for her infinite patience. In
addition to taking care of my toddler and infant sons, Brandon
and Joshua, she accommodated graciously the irritabilities of a
husband struggling to bring this book to its close. To her this
book is affectionately dedicated.

I thank James R. Andreas for permission to use portions of my
article "Representing the Other: *Othello,* Colonialism, Discourse,"
which appeared in *The Upstart Crow: A Shakespeare Journal* 13
(1993): 57–78. I also thank François Paré for permission to use
material from another article of mine, "Figuring Justice: Ideology
and the Discourse of Colonialism in Book V of *The Faerie Queene*
and *A View of the Present State of Ireland,*" which appeared in *Renaissance and Reformation* 19 (1995): 45–70. Part of chapter 5 of the
present work appeared in a slightly different version in "Adam,
Eve, and Biblical Analogy in *Paradise Lost.*" Reprinted by permission of *SEL Studies in English Literature 1500–1900* 30, no. 1 (winter 1990). A part of chapter 5 of the present work also appears
in a slightly different version in Robbie Goh, Ban Kah Choon,
and Robert Young, ed., *The Silent Word: The Role of the Unwritten
in the Production of Meaning* (in press).

The following publishers have generously given permission to
use extended quotations from copyrighted works: From Merritt
Y. Hughes, *Complete Poems and Major Prose: John Milton,* ©1957;
reprinted by permission of Prentice-Hall, Inc., Upper Saddle
River, N.J. From C. B. Macpherson, ed., *John Locke: Second Treatise
of Government,* ©1980; reprinted by permission of Hackett Publishing Co., Inc. From Ann Kibbey, *The Interpretation of Material Shapes
in Puritanism,* ©1986; reprinted with the permission of Cambridge
University Press. From Evelyn M. Simpson and George R. Potter,
ed., *The Sermons of John Donne,* 10 vols; reprinted by permission
of the University of California Press.

The Arts of Empire

Introduction

THE TWO CENTRAL COLONIAL PROJECTS OF ELIZABETHAN AND EARLY
Stuart England were Ireland and the New World. For Elizabeth
I, the colonization of Ireland constituted the more significant enterprise because of its particular history as well as geographical
proximity to England. By comparison, the advantages of the Atlantic ventures appeared much less certain. It was during the
reign of the Stuart monarchs that interest in the American colonies grew much stronger because of an emerging recognition of
their economic potential. Focusing on the subjects of Ireland and
the New World, this book sets out to explore the emergings of a
colonialist consciousness in the writings and political workings of
the English Renaissance. Any effort made to describe the awaken-
ings of this consciousness must take into account the uncertain
energies characteristic of a nation's nascent colonial ambitions.
Because late Tudor and Jacobean England did not possess a systematic and coherent colonial policy, the writings of the period
alluding and referring to England's settlement of colonies in the
New World or its colonial designs in Ireland offer multiple perspectives and attitudes existing in constant collision and negotiation. How do these collisions and negotiations shape and forge a
distinctly English colonial discourse?

During the reign of Elizabeth I, two very important activities
developed hand in hand: the rise of commercial activities across
the seas and an outburst of geographical interest.[1] The two are
interrelated, for geography was linked to cartography, a deep
knowledge of which was essential for navigating the oceans. The
younger Richard Hakluyt, a man who became a leading authority
in maritime economic enterprises, studied and taught the new
cosmography and cartography at Oxford. Like Dr. John Dee, he
recognized that control of the seas would make England a great
nation. In his dedication to Sir Francis Walsingham, in the first
edition of *The Principal Navigations*, Hakluyt elaborates on how
his interest in England's activities of ocean travel and their relation
to empire building was initiated by his cousin's knowledge of
geography:

13

Right Honorable, I do remember that being a youth, and one of her Majesties scholars at Westminster that fruitfull nurserie, it was my happe to visit the chamber of M. Richard Hakluyt my cosin, a Gentleman of the Middle Temple, well knowen unto you, at a time when I found lying open upon his boord certeine bookes of Cosmographie, with an universall Mappe: he seeing me somewhat curious in the view therof, began to instruct my ignorance, by shewing me the division of the earth into three parts after the olde account, and then according to the latter, & better distribution, into more: he pointed with his wand to all the knowen Seas, Gulfs, Bayes, Straights, Capes, Rivers, Empires, Kingdomes, Dukedomes, and Territories of ech part, with declaration also of their speciall commodities, & particular wants, which by the benefit of traffike, & entercourse of merchants, are plentifully supplied. From the Mappe he brought me to the Bible, and turning to the 107 Psalme, directed mee to the 23 & 24 verses, where I read, that they which go downe to the sea in ships, and occupy by the great waters, they see the works of the Lord, and his woonders in the deepe, &c. Which words of the Prophet together with my cousins discourse (things of high and rare delight to my yong nature) tooke in me so deepe an impression, that I constantly resolved, if ever I were preferred to the University, where better time, and more convenient place might be ministred for these studies, I would by Gods assistance prosecute that knowledge and kinde of literature, the doores whereof (after a sort) were so happily opened before me.[2]

The efforts made by men like Hakluyt in energizing and sustaining England's emerging geographical interest and curiosity played an important part in contributing to the notable increase in English maritime activities, especially in the 1580s. Richard Helgerson reminds us that with the focus on merchants and their activities in Hakluyt's writings, the concept of the nation emerges as a transcendent and uncontested point of reference. Hakluyt recognized that commerce would be the life of England and the world. And so, in order to describe the mercantile activities of the larger world and offer proof of England's active participation in them, Hakluyt brought merchants into the nation and gentry into trade. Hakluyt's narratives confer importance on the merchants who never occupied any significant place in the aristocratic ethos of classical epic.[3] According to Kim F. Hall, Richard Hakluyt's compilation of the narratives of English trade and travel inscribes the explicit political agenda of putting English exploration on the map of European expansionism.[4] In Hakluyt's sense of the destined order of the English empire, Hall argues, compiling manuscripts becomes a way of travelling, necessary for properly ordering the world, "subsuming both territorial property and literary propriety to the needs of the state."[5] The very act and practice of compilation cannot be separated from the desire and dream of ordering the knowledge made available of other geographical locations and trade routes for the consumption of the English reader. Hakluyt works with strict order and method to itemize knowledge for his reader, one whom he hopes to convince concerning the importance of England's potential as a colonial power.

Toward the end of the previous decade, in 1577, Francis Drake had already made his famous expedition, passing through the Straits of Magellan, sailing up the coast of America, and returning to England by way of the Indian Ocean and the Cape of Good Hope. At this point, Sir Walter Ralegh was pressing hard for English settlement of the New World; Ralegh obtained a patent for an American colony in 1584, and in the following year a settlement was established on Roanoke Island in the area he christened Virginia in honor of Queen Elizabeth. In 1585, the same year that Ralegh planted Virginia, Drake was waging war in the Caribbean. The ventures and ambitions of people like Drake and Ralegh were contributing, by the 1590s, to the exploration and exploitation of the wealth of the oceans.

In addition to its navigational and mercantile activities, England also started getting itself involved in many other projects: asserting its strength in the face of powerful Catholic Spain; settling plantations in the New World; thinking up ways to subdue a rebellious Ireland; even dabbling tentatively in the slave trade. Writers of the period showed keen awareness of England's promise as an emerging colonial power. John Donne, for example, enjoyed making use of navigational and cartographical figures in his poetry. Donne stands out prominently among his contemporaries for his ability to invoke figures linked to England's new geographical and navigational interest and to use these to tease out riddles and meanings from the then-prevailing Renaissance theory of correspondences. Other writers supported setting up colonies in the New World or drew up representational sketches of the native. Edmund Spenser produced an elaborate blueprint on how to control and subdue Ireland. William Shakespeare dramatized the figure of the exotic Other in Othello and that of the savage in Caliban.

Generally, however, and despite the enthusiasm expressed in much of the writings of the period, early efforts at pulling off a coherent colonial program in both Ireland and the New World were neither sustained nor coherent. The process of entrenching and consolidating English colonial power was a slow one. And even though ambitious efforts were made, for example, to settle the Virginia colony and establish effective governance there, it was not until the economic potential promised by tobacco planting was recognized, after the second decade of the seventeenth century, that England was confident of a permanent New World settlement. English adventurers might have participated in New World voyages and explored coastal areas from as early on as the end of the fifteenth century, but concerted attempts to colonize the Americas began in earnest only in the 1560s.

In the early seventeenth century, the colonial ventures undertaken by the Stuart monarchs, James I and Charles I, fared badly. But by the first half of this century, shifts in the historical register charting England's status as a growing colonial power, tied to reconfiguring political situations, were already perceptible. Examples include the stronger sense of the importance of mercantile commerce, an increasing recognition of the need to tap the wealth that the Americas offered, experience of the great migrations of the 1630s, and the devastating English Civil Wars of the 1640s. One of the most striking shifts in England's conception of itself as a colonial power at the start of the Jacobean period involved the recognition that trading activities were central to the building of empire. England was taken aback by the growing status of the monarchy in the Netherlands, a country that had until recently depended on the English for protection. This monarchy was now touted as potentially possessing the ability to rival England's own, a status derived very much from the growing commercial strength of the Dutch. When *The Merchant of Venice* was composed, probably some time in late 1596 or early 1597, Shakespeare allowed Antonio's trading activities to run into trouble, representing the tremendous uncertainties that evidently accompanied such ventures. Even though at the end of the play, "three of [Antonio's] argosies / Are richly come to harbour suddenly" (5.1.276–77),[6] a comic turn that links the Christian's merchandising enterprises to a providentially guided success, Shakespeare's play continues to maintain an ambivalent attitude toward the subject of bourgeois mercantilism. Bassanio pursues financing at the risk of suffering economic losses; he also borrows three thousand ducats from Antonio to woo a lady in Belmont and jeopardizes his friend's life as a result. Antonio's trading ventures, Bassanio's prodigal pursuit of profit, and the suitor's correct choice of the lead casket with its symbolic disavowal of greed, all point to what Thomas Moisan reads as "an ambivalence we find in Shakespeare's culture toward wealth and the 'venturing' for it in trade."[7]

In *Eastward Ho!* (1605)—a comedy jointly produced by Jonson, Chapman, and Marston—a character named Security speaks about trade in a way that recalls Shakespeare's ambivalent treatment in *The Merchant of Venice:*

> all trades complain of inconvenience, and therefore 'tis best to have none. The merchant, he complains and says, 'traffic is subject to much uncertainty and loss'. Let 'em keep their goods on dry land, with a vengeance, and not expose other men's substances to the mercy of the winds. (2.2.86–90)[8]

But Security's view does not represent changing attitudes toward trade by the start of the seventeenth century. Carole Shammas tells us that about the time James I became king and the Spanish war ended, "Colonization became identified with the general effort to build up English trade, hence attracting not only widespread public support but also the financial backing of merchants."[9] With "the commercializing of colonization," many who had previously been apathetic toward the Western planting now began giving public support to settling colonies in America.[10] We find the flamboyant buccaneering exploits of such Elizabethan adventurers as Drake, who were energized and swayed by romantic notions of emulating the exploits of Cortés in Mexico or Pizzaro in Peru, disappearing from the scene.[11]

In a cultural milieu evolving an understanding of its identity as a potential colonial power, it is not surprising to find much of its literature engaging such subjects as settling plantations in the New World, rivaling Spain in the creation and building of empire, defining the identity of the savage, and disseminating the gospel. In representing these subjects, literary works can serve to ratify a politics of marginalization and containment. When Africa, for example, gets represented in travel writings and dramatic performances, it obtains its symbolic identity from its reception by the reader or audience. Inevitably, any production of *Othello* in early seventeenth-century England must construct its meanings in relation to a culture's perceptions of Otherness and difference, influenced not only by literary texts but shaped through such ideologically laden actions as Queen Elizabeth's deportation of Blacks from England. Limiting a foreign people is achieved not only by creating myths of Otherness or amplifying the exoticism of cultural difference, but also by highlighting the terrors and

threats posed by such difference. The Irish people are portrayed
by Edmund Spenser less as exotic types than as the (un)natural
enemies of England, constantly threatening to undermine its authority. Spenser's *A View of the Present State of Ireland* calls for
England's cold-blooded colonial intervention in Ireland to bring
order out of a state of primal anarchy and chaos.[12]

Identifying the colonialist motifs and narratives in the writings
of Elizabethan and Stuart England does not limit or bound the
meanings encoded in literary texts. The presence of these motifs
and narratives informs us that the literature of late sixteenth-
and early seventeenth-century England cannot be divorced from
a people's awareness of their culture's expansionist potential. Expressions of that awareness are, however, complex; many literary
works complicate England's early development of its identity as a
colonial power by supporting as well as interrogating its expansionist ambitions. If there was support for the colonizing impulse
in the literary writings of Elizabethan and Stuart England, there
was also much internal critique. In relating and responding to
this moment of English nascent colonialist energies, literary texts
yielded a variety of contesting world pictures.

The subject of the Virginia colony was treated, to cite an example, with much ambivalence in the writings of the period. A character by the name of Seagull satirizes the commonplace figuration
of Virginia as female body in *Eastward Ho!*: "Come, boys, Virginia
longs till we share the rest of her maidenhead" (3.3.14–15). This
ambivalence is also present in William Shakespeare's *The Tempest*,
which alludes to the voyage undertaken by Sir Thomas Gates and
Sir George Somers to prop up John Smith's foundering Jamestown colony. At this point in my introduction, I wish to evoke and
briefly consider *The Tempest* as a play importantly situated at a
time when England was engaging in colonial activities in the New
World. Because this play is frequently considered in studies of
colonialism in Renaissance England, it serves well as a register
of the map of contemporary critical responses to its ideological
inscriptions; it also helps to position my own particular study in
relation to others written on the subject.

The Tempest is a play that heightens topical interest in the Virginia colony by dramatizing the savage, Caliban, who inscribes in
his representative body all the negative features found in depic-
tions of Otherness in travel literatures of the period. Through his
portrayal of the savage, Shakespeare engages in dialogue with
views in circulation concerning the project of settling the Virginia
colony. He first defines his savage by signaling an unbridgeable

divide separating nature and culture. Then, by making Caliban obey the dictates of his primal appetite divorced from the ordering codes of culture and civilization, Shakespeare interrogates implicitly Montaigne's assertion that because the savage is much closer to nature, both physically and ontologically, he occupies a world of innocence from which the European, burdened with the trappings of an artificial culture, is excluded. Montaigne's interest in the universality of human nature had expressed itself in his description of the contagion with which Europe had infected the Golden Age society of the New World.

Arguments offered in support of *The Tempest* as a protoimperialist text depend on revisionary readings often undertaken by postcolonial writers and critics who find in Shakespeare's portrayal of Caliban an important contribution to the discursive formation of the savage Other as a figure ripe for exploitation. It is normal for postcolonial readings to posit *The Tempest* as a colonialist text and its controlling figure Prospero as a colonizer. The discourse of colonialism in *The Tempest* has been cogently identified and studied, for example, by Paul Brown who writes about conceptions of masterlessness and savagism in the English Renaissance that offer useful pretexts for enacting the colonialist project.[13] In his theoretical reading, following Homi Bhabha, Brown writes about how the struggles to restrict the savage Other's propensity for disruption can never enjoy complete success because discursive modes of containment always possess the seeds of their own subversion. If the imposition of restrictions is not a one-time affair, but requires continual (re)production, each successive repetition also enlarges the space available for resistance. Caliban is able to curse his master, forcing Prospero to curse back in his turn and thereby effecting a "degeneration" from the level of the civilized discourse he is supposed to have brought from the European world. Bringing into alliance the deconstructive and postcolonialist projects, Paul Brown concludes with what can be read as an interrogative reading of Prospero's colonialist and hegemonic discourse: another example of the criticism of intervention and resistance.

Politically conscious readings of the kind practiced by Brown are important and necessary, but they sometimes yield interpretations that elide the complexities embedded in the text's response to specific social currents and interests emerging and taking form in its day. I propose, for example, that while there is no doubt that *The Tempest*'s allusions to the shipwreck off the Bermudas in 1609 aroused topical interest on the part of Shakespeare's audience, the treatment of Caliban is an extremely ambivalent one when situated against recognizable expansionist paradigms of the period. That Shakespeare enjoyed patronal relations with prominent members of the Virginia Company does not necessarily mean that he was fully comfortable with England's colonial undertakings in the New World. Shakespeare's allusion to the unstable state of affairs in the Jamestown colony and the imagined encounter between Prospero and the savage do not necessarily translate into an endorsement of the colonialist project.

Where an older criticism has generally read *The Tempest* as a humanist play in which the cabbalistic Prospero harnesses his power to bring about good in society, more recent readings—particularly those offered by the new historicists—have been especially interested in analyzing the ways in which he exercises this power. Analogies have been drawn between Prospero and James I because both figures cultivate anxieties in their subjects in order to procure consent and contain dissent.[14] The need to exert control over the potentially disruptive forces of masterlessness and savagism involves not only finding a pretext to contain and subordinate Otherness, but entails enacting a politics of class difference and expansionism. There are discernible similarities shaping Prospero's treatment of Trinculo and Stephano and the English efforts to contain Irish masterlessness in the penultimate phase of the Elizabethan expansionist design in Ireland. Paul Brown has commented that, in *The Tempest,* members of the aristocracy put aside their internecine quarrels in a show of solidarity when faced with the threat of the masterless man. Interestingly, of course, the power Prospero exercises is extended to control even members of the aristocracy: Sebastian, Antonio, Alonso, and Ferdinand. In the betrothal masque, presented as a gift to Ferdinand and Miranda in anticipation of their forthcoming marriage and dynastic union between Milan and Naples, Prospero interrupts the spectacle to draw attention to the conspiracy that is under way to destroy his authority. Prospero's lapse in memory recalls for the audience the propensity of the dispossessed duke to lose himself completely in the pursuit of particular projects; it also, as Curt Breight suggests, affords an opportunity for him to impress on aristocratic types like Ferdinand that he is in control of a power that cannot be controverted. Masterless men like Trinculo and Stephano serve as exemplars for Prospero to impress on the aristocrats his absolutist authority and power.[15]

The same power that Prospero exercises over recalcitrant aristocrats and masterless men is employed to control the savage Other in a play that can be read as a fantasy of English colonialism in the New World. What is interesting is that at the end of this display of authority, one that cannot be extricated from Prospero's need to control the passions within himself, there is a highly ritualistic and symbolic repudiation of power. Prospero's preparation to (re)-enter the deeply personal space of retirement and meditation upon death effaces not only individual power, but marginalizes any interest raised in the play concerning English colonial activities in the New World.

Various moments in *The Tempest* reveal Shakespeare's ambivalence toward the project of English colonialism in the New World. Once Shakespeare's Caliban shows himself impermeable to the effects of culture and civilization, no further project is proposed and undertaken for his transformation: he is simply enslaved. *The Tempest* is a text that registers very little interest in the topoi of converting, exterminating, or transporting the Other. Channeled toward the intensely personal domain of retirement and the equally introspective meditations on mortality, the concluding energies of *The Tempest* produce the effect of marginalizing the concerns with Europe's colonial encounter to which the play alludes. By leaving Caliban behind on the island, Prospero rejects the only means possible for him to maintain connections between the New World which he is leaving and the Old World to which he is returning. Prospero does not bring the savage back to Europe as a token of difference and sign of his encounter with a foreign and as yet uncharted land. Such a conclusion disrupts the teleology of any ostensible colonial project suggested or hinted at by the play. We remember that in the history of early European imperialism, natives have always been selected and brought back to Europe to be turned into translators, employed subsequently to facilitate some level of communication between the colonizing power and the inhabitants of foreign lands. Because the figure of Caliban incorporates the dark and negative meanings and associations given to the savage Other in colonial literatures, and because this existential condition cannot be revised and rewritten through any reformative scheme, Shakespeare may be suggesting that there is really no point attempting to assimilate the Other into English domestic and political life.

By giving to the audience a portrait of the uncivilizable savage, *The Tempest* may be said to function as a dramatized travel narrative eliciting from its audience a sense of wonder. Wonder, in this instance, is the experience of delight and fascination of the Jacobean theatergoer reacting to the exotic, unfamiliar, and new in the figure of Caliban. If Shakespeare dramatizes a subject of topical interest knowing full well the kind of audience response to be expected, he also appears to offer a corrective for such a response. The two characters in *The Tempest* who are especially keen to bring the savage back to the European world as proof that they have journeyed to faraway lands are Trinculo and Stephano; they nourish the mercenary dream of profiteering by putting the savage on display before curious multitudes (2.2.24–34, 2.2.66–72). Trinculo and Stephano recognize that there is always a market for displaying the marvelous and the monstrous. They know that people will pay to witness any token of the exotic or spectacle of the Other. Even Antonio recognizes this when he intimates to Sebastian: "Very like; one of them / Is a plain fish, and, no doubt, marketable" (5.1.265–66).

Significantly, the characters who talk about Caliban's marketability are the lower-class drunk and the villain, not members of the nobility. Whatever wonder Prospero might have initially experienced at the sight of Caliban no longer exists after the savage has proved himself impervious to the effects of culture and civilization. Prospero never registers any desire to bring Caliban back to Europe with him. If the play mirrors different audience responses to the figure of the savage Other, it also appears to want to intervene in the social and cultural reflexes generating them.

Shakespeare's play may evoke topical interest in its portrayal of Caliban, but it specifically centers the experience of wonder on objects other than the spectacle of the savage. Shakespeare makes wonder an experience of the meeting between the sexes: Ferdinand responding to Miranda and Miranda responding to Ferdinand. Sexual attraction generates wonder; and so does listening with thrill to the music of one's own native tongue (1.2.424–36). Fascination with the savage as token of difference and sign of the marvelous or monstrous is replaced by an interest in the more important promise and great potential of the European world, the one to which the entire court party returns at the end of the play. It is possible that despite the play's allusions to colonial commonplaces—the voyage to a new land, the encounter with the native, talk on transporting the Other back to the European world—the project of settling colonies is not its all-consuming and overriding concern.

It is generally recognized that *The Tempest* points to the larger world of England's Atlantic activities. It situates the island on the map of the New World near the Bermudas and celebrates the shaping powers of the poetic imagination.[16] But the imagination, as *The Tempest* makes explicit, is ambiguous. It is celebrated for its ability to entertain, but also distrusted as the originating source of fictions rather than truth. The island that the poet-dramatist's imagination bodies forth, like the narrative world created by Prospero's magic conjurations, is both present and absent, here and nowhere. At the end of the play, Shakespeare's subsumption of even the powers of the dramatic imagination under the tyranny of transitoriness—"We are such stuff / As dreams are made on; and our little life / Is rounded with a sleep" (4.1.156–58)[17]— prepares for the inevitable dissolution of the glimpses given of Virginia in the New World.

Ambivalences of the kind present in a play like *The Tempest* can be traced to a culture's larger response to overseas projects whose outcomes can only be unpredictable. There may be radically different opinions about the forms to be assumed by a viable English colonialism, as Ralegh and Spenser find out in relation to their queen. And this is, of course, further complicated by the interplay of commercial and theological interests in the formulation of a coherent program of colonial expansion.

Anyone who proposes to undertake the task of writing yet another book on the poetics and politics of colonialism in the period of the English Renaissance feels called upon to explain the choice, given the staggering amount of scholarly materials that have recently come into print. The purpose of my particular project is first and foremost to call attention to the presence of a tremendous sense of England's potential as an emerging colonial power in the reigns of Elizabeth I and the Stuart monarchs. This sense permeates the writings of the period in all the different genres: love lyric, religious lyric, romance, epic, comedy, tragedy, homily, sermon, travel narrative. Whenever the project of Virginia, Guiana, or Ireland is portrayed and represented in these writings, a dialogue ensues between subject matter and literary text, ratifying and contesting the scope and articulations of what constitutes the English nation and its expansionist ambitions. The vast scholarship available on the discourse of colonialism and imperialism has offered much theoretical material to frame discussions of the subject in general and readings of a period or literature in particular. But even in studies of particular periods and literatures, the scope of inquiry has been quite focused and specific. Stephen Greenblatt's *Marvelous Possessions,* for example, centers on the moment of originary encounter between Christopher Columbus and the native of the New World, setting it up as a paradigm for considerations of future colonial encounters.[18] In *Epic and Empire,* David Quint has given a detailed and thorough account of the inextricable links existing between the epic genre and the imperial theme; Quint considers epics written in different epochs and cultures, including Roman, Portuguese, Italian, and English.

In *Milton's Imperial Epic*, J. Martin Evans offers a detailed analysis of Milton's interest in the New World, as made amply evident in *Paradise Lost*.[19] As Evans convincingly shows, even a poem like *Paradise Lost*—often read as a text that encodes the anxieties of a poet relating to the bitter experience of political defeat—registers its author's awareness of English activities taking place in the New World. In this study, he describes in detail how *Paradise Lost* inscribes many of the tropes found in the discourse of English involvement in settling colonies in America. Clearly, the presence of the New World is alive and well in Milton's major epic: God is the master colonist, while Adam and Eve are in the position of indentured laborers; Satan is the archetypal imperialist and colonist; Columbus's encounter with the American native is evoked by Milton to describe Adam and Eve's condition of innocence and fall; Adam and Eve even accrue to themselves, in the dominion they enjoy over Eden, the identity of colonists. Evans's point is that much of Milton's epic narrative is constructed upon allusions and references made to such contemporary colonial activities. Evans's book appeared after I had completed my own consideration of Milton's place in relation to the discourse of colonialism in early modern England, the subject of the concluding chapter of my book. There are areas of overlap in his project and my own, but the differences in emphasis are notable. Where Evans has, for example, concentrated on the significant and important presence of America in the epic, I have concentrated on both the New World and Ireland. This means that my examination of the inscription of colonial tropes in *Paradise Lost* includes readings of a prose work like *Observations Upon the Articles of Peace*, which tells Milton's reader much about the polemicist's attitude toward the subjugation of the Irish. Furthermore, I am interested also in considering how Milton writes about the colonial motif in *Paradise Lost* through a reflexive gesture inseparable from his socialized position and identity as a Puritan living in Renaissance England. My point is that Milton's colonial and imperialist temperament must be accounted for in relation to the rhetoric of exclusivism that he employs, for implicit to this rhetoric are strategies enabling the demonization of difference. These strategies mark the polemic thrust of the production of Milton's entire corpus: the antiprelatical tracts, the regicide pamphlets, and the major poems.

In another but more general study, *An Empire Nowhere*, Jeffrey

Knapp focuses on Renaissance England's conceptions of and expansionist designs in the New World.[20] In his provocative reading of the presence of colonial tropes in the literature of early modern England, Knapp cautions the reader against making the erroneous assumption that there was such a phenomenon as a sustained expansionist agenda in the period. As he puts it, England's continued failure to establish a stronghold in the New World, something that stands out in great contrast against the Spanish success, created the historical reality of England's "frivolous"[21] relation to the New World. Knapp elaborates: "Yet if England's colonial trifling makes the discovery of America seem an unlikely source of inspiration for a burgeoning English literature, neither on closer inspection do the other traditional sources for England's literary Renaissance look especially capable of having taught English literature an expansive lesson."[22] Based on this central premise, he then proceeds to read a wide range of authors (including Ralegh, Spenser, and Shakespeare) by situating them in relation to accounts and manuscripts of England's colonial endeavors in America, a move that shows affinities with the new historicist characteristic of dismantling the generic distinctions traditionally accepted as separating literary texts from other cultural documents. *An Empire Nowhere* then proceeds to highlight the presence of a powerfully emerging colonial consciousness in English Renaissance texts, but almost always deconstructing this foregrounding by evoking its ephemeral identity and intangibility: efforts to ground England somewhere leads to its presence "nowhere"; and attempts to celebrate Queen Elizabeth's identity as a monarch concludes with the affirmation of her otherworldliness—a transcendent identity that is, at the same time, nonpresent.

My own study moves in a different direction from Knapp's in its analysis of the presence of colonial themes, tropes, and motifs in the literature of late sixteenth- and early seventeenth-century England. In my emphasis, England's nonviable position as a colonial power in the period finds itself expressed in literary texts very much concerned with the possibilities of revising such a position. As some powerful meditations concerning the logic and viability of English expansionism ensued, voices of doubt engaged other more-affirmative voices, so that individuals sometimes found themselves challenging assumptions held by the monarch relating to England's potential as a colonial power. In these dialogues, debates, and discussions, terms are set and discursive boundaries established to facilitate what might effectively be called the discourse of nascent English colonialism.

The status of England as an emerging colonial power cannot be separated from the conceptualization of itself as a sovereign state and even as an "empire" in the early modern period. This definition of its national identity is complex, forged in relation to such diverse political signifiers as the monarch, the people, or "the cultural system as figured in language, law, religion, history, economy, and social order."[23] The Elizabethan writing of England as a nation, as Helgerson argues, is far from monolithic. National identity—whether defined in relation to linguistics, literary and cultural achievement, or political and military viability—is, at its most basic, constructed and constituted with reference to other realities: examples include Italy's possession of a mellifluous language that lends itself naturally to the creation of great literature, Spain's possession of a large overseas empire, and Europe's lucrative participation in overseas trade and commerce. The forging of a national identity is, in short, inseparable from the need of a people to come into their own, to define their own center instead of being defined by others. Cultural clout comes not only by saying that what one does is better than others, but it also needs reinforcement through viable and tangible gains and accomplishments. One such gain that would be immediately visible to the outside observer is the acquisition of foreign lands and territories.

The dream of territorial acquisition and expansion began to make itself palpably felt in the period considered in this book. In recent years, interest in England's conceptualization of its national identity is clearly present. In *Literature, Politics, and National Identity*, for example, Andrew Hadfield sets out to examine the links between literature, politics, and national identity in sixteenth-century England.[24] Together with Brendan Bradshaw and Willy Maley, Hadfield has also edited another book, a collection of essays, titled *Representing Ireland*.[25] The recognition exists that, in addition to writing the English nation, as Helgerson puts it, there is also the vitally important writing of Ireland into English Renaissance literature. The emphases in *Literature, Politics, and National Identity* and *Representing Ireland* draw attention to the politically-conscious bent of a historical criticism. There is a sustained effort made to foreground what had previously been submerged: that interpretations of the construction of English Renaissance literature must take into consideration the fact of its early colonial and expansionist ambitions.

In this book I will consider early English expansionism in America in relation to the efforts made to bring about the effective colonization of Ireland because the project of expanding England's political body into one place often provides object lessons for penetrating into the space of the other. What this book therefore sets out to do is consider the joint places of America and Ireland in the dreams of Elizabethan and Stuart expansionism. It looks at how awareness of settling colonies in the New World and the Irish question contributes toward forming the literary output of such different figures as Sir Walter Ralegh, John Donne, William Shakespeare, Edmund Spenser, and John Milton.

Critical studies on the politics of colonialism have focused a great deal of attention on the tropes frequently found in colonial texts: the land as desiring female body and object of desire; gold and transaction; the masculinist gaze responding to exotic spectacles and signs of the marvelous; and the experience of the thrilling sensations of wonder. I discuss the presence of these tropes in different writings of the English Renaissance, examining how their inscriptions in texts create understandings of the scope of Renaissance England's dreams of colonial expansion. These inscriptions reveal general cultural perceptions of England's status as an emerging colonial power; and they also locate specific consciousnesses engaging with this new emerging discourse. The dreams of expansionism are then both individual and social. They are articulated, formed, and forged as different figures in Renaissance England respond to the particularities of their private and social situations: Sir Walter Ralegh responding to an irate queen; John Donne never fulfilling his ambition to be actively involved in settling the New World; Edmund Spenser developing a cynicism as he discovers his dreams of advancement in court receding steadily; John Milton finding that England has lost its cultural mandate and therefore any right to expand its political boundaries.

This book has five chapters. Chapter 1 is titled "'To Seeke New Worlds': Ralegh's *The Discoverie of Guiana*, Subjectivity, and the Politics of Colonial Expansion." I begin this book by considering Sir Walter Ralegh as a pivotal and representative figure living in an England surging with new energies and a powerful sense of its own potentiality. Energies of this kind, forged out of a romantic sense of possibilities and enabled by mythmaking, are also powered by England's presiding genius, Elizabeth I. With the power of her royal charisma generating much-needed inspiration, a courtier like Ralegh is able to nourish dreams of setting forth and colonizing the Americas. But the Virgin Queen who is England's source of inspiration and the center of its national identity is also the focus of a deep ambivalence based on a culture's perceptions of gender difference. When Ralegh wrote *The Discoverie of Guiana* to try and get highly desired endorsement for his colonial ambitions, he responded to the queen as a subject and a male lover pining for the beloved's attention. *The Discoverie of Guiana* is an important and paradigmatic text in the discourse of colonialism in Renaissance England because it identifies the cultural framework within which the courtier moves and has his being. It also registers differences in opinion on what constitutes a viable colonial project. Ralegh's struggles to garner support point to the absence of a consensual position on the ambitions of colonial expansion in Elizabethan England. But what it also shows are the beginnings of an emerging colonial consciousness that, in negotiating complex and contradictory responses to English overseas engagements, contribute toward forging a more distinct and coherent discourse.

Chapter 2 is titled "'Let Us Possess One World': John Donne, Rationalizing Theology, and the Discourse of Virginia." In the sermons of John Donne, the viability of settling the Virginia colony was imagined and rationalized. As Donne thought about English colonial activities in America, he found himself inevitably coming to terms with the figure of the native/savage and working to accommodate him in his theological universe. He also found himself having to define further a way of relating to the natives after a brutal massacre of the Virginia colonists took place in 1622. Not everybody responded as did Donne, for whom the sword was not a viable option in the conversion of the native. The massacre gave other people like Samuel Purchas the opportunity to flesh out a distinct rationale for dislodging a people from their land. Purchas's "Virginias Verger" is a text that offers a revealing comparison with Donne's understanding of the proselytizing mandate. In "Virginias Verger," Purchas intertwines the distinctively secular ambition of making Virginia yield its material bounty with a theological conception that endorses the need to inflict rough justice on the bodies of the savage and less-than-human natives. In the course of using a theological worldview to relate to a native people and their land, concepts like Natural Law and the Law of Nations are given specific emphases designed to support and enact the politics of dispossession. This chapter concludes by drawing analogies between the "theological" discourse of Virginia and Puritan rationale for forging the beginnings of New England.

Chapter 3—"'More Fair Than Black': *Othello* and the Discourse of Race Relations in Elizabethan England"—situates Shakespeare's creation of *Othello* against a culture's general perceptions of the African and the Moor. Significantly, the play engages themes and motifs found in travel narratives popular in late sixteenth- and early seventeenth-century England. The presence of these themes and motifs shows Shakespeare depicting the problematics of miscegenation through the mediating narratives of a familiar European colonial experience. *Othello* then engages the politics of both race and gender, inscribing in its dramatic narrative the cultural ambivalences of responding to figures of Otherness and difference.

The fourth chapter is "Figuring Justice: Imperial Ideology and the Discourse of Colonialism in Book 5 of *The Faerie Queene* and *A View of the Present State of Ireland*." It examines Spenser's views on the nature of justice and effective ways to subjugate the Irish. Where Spenser is concerned, the prerogative of law and justice that proceeds from the monarch constitutes the foundation and basis of social order; it is this justice that enables the creation and consolidation of order which Spenser desires visited on the recalcitrant Irish. Even as Spenser articulates his vision in book 5 and the *View*, he finds himself reacting to what he perceives to be the queen's ineffective conducting of foreign policy—protecting the interests of the Protestant Church abroad and quelling the rebellious Irish. His *Faerie Queene* and *View* then become texts that communicate these reactions within the limits and constraints imposed by narrativity and, of course, by censorship. What Spenser ultimately reveals is his inscription in an absolutist ideology. His criticism of Elizabeth's conduct of foreign policy cannot be separated from his validation of this ideology.

The last chapter—"'Space May Produce New Worlds': Theological Imperialism and the Poetics of Colonialism in *Paradise Lost, Paradise Regained,* and *Samson Agonistes*"—considers the reason Milton depicts Satan's journey across Chaos to destroy God's newly created Eden with reference to metaphors linked to the designs and practices of European imperialism and colonialism. Representing the Satanic journey as a colonizing venture has the effect of rhetorically demonizing the imperialist tropes central to fantasies of European expansionism. Does this particular representation convey Milton's critique of imperialist and colonialist undertakings in general? And, if so, why? I will respond to these questions by proposing that *Paradise Lost*'s representation of Satan's journey, and the associative links forged between colonialism and the demonic, can be traced to Milton's experience of disillusionment after the collapse of the English Commonwealth and the failure of the Puritan experiment. That representation also encodes a critique of the concept of *imperium,* a critique that entails an interrogation of the encomiastic narrative of Virgil's *Aeneid* and is enforced even further in Jesus' repudiation of the political structures that Rome embodies in *Paradise Regained.* If *Paradise Lost* and *Paradise Regained* register Milton's interrogation of England's aspiration to be a colonial power because of its deep-seated political problems, they do so in poetic narratives controlled by a dominant rhetoric of theological imperialism. This rhetoric, predicated on the biblical conception of exclusivism, is especially central to the (re)definition of self-identity in *Samson Agonistes.*

Each of the five chapters above focuses on one aspect or expression of England's emerging colonial consciousness: white/black social relations; the politics of the colonization of Ireland; imagings and figurations of overseas expansionism; the relationship between culture, theology, and colonial expansion. Starting with Ralegh and ending with Milton, the chapters also aim to give a sense of diachronic development as different political and social pressures existing in the respective reigns of Elizabeth I and the Stuart monarchs contribute to effecting change in the expressions of Renaissance England's colonial dreams and ambitions. The focal terms I have adopted for this study—"colonialism" and "imperialism"—need definition and contextualization because England in the period I am considering, from about 1558 (Elizabeth's accession) to 1674 (Milton's death), is far from being a colonial power; and it is certainly far from possessing that consolidated political identity known as empire, capable of uniting its different parts for the purposes of warlike defense, internal commerce, and the acquisition of colonies. Imperialism, in the strict sense of the word, cannot be said to exist in England until at least the mid-seventeenth century. But the point is that the fantasies of Renaissance England involve the dreams of colonialism and imperialism. And what we witness as we read Ralegh, Donne, Shakespeare, Spenser, and Milton are how such diverse people in Renaissance England engage a culture's dreams of transforming England into a colonial and imperial power. The fantasies of colonial expansion and empire building intertwine, and even before the close of the sixteenth century, the epic poet Edmund Spenser had already begun conceptualizing England as *imperium.* Before reality exists the dream, and this book seeks to analyze this dream before its materialization in empire.

1

"To Seeke New Worlds": Ralegh's *The Discoverie of Guiana,* Subjectivity, and the Politics of Colonial Expansion

IN THE REIGN OF ELIZABETH I, THE SENSE OF MOUNTING EXCITE-
ment attending prospects of the building of empire was generated
by the experience of entering into an era brimming with cultural
potential. England even felt courageous enough to contest Spain
for the territorial possession of foreign lands. Sir Francis Drake—
the man whom the Spaniards referred to with a certain terror as
"El Draque" because of his uncanny ability to checkmate many of
Spain's offensive strategies aimed at undermining England's contest for the privilege of the seas—exemplified England's spirit of
high adventure when he plundered the Spanish Main as a bucca-
neer, harassing and pillaging Spanish ships. He was an active par-
ticipant in the famous raid on Cadiz; and he also succeeded in
blocking Spain's mobilization of the Armada in the harbor in Lisbon by seizing the fortress of Cape St. Vincent. Activities of the
kind undertaken by Drake always held a romantic fascination for
Elizabethan England. Sir Philip Sidney had, for example, planned
to get himself involved in the 1595 expedition that Drake undertook to the West Indies; Sidney never made the trip because of
the queen's timely intervention commanding him by royal decree
to return to the court.

Drake's buccaneering activities enjoyed the implicit, if not explicit, endorsement of Elizabeth I, who always made an outward
show of officially disapproving of the activities of the English privateers; in reality, however, her policy was one of encouragement.
Elizabeth recognized accurately that the engagements of the English privateers could only disrupt Spain's hegemony in the high
seas. It is not surprising, therefore, that after the 1560s, the English began actively trading and raiding in the Caribbean, making
the area of the West Indies abuzz with activity. The half dozen

31

fleets that Sir Walter Ralegh dispatched to Virginia between 1584 and 1602 all touched the islands of the West Indies in passing. Ralegh himself had also explored Trinidad and Guiana; in 1595, he captured the Spaniard Antonio de Berreo in Trinidad and obtained from him firsthand stories of the much sought after treasures in the legendary city of Manoa. The governor of Trinidad, de Berrio had spent a lifetime seeking El Dorado and died still believing in its existence. It was also in the Caribbean that Francis Drake stole £40,000 in silver, gold, and pearls in 1573; in 1585, he returned with thirty ships to sack Santo Domingo and Cartagena. During the war years, between 1585 and 1604, English privateers captured hundreds of enemy ships and carried home a veritable fortune in sugar, hides, logwood, indigo, silver, gold, and pearls.[1] Richard Dunn surmises: "It is probable that English investors—chiefly London merchants—put more money into commerce and piracy in the Caribbean from 1560 to 1630 than into any other mode of long-distance, overseas business enterprise, even the East India Company."[2]

The patriotic motive of enabling England's national and militaristic empowerment is often intertwined with the workings of court politics. Ralegh's propagation of the conquest of Guiana, like his christening of Virginia in the New World after the symbolic namesake of his queen, augments the ambitions of English colonialism. It also obtains its meanings and significance from the elaborate fictions of courtship played out between the courtier and his monarch. In this fiction, Ralegh figures himself as the male lover wooing his courtly mistress. He yearns for her affection and is especially anxious about the possibilities of losing her favor. In Ralegh's court poetry, the courtier woos the queen—his royal mistress—by producing encomia and valorizing her attributes.

In the courtly love convention that Ralegh uses to define his relationship with his queen, the elevation of the desired mistress on a pedestal gives the woman a great deal of power over the man, but the very act of representation itself guarantees male control of language and narrative. In *Ocean to Cynthia*, for example, Elizabeth is portrayed as the desired mistress of the courtly love tradition because Ralegh wants to demonstrate the suffering he is undergoing, pining for her. And she is also Cynthia, the goddess of the moon, existing beyond the particular contingencies of time and history that shape mortal affairs in the sublunary world. It is important to note that the context and occasion for scripting *Ocean to Cynthia* was Ralegh's imprisonment in the Tower by the queen in 1592 for marrying one of her maids of honor, Elizabeth Throckmorton. In the 21st Book of *Ocean to Cynthia*,

Ralegh expresses his shock at the queen's violent response to his clandestine marriage in a series of oxymora that describe his own powerful feelings and perceptions of the queen. These draw attention to a self constructed on a crisis of identity and the shifting winds of political favor. Ralegh has lost the favor of his beloved and is plunged into a state of despair: "I hated life and cursed destiney" (line 165).[3] The poem predicates its representation of despair on the relationship between past and present, memory and desire. Things had been so unbelievably good in the past; the present is a nightmare in which all desire is crushed: "the thoughts of passed tymes like flames of hell, / kyndled a fresh within my memorye / the many deere achiuements that befell" (lines 166–68). Even as the narrator of *Ocean to Cynthia* bemoans the agony of lost love, he transforms the specificity of individual experience into the universal. In the 21st Book, Ralegh subsumes the pain of individual experience under the ravenous jaws of devouring time: "Loves grovnd, his essence, and his emperye, / all slaues to age, and vassalls vnto tyme" (lines 178–79). If losing the favor of the courtly mistress translates itself into a metaphysical affirmation of the reality that all things end in the grave, the poignant sense communicated of the meaninglessness of human existence also engulfs the queen in humankind's "frayle mortallety" (line 186). Ralegh's poetic fragment intimates that even Eliza herself is dust, a critique of the myth of immortality that frames the construction of the monarch's iconic identity. A cautionary wedge is inserted between the symbolic constructions of immortality and the fact that the queen cannot convincingly conceal her decayed teeth and her age behind the red wig she wears and the cosmetic plaster she applies. Ralegh's awakening call to reality exposes the making of fictions that is the tradition of courtly love.

What we find then is that the power Ralegh accords his royal mistress in his poetic fragment, the same power whose celebration he hopes will soften her attitude toward him, also has the effect of reinforcing her implacable cruelty: the plea for the bestowal of royal favor cannot be separated from trenchant criticism. Tyranny is the best description that Ralegh can evoke to emphasize the monarch's cruel treatment of her subject:

> Thes be the Tirants that in fetters tye
>
> their wounded vassalls, yet nor kill nor cure,
> but glory in their lastinge missery
> that as her bewties would our woes should dure
> thes be th' effects of pourfull emperye . . .

(lines 196–200)

Importantly, *Ocean to Cynthia*'s designation of Elizabeth as a tyrant is not limited to the suggestion that, in one way or another, the queen had scrambled the codes defining the game of courtly love, so that the courtier is now unable to operate with established rules; it identifies the queen's act as a violation of virtue: "So douth shee pleas her vertues to deface" (line 204). After the negation of these virtues, all that is left is profound disappointment and cynicism that extend beyond the immediate occasion or lesson of the transience and unpredictability of princely favor. In his poem, Ralegh implicates the queen in the tyrannical practices of princes in general. The use of the pluralized form, "Tirants," enables a general observation to be made on the exercise of a power that finds great pleasure in the sufferings of the subject. Elizabeth, as Ralegh's poetic fragment makes no effort to conceal, luxuriates in this pleasure. And she is not alone in performing acts of cruelty: all monarchs do the same thing. One can argue that in *Ocean to Cynthia*, Elizabeth's very identity as England's Virgin Queen and Ralegh's beloved is made to lose its specificity and individuality when she is portrayed as indistinguishable from any other prince.

In his preface to *The History of the World*, Ralegh goes to great lengths to highlight the destructive tyranny of monarchs and corruption of worldly power; the retributions that are shown to follow the cruel acts of kings draw attention to the fragility of all human ambition. Ralegh's criticism of the Jacobean regime is obvious in *The History*, and James I responded to its treatment of monarchs by forbidding its sale in 1614.[4] *Ocean to Cynthia* also highlights the fragility motif but relates it to the queen's mortal body in order to counterpoint her mystified and iconic identity. The involved and deeply personal nature of Ralegh's portrayal of his relationship with the queen then gives way at different and unexpected moments in the poem's narrative to a critique of political power in general. The tyrannical Elizabeth is not only the cruel mistress, but also the consummate politician. Ralegh finds himself compelled to recognize that he is nothing more than a subject in the manipulative world of power. Ironically, this courtier who enjoys playing with power, a capacity that facilitated his meteoric rise in the queen's court in the first place, now finds himself an object of play in its treacherous domain. It is with this full awareness of the insidious ways in which authority and power operate that Ralegh produces *The Discoverie of Guiana*, first and foremost a transacting and negotiating text. The *Discoverie* is a text written with the design to obtain Elizabeth's endorsement and support for his desire to colonize the Orinoco basin.

The reasons Ralegh gives for his colonial dreams cannot be separated from a desire to place England on the map as a powerful nation. From the start then, the quest for gold with which Guiana is rumored to be saturated is a trope used in Ralegh's text to designate England's larger national interests of which Elizabeth I, as custodian, is natural protector: "The countrey hath more quantity of gold by manifolde, then the best partes of the Indies, or Peru."[5] In his address to the reader, Ralegh elaborates:

> I wil hope that these provinces, and that Empire now by me discovered shal suffice to inable her Majestie & the whole kingdome, with no lesse quantities of treasure, then the king of Spaine hath in all the Indies East and West, which he possesseth, which if the same be considered and followed, ere the Spaniards enforce the same, and if her Majestie wil undertake it, I wil be contented to lose her highnesse favour & good opinion for ever, and my life withall, if the same be not found rather to exceed, then to equal whatsoever is in this discourse promised or declared. (*DG* 10:348)

Behind Ralegh's demonization of imperial Spain lies the implied message that Elizabeth, as professed protector of the Protestant Church in Europe, has the obligation to carry out her political and "spiritual" duties. Ralegh himself does not explicitly appropriate the language of theology to frame his anti-Spanish rhetoric and sentiments. His desire not to have an England lagging behind as a peripheral and backward nation is made to resonate with a kind of political pragmatism: to adjust England's peripheral status requires making an urgent effort to penetrate into and appropriate the wealth of Guiana. The value of Guiana for Ralegh resides in the abundance of its legendary wealth and not in any notion that God has given this land to the English by divine dispensation.

In *The Discoverie of Guiana*, Ralegh demonizes imperial Spain to reveal to the queen his loyalty: the Ralegh who has the best interests of his queen at heart is also the avowed nationalist. Part of the pressure Ralegh exerts on the queen to support his colonial ambition is found in *The Discoverie of Guiana*'s constant reminder that Spain owns a substantial chunk of the New World and it is about time for some reapportioning of territory and property. Ralegh's rhetorical attacks on the brutality of Catholic Spain can be read as encoding an implicit critique of Elizabeth's handling of foreign policy. Ralegh once made the comment that Elizabeth "did all by halves."[6] In other words, she is undecided, unfocused, and as he finds himself learning firsthand from the loss of princely favor, whimsical. By fashioning himself as a nationalistic subject, and giving to his projection of the colonization of Guiana the focus of English contestation with Spain for the building of empire, Ralegh makes full use of his text to pressure the queen into endorsing his ambitions.

Even Ralegh's recounting of the experiences of the Spanish colonists who had set out to discover Guiana contributes to this application of pressure for endorsement. The catalogue of men who have done so much for Spain and who are driven by their conviction must surely reveal something about the inherent and material value of Guiana. Having had the privilege of learning about these narratives of travel and discovery, a great deal would be lost if nothing were done to undertake a similar journey. The Spaniard's place in the text is partly to embellish and lend credence to the legend of Guiana's tremendous wealth.

Ralegh's lieutenant, Laurence Keymis, specifically adds the theological emphasis to the anti-Spanish rhetoric in *A Relation of the Second Voyage to Guiana* (1596), a text produced for Sir Walter Ralegh who had instructed him to perform a "second Discoverie":[7]

> If wee doe but consider, howe unhappily Berreo his affaires, with his assistants have of late yeeres, in our owne knowledge succeeded: who can say, if the hand of the Almighty be not against them, and that hee hath a worke in this place, in stead of Papistrie, to make the sincere light of his Gospell to shine on this people? The effecting whereof shall bee a royall crowne of everlasting remembrance to all other blessings, that from the beginning the Lorde hath plentifully powred on our dread Soveraigne, in an eminent and supreme degree of all perfection. If the Castilians, pretending a religious care of planting Christianitie in those partes, have in their doings preached nought els but avarice, rapine, blood, death, and destruction to those naked, & sheeplike creatures of God; erecting statues and trophees of victorie unto themselves, in the slaughters of millions of innocents: doeth not the crie of the poore succourlesse ascend unto the heavens? Hath God forgotten to bee gracious to the workemanship of his owne hands? Or shall not his judgements in a day of visitation by the ministrie of his chosen servant, come on these bloodthirstie butchers, like raine into a fleece of wooll?[8]

Ralegh had never used the language of proselytization to frame his argument for the colonization of Guiana. By contrast, when

Keymis looks at the problems besetting de Berreo and his men, he reads these as signs of God's displeasure acted out on the bodies of the Spaniards—for planting "Papistrie" and for committing acts of brutality on "those naked, & sheeplike creatures of God." Any claim that the Spaniard has to the land through right of conquest is forfeited as a result of colonial violence, an argument also used by members of the Virginia Company to dislodge the natives from their natural links to land after the infamous 1622 massacre of the Jamestown colonists. The native of the New World is a flexible figure used either to legitimize England's ambition for territorial appropriation or to remove the Spanish presence from the land. If the native exists in a discourse aimed at obliterating the presence of the Spaniard from the literal and discursive space of the New World, he/she can be made to assume an identity as the innocent victim of Spanish imperial cruelty. The native enjoys a functional identity, which can be made to shift according to the needs of rhetorical and discursive demands.

I began by saying that *The Discoverie of Guiana* is a negotiating and transactional text, with Ralegh offering the (symbolic) gift of Guiana and its gold to win back the queen's favor and to fulfill individual desire. The fact that Elizabeth gave her consent in the first place for Ralegh to undertake his voyage to Guiana in 1595 suggests that she had already cooled off somewhat in her anger toward him. But if Ralegh could get the queen to support his plans for Guiana's colonization, that would enforce the knowledge he needed that she had forgiven him. The advancement of England's national interests cannot be separated from the furthering of Elizabeth Tudor's own as head of the body politic. If "Charles the 5 . . . had the maidenhead of Peru" (*DG* 10:346), England must make it its prerogative to obtain the maidenhead of Guiana. It is Spain's "Indian gold that indangereth and disturbeth all the nations of Europe, it purchaseth intelligence, creepeth into counsels, and setteth bound loyaltie at libertie, in the greatest Monarchies of Europe" (*DG* 10:347). And rewriting, through the terms of a colonialist rhetoric, Sir Philip Sidney's humanist discourse in which "those skills that most serve to bring forth [virtuous action] have a most just title to be princes over all the rest,"[9] Ralegh concludes: "Those princes which abound in treasure have great advantages over the rest" (*DG* 10:347). Of course, the furthering of England's national interests cannot be extricated from the advancement of the subject's own: Ralegh's desire to be restored to royal favor. Restoration to Elizabeth's favor, or the knowledge of such restoration, involved nothing less than pleading with the monarch to sanction by royal decree the rape of a land and its people. The self in Ralegh's case is legitimized—or at least he hopes it would be so—through the suppression and annihilation of Amerindian culture.

If the aim of Ralegh's dream project in Guiana is to enact the rape of land, people, and culture, then his encounter with the natives of Guiana is to help pave the way for future colonization. Ralegh first presents himself to the natives as the emissary of a great monarch, come to bring deliverance and liberation:

> . . . by my Indian interpreter, which I caried out of England, I made them understand that I was the servant of a Queene, who was the great Casique of the North, and a virgine, and had more Casiqui under her then there were trees in that yland: that shee was an enemie to the Castellani in respect of their tyrannie and oppression, and that she delivered all such nations about her, as were by them oppressed, and having freed all the coast of the Northren world from their servitude, had sent mee to free them also, and withall to defend the countrey of Guiana from their invasion and conquest. I shewed them her Majesties picture which they so admired and honoured, as it had bene easie to have brought them idolatrous thereof. (*DG* 10:353–54)

One of the most elaborate accounts given by Ralegh of his interactions with a native chief, one registering the complex workings of power between colonist and Other, is found in his discourse with Topiawari. In his narrative of this encounter, Ralegh elaborates on the great hospitality he receives from the old king who "came to us on foote from his house, which was fourteene English miles (himselfe being a hundreth and tenne yeeres olde) and returned on foote the same day" (*DG* 10:398–99). A statement about power is revealed in Topiawari's visit to Ralegh, who enjoys symbolic superiority. The retinue Topiawari brought with him on the visit, besides bringing gifts, "came to wonder at our nation" (*DG* 10:399). Wonder, the experience of the native responding to the newness of the Old World, is set in a text dilated for the wonder of Ralegh's English reader. In colonialist discourse, the wonder experienced by the native is itself a source of wonder for the European beholding native gullibility, which, in turn, is the site of vulnerability for colonial penetration into the space of the Other.

Once Ralegh has set up this relationship between the old king of Arromaia and himself, he introduces by "dilating at large" (*DG* 10:399) on the greatness of his queen, "her justice, her charitie to all oppressed nations, with as many of the rest of her beauties and vertues" (*DG* 10:399). This *dilation* is not meant solely for the benefit of Topiawari and the forging of his confidence, but for the reception of Elizabeth I herself. Inscribed in the design to win the trust of Topiawari is encomium directed at softening the queen's anger. Topiawari responds to Ralegh by expressing admiration for Elizabeth. Once a certain level of trust is established, Ralegh proceeds to learn as much as he can about the state of Guiana, the interactions between different tribes and peoples, the nature of their defence mechanisms, and their modes of government. Ralegh is on track in his colonialist project, recognizing the importance of communication skills in interacting with the natives. Possessing these skills is necessary for the European colonist who wants to gain access into the secrets of the landscape as well as the dark space of the native Other. The name of the game is reconnaissance, and this Ralegh learns from Cortés to whom we owe, as Todorov tells us in *The Conquest of America,* "the invention, on the one hand, of conquest tactics, and on the other, of a policy of peacetime colonization." Todorov elaborates, "What Cortés wants from the first is not to capture but to comprehend; it is signs which chiefly interest him, not their referents. His expedition begins with a search for information, not for gold. The first important action he initiates—and we cannot overemphasize the significance of this gesture—is to find an interpreter."[10]

A second conference with Topiawari takes place shortly after. This conference transpires in a private space occupied by Ralegh, Topiawari, and an interpreter. It starts off with Ralegh showing his support for old Topiawari by telling him that both the Epuremei, another tribe, and the Spaniards are his enemies. This revelation serves to forge a symbolic alliance and friendship. Mary Campbell tells us that Ralegh pays close attention to native discussions because he knows that he would be unable to colonize Guiana without the alliance and friendship of some of the natives.[11] Almost immediately after this, Ralegh asks Topiawari to give him instructions on how to locate "the passage into the golden parts of Guiana" (*DG* 10:410). Topiawari's response is a fascinating one, for it stresses all the difficulties that can be encountered in any effort to find the way into Guiana: the time of the year is wrong, weather conditions are hostile, and there are simply not sufficient men and the undersized party may "bee buried there" as the result of a massacre (*DG* 10:410). Topiawari's point is that there will be an opportune moment for such an enterprise, but one that can only materialize through the happy confluence of weather conditions and logistical preparedness.

On the surface, Topiawari's narrative of hardship and impossible endeavor suggests that he has the best interests of Ralegh and his expeditionary force at heart. But the catalogue of obstacles he lists and his almost strident plea for Ralegh not to make the journey have all the features of negotiation and transaction, undertaken singlehandedly by an old native chieftain who, quite possibly, has the prescience to see the larger picture and colonial motivations of Ralegh's dark interest in Guiana. We recall here de Berreo's own attempt to prevent Ralegh from undertaking the journey to Guiana. The Topiawari who brings a retinue and gifts to greet the English visitor is perhaps not as gullible as he may appear to be.

Topiawari and Ralegh end up performing a highly symbolic exchange of gifts. The lord of Arromaia gives to Ralegh his son to bring back to England and Ralegh leaves behind one Francis Sparrow, the servant of a captain, and another boy, Hugh Goodwin. Once again, this exchange, betokening friendship, cannot be extricated from the complex interplay of power. Topiawari, in giving his son to Ralegh, hopes to make use of the "meanes" (*DG* 10:414) of the Englishman to set his son up as lord of Arromaia after his death. Topiawari has taken into consideration his old age and his enemies. For Ralegh, the men he gives in exchange are in a sense expandable: one is a servant who, Ralegh tells us, "was desirous to tarie, and could describe a countrey with his pen" (*DG* 10:414); the other, Hugh Goodwin, was specifically given instructions to learn the language of the natives. In *A Relation of the Second Voyage to Guiana*, published shortly after *The Discoverie of Guiana*, Laurence Keymis reports learning that Topiawari had fled to the mountains and died there while Hugh Goodwin had been killed by a tiger.[12]

In the moments of early encounter, interactions between the English colonist and the native of the land he wishes to conquer do not always occur in a transactional space in which the European bargains from a position of innate superiority and advantage. Ralegh makes a special effort to cultivate Topiawari's friendship not only because he responds to the old chief as another vulnerable member of the human family, but because he recognizes the need for friendship and alliance in any projected design for the conquest of Guiana. In addition to the dangers posed by the numerous enemies that will abound in any ambition to enact the colonial rape of a land, there is always the presence of the treacherous and hostile landscape, a topos as well as reality in travel narratives. Against the hostility of the landscape, the English intruder, disguised as visitor and ambassador, is powerless.

The realization comes as a shock to Ralegh who reveals vividly an experience that will plague, in different circumstances, the English colonists who went over to settle the Jamestown colony a few years later. In *The Discoverie of Guiana,* Ralegh recounts one incident in which he finds himself depending completely on an old pilot to lead him to a small town along the river:

Our olde pilot of the Ciawani (whom, as I sayd before, wee tooke to redeeme Ferdinando) tolde us, that if we would enter a branch of a river on the right hand with our barge and wheries, and leave the galley at anker the while in the great river, he would bring us to a towne of the Arwacas, where we should finde store of bread, hennes, fish, and of the countrey wine; and perswaded us, that departing from the galley at noone, we might returne yer night. I was very glad to heare this speech, and presently tooke my barke, with eight musketiers, captaine Giffords whery, with himselfe and foure musketiers, and Captaine Calfield with his whery, and as many; and so we entred the mouth of this river: and because we were perswaded that it was so nere, we tooke no victuall with us at all. When we had rowed three houres, we marvelled we saw no signe of any dwelling, and asked the pilot where the towne was: he tolde us a little further. After three houres more, the Sun being almost set, we began to suspect that he led us that way to betray us: for hee confessed that those Spanyards which fled from Trinidad, and also those that remained with Carapana in Emeria, were joyned together in some village upon that river. But when it grew towards night; and wee demanded where the place was; hee tolde us but foure reaches more. When we had rowed foure and foure; we saw no signe; and our poore water-men, even heart-broken, and tired, were ready to give up the ghost: for wee had now come from the galley neere forty miles.

At the last we determined to hang the pilot; and if wee had well knowen the way backe againe by night, hee had surely gone; but our owne necessities pleaded sufficiently for his safety: for it was as darke as pitch, and the river began so to narrow it selfe, and the trees to hang over from side to side, as wee were driven with arming swords to cut a passage thorow those branches that covered the water. Wee were very desirous to finde this towne, hoping of a feast, because wee made but a short breakefast aboord the galley in the morning and it was now eight a clocke at night, and our stomacks began to gnawe apace: but whether it was best to returne or goe on, we beganne to doubt, suspecting treason in the pilot more and more: but the poore olde Indian ever assured us that it was but a little further, but this one turning and that turning. (*DG* 10:386–87)

The would-be colonist finds himself in a completely powerless position, lacking the means to bargain and negotiate with his guide. At this moment, his life is at the mercy of the native. The narrative has a happy conclusion: Ralegh managed to arrive at his destination because it was the difficulty of negotiating the terrain, rather than any treachery designed by his guide, that made the journey appear endless.

Ralegh's experience is significant because it reveals one important aspect of early English colonial experiences in the New World, in which survival in an alien land is fraught with dangers and uncertainties. A well-known experience is the complete disappearance of the English colonists on Roanoke Island. In this particular example, it is believed that the Roanoke colonists had alienated the native people by their cruelty, so that when the invasion of the Spanish Armada prevented the sailing of supply ships in 1588, they received no help and literally starved themselves into extinction. The European colonist may come with the superior technology of his weaponry, but that in itself cannot guarantee his survival. In the Jamestown colony, for example, transactions and negotiations went on constantly between colonist and Amerindian. The dependence of the English colonist on the American native for food and for living in a completely foreign environment means that the balance of power was not so lopsided at the start of the settlement of the Jamestown colony.[13] The colonist needed the skills and the knowledge of the native—and got them by making contact—but only to turn that knowledge back against its teachers: this is the basic narrative of Richard Slotkin's *Regeneration Through Violence.*[14]

The Proceedings of the English Colony in Virginia also records that much of the negotiations and "trafficking" going on and conducted between the Amerindians and the colonists centered on the recognized necessity of "victuals" for survival. "Trafficking" assumed different forms: friendly exchange, devious barter, and the inducement of fear and terror. As Powhatan, the great overlord of tidewater Virginia and renowned Algonquian despot, once said to Captain John Smith:

[W]hat will it availe you, to take that perforce, you may quietly have with love, or to destroy them that provide you food? what can you get by war, when we can hide our provision and flie to the woodes, whereby you must famish by wronging us your friends. . . .[15]

Powhatan was especially astute in recognizing the dire need of the colonists for his corn and, as such, often bartered for costly possessions owned by the colonists. Possessing the knowledge and means of survival, Powhatan ensured that the balance of power never shifted to the complete advantage of the colonists. The advantage Powhatan possessed that Shakespeare's Caliban lacked was the faculty and ability to engage in contestation with the European colonist: like threatening to withhold the means of survival in order to readjust an unfair power relationship that had been forcibly or violently imposed. Shakespeare grounds Caliban's inability to pose any form of effective resistance to Prospero's appropriation of his island in the simple trust he exhibits at the moment of original encounter.

Despite the reality that the possession of superior fire power itself was no guarantee of survival in the hostile land of the New World, the English colonists needed to create fictions for themselves and their audience back in England that they were, from the start, superior to the Amerindian in every way. For Ralegh the experience of dependency when he thought he was completely lost through the treachery of his guide also gave him an occasion for creating fiction. Ralegh elaborates for the benefit of his queen on the extreme difficulties he encounters when journeying on the Orinoco with Arwacan guides who are not always very effective. The fear and real danger of becoming lost in the dense forests of the Orinoco basin, Ralegh details, are exacerbated by harsh climatic conditions and far from hospitable environment: oppressively hot weather, a river completely unblessed by any refreshing breeze, starvation, and extreme weakness. The force of this barrage of detailed descriptions of the Orinoco and its hostile landscape is to draw the queen's attention to the hardships he is willing to suffer to further her interests. The disgraced courtier negotiates the treacherous Orinoco in the hope that the queen will give due recognition to an undertaking that can easily cost him his life. Ralegh constantly draws attention explicitly and implicitly to the extent of the sufferings he is willing to undergo for the interests of his queen. As Ralegh expresses in his address to Lord Charles Howard and Sir Robert Cecil:

I did therefore even in the winter of my life, undertake these travels, fitter for bodies lesse blasted with mis-fortunes, for men of greater abilitie, and for mindes of better incouragement, that thereby, if it were possible, I might recover but the moderation of excesse, & the least tast of the greatest plenty formerly possessed. If I had knowen other way to win, if I had imagined how greater adventures might have regained, if I could conceive what farther meanes I might yet use, but even to appease so powreful displeasure [referring to the

Queen's response to his marriage], I would not doubt but for one yeere more to hold fast my soule in my teeth, till it were performed. Of that litle remaine I had, I have wasted in effect all herein. I have undergone many constructions. (*DG* 10:339)

The primary aim of *The Discoverie of Guiana* is to convince Elizabeth I of the trials experienced and undergone by the courtier in the service of his queen, as well as to give ample proof that the Eden of Guiana does in fact exist.

How does Ralegh present the Orinoco basin and Guiana for the gaze of his queen? First, he must uncover for the royal gaze the hidden spaces of the New World he had the privilege of "discovering." And he does so by representing the New World as the female body, a figuration that Patricia Parker argues is tied to the inextricable links between rhetoric and property.[16] The division of the woman's body into parts is central to the tradition of the blazon, Parker elaborates, in which the detailing of parts enables distribution and amplification. The blazon that "blazes" the wonders of the woman to the world also serves to distribute and dilate on the wonders of the New World to a curious and mercantile-minded people. The tradition depends on the presence of the gaze, the ocular receptor of the wonders of the woman as New World and the New World as woman, a gaze primarily male. What the blazon is capable of doing is bring the wonders of the New World directly to an audience, most of whom do not have the privilege of being "literally" there. Distribution and amplification must then depend on more than an appeal to the ocular or auditory faculties; convincing the auditor that America is a land of plenty also makes use of the figure of the inventory central to the lexicon of merchandising. The spirit of commercialization and desire for the creation of property, Parker further elaborates, is inscribed in the very use of the blazon, for not only are the different parts of the female body the "property" of the writer or poet who represents it in language and discourse, but the entire purpose of distribution and amplification is to proffer an object to a third party for purchase.

Patricia Parker also comments on how the blazon sells the idea of the value of the object it seeks to distribute by relying not only on ocular proof for amplification, but also on its substitutive *enargeia* or *evidentia*.[17] *Enargeia* or *evidentia* is a form of description that raises the visual aspect of the object: it aims to offer and communicate to the gaze the sensuous immediacy of the object. The terms that Parker employs to discuss the blazon and its complicity in the designs of empire building can be usefully evoked to frame the discussion of the relationship between Ralegh and his intended audience in *The Discoverie of Guiana*. This text is addressed directly to Lord Charles Howard and Sir Robert Cecil, figures of great power and tremendous influence in Queen Elizabeth's court. And there is, following this, also an address "To the Reader," that Louis Montrose identifies as the encapsulated form of all "Elizabethan masculine subjects—gentlemen, soldiers, potential investors, and colonists."[18] And, of course, oblique but palpable, the text is primarily designed for her majesty's consumption. Ralegh's address to Lord Charles Howard and Sir Robert Cecil has an obvious purpose: if these two men, among the most powerful in England, can be persuaded by the argument and proofs of his text, then it is hoped that they may be prevailed upon to convince Elizabeth of the wisdom and logic of undertaking the colonization of Guiana. Working with rhetorical structures that function like that of the blazon, *The Discoverie of Guiana* distributes, dilates, and amplifies the feminized body of one very important region in the Orinoco. The "parts" of Guiana are described for the reader with reference to the *materia* of the land, one inseparable from a vision of natural plenitude. Typically, in travel narratives, this vision of plenitude is based upon a cultural desire to seek out and recover the Eden that has been lost through the original and theological transgression recorded in Genesis. Once paradise is imagined, then discovery and hence materialization can take place, but only at the close of a ritualistic sojourn through extremely harsh physical terrain.

The ideal reader of Ralegh's text is the Virgin Queen herself as Elizabeth possesses the royal prerogative of sanctioning or not sanctioning any colonial project. The immediate task for Ralegh is, therefore, to undertake what in a different context Kenneth Graham has called "the performance of conviction."[19] Ralegh must convince the queen that Guiana is literally paved with gold and he must communicate effectively his own conviction of its veracity. Obviously the way to do so is to provide *enargeia* and *evidentia*. The beholder must be dazzled by the imagings and sight of Guiana's gold through the sensuous immediacy communicated through language.

The Discoverie of Guiana effects this by offering the reader catalogues and lists of people who have come into contact with the fabled wealth of El Dorado: Juan Martínez, reputed to be the first man to see Manoa and also the one to confer upon it the name of El Dorado, was given as much gold as he could carry when he left (*DG* 10:359–60); the natives of Guiana, or so De Oviedo reports, get themselves inebriated in a state of nakedness, their bodies covered with gold dust: a literal reenactment of the myth of "the gold-man," El Dorado (*DG* 10:361); and different Indian tribes are found to have in their possession gold from Guiana, powerful evidence that some form of tribal "economic" exchange existed. And the gold is found available in different forms: images in temples, plates, armors, shields, and even dust acting as powder for the body. The overabundance of gold that makes this commodity valueless in Sir Thomas More's *Utopia* makes it the first and final object of desire in *The Discoverie of Guiana*.

Ralegh's text provides much cataloguing, itemizing, and projecting of images of things golden. Its claims to verifiability and reliability depend very much on the reception of the reader, bringing with him/her a society's cultural fantasies of discovering cities of gold: in other words, experiencing vicariously the exhilaration of discovery. The dreams to replicate and reenact the exploits of Cortés and Pizarro in Renaissance England are powerful ones. Any nation that possesses Guiana, Ralegh tells the reader in *The Discoverie of Guiana*, inherits an empire even greater than that of Peru's: "The Empire of Guiana . . . hath more abundance of golde then any part of Peru, and as many or moe great Cities then ever Peru had when it flourished most. . . . [A]nd I have bene assured by such of the Spaniards as have seene Manoa the Imperial Citie of Guiana, which the Spaniards call El Dorado, that for the greatnesse, for the riches, and for the excellent seat, it farre exceedeth any of the world, at least of so much of the world as is knowen to the Spanish nation" (*DG* 10:356); for England, it means "a better Indies for her Majestie then the King of Spaine hath any" (*DG* 10:342).

But *The Discoverie of Guiana* does not obtain the closure it desires: materialization of the dream of Guiana. Its declaration to offer "a relation of the great and golden citie of Manoa" found in the title is left unfulfilled by the immateriality of Ralegh's performance. The last site in the Orinoco that Ralegh visits is Morequito, not Guiana. Mary Campbell refers to Ralegh's failure to arrive at Guiana as "an absolutely central absence" in the text.[20] And Mary Fuller comments that "Ralegh wrote *The Discoverie of Guiana* about not discovering Guiana. . . . The *Discoverie* suggests a succession of terms for the place of the hidden deposit. Ralegh composes lengthy apologetics for not having investigated Spanish gold mines of which an Indian pilot informed him."[21] Fuller rightly identifies Ralegh's use of the strategies of deflection in *The*

Discoverie. But Fuller's "deflection" and Campbell's "absence" do not fully account for another rhetorical maneuver Ralegh employs in his text to create the illusion of presence.

To enforce on his reader the materiality of the existence of Guiana, Ralegh couches the record of his failed performance in a narrative that embeds the exhilaration of fulfillment. Evoking spatial dimensions and even making the outright declaration that he has been on the ground of the land sought after aim to reinforce the sense of the immediacy of presence. Examples of such narrative moments include the following:

> But seeking after the Spanyards, we found the Arwacas hidden in the woods, which were pilots for the Spanyards, and rowed their canoas; of which I kept the chiefest for a pilot, and *caried him with me to Guiana*, by whom I understood where and in what countreyes the Spanyards had laboured for golde, though I made not the same knowen to all. (*DG* 10:389; italics mine)

> . . . but we fastened an ancker upon the lande, and with maine strength drewe her off: and so the fifteenth day *wee discovered afarre off the mountaines of Guiana* to our great joy, and towards the evening had a slent of a Northerly winde that blew very strong, which brought us in sight of the great river Orenoque. (*DG* 10:392; italics mine)

> When I came to Cumana in the West Indies afterwards by chance I spake with a Spaniard dwelling not farre from thence, a man of great travell, and *after hee knew that I had bene in Guiana*, and so farre directly West as Caroli, the first question hee asked me was, whether I had seene any of the Ewaipanoma, which are those without heads: who being esteemed a most honest man of his word, and in all things else, tolde mee that hee had seene many of them: I may not name him, because it may be for his disadvantage. (*DG* 10:406–07; italics mine)

The reader responds to Ralegh's statement that he had carried with him an Arwacan pilot "to Guiana" and that he had told a Spaniard that he had "bene in Guiana" by absorbing them in the process of digesting the narrative of a travel that includes meetings with natives, dialogues with captive Spaniards, and anthropological accounts of the cultures and customs of tribal life. Even the evocation of the prospect topos—"wee discovered afarre off the mountaines of Guiana"—dilates on and uncovers for the masculinist gaze the exciting landscape of a new land. Vicarious engagement in experiencing the closeness and actual presence of Guiana is elicited. The end of the journey is not only anticipated, but imminent. At the same time that Ralegh's narrative documents his failure to arrive at the site of desire, it interweaves into its narrative the fictions of success. Those fictions involve nothing less than announcing his presence in Guiana to various characters he meets in his travels.

The rhetoric of conviction that Ralegh manipulates to reinforce for his reader impressions of the materiality of Guiana's immaterial wealth is necessarily situated against the presence of an anti-Spanish discourse that links the thirst for gold to Spanish rapaciousness and greed.[22] In order to distinguish himself from the much-hated Spaniard, the English colonist must, at least on the surface, show himself unmotivated by the allure of gold. But Ralegh is not in a position to adopt a posture of indifference to the possibility of obtaining the fabled wealth of Guiana. In fact, he offers no pretence whatsoever about his deep need and desire to obtain possession of this gold because it is a necessary item not only for effecting his literal and symbolic negotiations with his queen, but also for empowering the self. Ralegh harbors fantasies of being immortalized as the discoverer of a new land and possessor of its immense wealth. His approach to the entire subject of Guiana's gold is shaped by immediate and pragmatic concerns. He needs first and foremost to get back on a right footing with his queen; and the way to do so is to feed Guiana's wealth into the royal coffers and state treasury. But Ralegh's desire is also informed by his view that England is a nation that needs to enter into contestation with nations like Spain in order to etch out a place for itself in the international political arena. For England to make its mark and consolidate a distinct and national identity, it must be remorseless in ravaging another land and hoarding more gold than that already appropriated shamelessly by the Spaniards. It is ironic that even as Ralegh envisions a significant place for England in the world of nations, he can only imagine the possibilities of its fruition in terms of securing wealth through pillaging another's possession. In *The Discoverie of Guiana*, the discourse of merchandising and mercantile engagements does not figure in Ralegh's conception of the emergence of England as a viable political entity.

Ralegh does everything to impress upon his reader the proximity and actuality of Guiana's presence because he can, at a very basic level, only offer accounts by people who claim to have experienced the materiality of Guiana. The reader of *The Discoverie* receives in effect an account of accounts, sometimes even an account of accounts of accounts. Distance appears to be the inevitable experience of reading Ralegh's text. The efforts expanded to close that distance, like Ralegh's very own experience in the Orinoco, only make the end in sight recede further: eternally deferred, to borrow a Derridean formulation. Ralegh's statements suggesting he has been in Guiana register a rhetorical effort to annihilate the experience and sensations of distantiation. It aims to communicate the impression of concreteness and materiality. If the stories given by the Spaniards and the Indians Ralegh recounts in his narrative are shaped in part or to a large extent by the author's own projections of El Dorado, then they are in a very real sense Ralegh's own story: his dreams and his fantasies. Ralegh's intermittent claims to being there in Guiana reveal the core of those fantasies without the interruptive and mediating figures of captive Spaniards and Indian chieftains, figures whose very presence prevents the text from escaping the impressions of absence.

How do veracity and truth, and together with that the whole subject of verifiability, figure in a text constantly negotiating the spaces of materiality and immateriality, presence and absence, success and failure, fact and fiction? To begin, it is interesting to note that "honest" and "true" are operative words in *The Discoverie of Guiana*. Toward the close of the document, Ralegh enforces the "veracity" of his claim that there is abundant gold in Guiana through assertion. He protests "before the Majestie of God [that what he says about the state and condition of Guiana are] true" (*DG* 10:431). And in the last paragraph of *The Discoverie of Guiana*, the reader is told: "I trust in God, this being true, will suffice" (*DG* 10:431). But the history of the reception of Ralegh's text tells us there were skeptics who did not believe in Ralegh's "truth," questioning if he had even set foot on the Orinoco instead of hiding out somewhere in Cornwall. The *evidentia* Ralegh brings back from the Orinoco fails to validate the language of performance in the *Discoverie* for many people, including the queen herself, calling into question the claims made to "truth" and "honesty." Ralegh has made accommodations to the possible disbelief of his reader by shifting the focus of his propaganda from gold to the figure of Elizabeth I. If material *evidentia* fails to validate the language of performance, then encomium may just succeed in doing so.

Toward the conclusion of *The Discoverie of Guiana* Ralegh delivers his famous statement, "Guiana is a countrey that hath yet her maydenhead" (*DG* 10:428) and reasserts his relationship to his monarch:

> This Empire is made knowen to her Majestie by her owne vassall, and
> by him that oweth to her more duetie then an ordinary subject, so
> that it shall ill sort with the many graces and benefites which I have
> received to abuse her Highnesse, either with fables or imaginations.
> The countrey is alreadie discovered, many nations wonne to her Maj-
> esties love and obedience, and those Spaniardes which have latest and
> longest laboured about the conquest, beaten out, discouraged and
> disgraced, which among these nations were thought invincible. Her
> Majestie may in this enterprize employ all those souldiers and gentle-
> men that are younger brethren, and all captaines and chieftaines that
> want employment, and the charge will be onely the first setting out
> in victualling and arming them: for after the first or second yeere I
> doubt not but to see in London a Contractation house of more receipt
> for Guiana, then there is now in Sivill for the West Indies. (*DG* 10:430)

In this passage, Ralegh refers once again to his expedition as a
duty performed by a loyal courtier in the interests of his royal
mistress. He affirms that the empire of Guiana is already discovered, a declarative statement that, as similarly elsewhere at various
moments in the text, remains unsupported by the finality of
performance. With this assertion, he proceeds to generating encomium in which the queen is told she has won the love and obedience of "many nations." This is thanks, of course, as the
implication goes, to the efforts of the courtier. England's Virgin
Queen has succeeded in winning the affections of these different
nations where the Spaniards have been "beaten out, discouraged
and disgraced." Ralegh announces the extension of Elizabeth's
symbolic sovereignty to large areas of the New World; but what
is not established is whether Elizabeth will realize that symbolic
sovereignty as literal authority, a materialization that can only be
enabled through colonization. Ralegh says that all that is required
to literalize this symbolic sovereignty is to provide assistance in
basic logistical support.

Ralegh's hyperbolic praise continues. Elizabeth's authority is
even oracled in Peru, a reference that assimilates to itself the
heroics of the Spanish conquistadors and epic foreshadowing of
a new emerging *imperium*. The gods themselves have prophesied
the greatness of Elizabeth and England, which like the first Rome
celebrated by Virgil, is about to fulfill its destiny as a mighty imperial power headed by a Virgin Queen. Mary Campbell percep-
tively observes that this queen admired with a kind of idolatrous
awe by the Indians at the close of the *Discoverie* is none other than
Gloriana, Spenser's "faerie queene."[23] And once England's great
Virgin Queen fulfills her place in prophecy and history, the exten-

sion of her literal and symbolic body across the far reaches of the
Americas will impel even the Amazons to learn of and celebrate
her name. The figure of the Amazon occupies an interesting place
in Ralegh's text. Louis Montrose has commented on the Amazon
as the "radical Other figured but not fully contained by the collec-
tive imagination of European patriarchy."[24] Part of their destabilizing effect on conceptions of gendered and political power
relations is that, in the Amazonian economy, the women are synonymous with the political nation.[25] Montrose cautions against an
overreadiness to link figures of the Amazon to the praise of a
female ruler; but he then proceeds to evoke a paradigmatic moment in which the queen at Tilbury before the Armada strikes
her male soldiers as resembling the Amazon in her martial stance.
It appears that this "androgynous personal symbolism" fleshed
out in the literal body of a woman wearing a steel corselet over
her white velvet dress proved disorienting to, if not disconcerting
for, England's male soldiers.[26] Given that the figure of the Amazon
can signify either as radical Other or as mighty prince in the
English cultural imagination, it is tempting to read Ralegh's situating of Elizabeth as paradigm of female rule and authority for the
Amazons as inscribing both encomium and critique. The queen
he celebrates as England's great monarch also possesses all the
dispositions of the erratic and unpredictable woman. Ebullient
praise always has the ability to mask political criticism.

Ralegh's first voyage to Guiana in 1595 constitutes a disgraced
courtier's expedient response to the exigencies of an unfavorable
situation. Having incurred the monarch's displeasure, Ralegh had
attempted to set up a colonial space at the periphery of civilized
society, a necessary move designed to reinscribe himself at the
center of life in the court. Ralegh's venture to Guiana cannot be
divorced from a deep desire for restoration after the experience
of disgrace, and also for an empowerment of the self that he
hoped might transcend the restrictive pressures exerted by a tem-
peramental monarch and her court. Fused with the ostensible
motif of carving out a new space in the interests of the monarch
that he served was the implicit recognition that any success in
establishing oneself as the discoverer of a new world would bring
with it not only fame and glory, but security against the giddy
whims and unpredictable workings of princes. In the case of Ralegh, the motives of expansionism are inseparable from fantasies
to advance the interests of the self. Obviously, if Ralegh succeeded
in obtaining the wealth of Guiana, he would, in addition to fulfilling his goal of offering a priceless gift to the queen, also bestow

upon himself the gift of a certain political freedom. If the queen were given the wealth of Guiana, she would reciprocate in kind by reinstating the courtier to the privileged position he once enjoyed. It is important to remember, however, that Ralegh's desire for restoration to royal favor cannot be extricated from his trenchant criticism of the queen, criticism that had the effect, if considered closely, of jeopardizing the ostensible narrative of praise and encomium. Stephen Greenblatt reminds us that it is significant that the queen probably never read, for example, *Ocean to Cynthia;* for this poetic fragment contained powerful criticism of Elizabeth that could only have been ill received by her.[27] Even as Ralegh labored to be restored to royal favor in the midst of his deep feelings that he had been unjustly treated, other observers commented on the power politics at play between subject and monarch. One important poet who revealed some of his perceptions of Ralegh's relationship with his queen was Edmund Spenser.

In the same year that Sir Walter Ralegh undertook his voyage to Guiana and published *The Discoverie*, Edmund Spenser published *Colin Clouts Come Home Againe*, a pastoral narrative that rehearses Colin's meeting with another shepherd, significantly named "the shepheard of the Ocean."[28] This shepherd is a transparent reference to Ralegh, while Colin is the poet's persona. In this poem, Cynthia (Elizabeth I) had assigned the charge of the ocean to the shepherd (Ralegh). In pursuit of his duty, this shepherd characteristically expresses his undying devotion: "Where I will liue or die at her beheast, / And serue and honour her with faithfull mind" (lines 254–55). The queen, who is the royal mistress of her subject and the head of England's body politic, is also the genius of her nation's expansionist ambitions: "Those be the shepheards which my *Cynthia* serue, / At sea, beside a thousand moe at land: / For land and sea my *Cynthia* doth deserue / To haue in her commandement at hand" (lines 260–63).

Colin Clouts identifies itself as a poem that celebrates the greatness of England's Virgin Queen. But it must also express support for Ralegh, who is having difficulties with his queen. Ralegh had earlier visited Spenser at Kilcolman in the early autumn of 1589; and he had also, before the close of that year, presented him to the queen, a kindness Spenser responds to with immense gratitude in *Colin Clouts:* "The shepheard of the Ocean . . . / Vnto that Goddesse grace me first enhanced, / And to mine oaten pipe enclin'd her eare" (lines 358–60). Spenser's pastoral narrative registers a sympathetic response toward Ralegh's particular situation, but it tries instinctively not to engage itself in criticism of the queen or her court. Ebullient encomium must be sustained by a poet harboring a desire to obtain preferment in the court. The attempt is, however, only partially successful, for the poem makes vivid distinctions between an idyllic world of pastoral and the political world of the court. Colin tells another shepherd named Thestylis that he needs to correct the perceptions of young shepherds who are all too eager to leave their "quiet home" (line 686) to find a good life in the court. In this poem, the idyllic world of pastoral celebrated by Colin also stands for the Ireland Spenser momentarily left when he came to London to be introduced to the queen. Returning to England proper from the margins of civilized society, Spenser nevertheless writes about the pull exerted by an Ireland that has ironically become "home"; referred to as "this barrein soyle" (line 656), Ireland is a better place to be in than the court.

Pastoral is also a literary genre Spenser employs in order to highlight how different shepherds/poets fail to find fulfillment in the service of the shepherdess Cynthia. Spenser has Ralegh in mind when he provides his list of forsaken shepherds: Harpalus, Corydon, Alcyon, and others. Standing for the transcendent and otherworldly identity of the monarch, the "diuine" (line 345) and "sacred' (line 349) Cynthia is also the object of desire in pastoral, but one that is distant and cruel. Significantly, this Cynthia is excluded from the poem's concluding vision of pastoral, replaced by Rosalind; at the same time, the central authority on the questions of love is no longer the shepherd of the ocean, but Colin himself. Cynthia's disappearance before the emergence of Rosalind replaces the queen's transcendent mythological identity with a vision of pastoral centered on Colin as Cupid's priest. Ultimately, for Spenser, the court continues to be the real center for legitimating individual and social identity. It is when this court does not fulfill Spenser's dreams of advancement that it is subjected to the critique found in *Colin Clouts,* or to the much more trenchant interrogation encoded in the second installment of *The Faerie Queene.* In the 1596 supplement to the first three books of Spenser's epic project, Gloriana—the final vision of the romance quest—is never attained, locking all the six books and "Two Cantos of Mutabilitie" forever in an endless quest. Spenser, like Ralegh, cannot divorce himself from considerations of power in the production of poetic encomia.

Sometimes poetic praise is inadequate to accommodate the particularities of a certain political situation. Ralegh, for example, found that he had no recourse to a convincing rhetoric of praise in relating to the first Stuart monarch; all he could ask for at the end of a long thirteen-year imprisonment in the Tower was that James I grant him the permission to repeat the project of journeying to Guiana to appropriate its gold. The king consented to the request. If Ralegh had figured himself in the earlier *Discoverie of Guiana* as an enemy of Spain, he would conclude his second voyage with an altercation with Spanish settlers in the Orinoco. Ralegh undertook his second voyage to Guiana fully aware he had to negotiate a political minefield because the area of the Orinoco he must necessarily traverse was laid claim to by the Spanish empire. He knew that the potential for a clash between the English and the Spanish was extremely high. James I could not afford to have any altercation take place between the English and the Spanish in Guiana because that would seriously compromise the hard-bought peace that he had managed to conclude with Spain at the beginning of his reign. Furthermore Gondomar, Spain's ambassador to England, was also visibly anxious about the possibility of an outbreak of hostility. Ralegh was undertaking an expansionist venture in a region that was understood to belong to Spain. Unable to get James to rescind his decision to endorse Ralegh's projected journey to the Orinoco basin, Gondomar instead forced the English monarch to subject Ralegh to a series of harsh and close-to-impossible conditions. Ralegh had to pledge with his life that not a single Spanish subject would be harmed, and also that the English party he led would not set foot on Spanish territory. The latter condition created an immediate conundrum because Spain claimed the entire Orinoco region for its own. Ralegh responded strategically by accepting Spanish control over the Orinoco, with the exception of its right bank. The right bank, he insisted, belonged to the English, and Spanish presence in this particular area constituted an infringement of territorial rights. Any gold discovered in the area staked out by the English belonged rightfully to the crown.

If Ralegh succeeded in enriching the impoverished crown treasury with the pure gold of Guiana, he could expect to be pardoned by James for his capital crime of treason and restored to his old glory. But if he failed in his enterprise, he would be completely ruined, especially if that failure was further contaminated by so much as the shadow of a scuffle between the English party and the Spanish colonists. Unfortunately but predictably, a catastrophic confrontation did take place. Ralegh's eldest son, Wat, attacked the Spanish settlement at San Thomé. The town was taken by the

English but Wat was killed. When Ralegh learned about the attack on San Thomé, he knew that he had forfeited his life.

The significance of Ralegh's desire to undertake the second voyage to Guiana requires further commentary. According to Stephen Greenblatt, Ralegh sincerely believed in the existence of the fabled mines and was convinced that he would deliver to the crown treasure that would enrich the royal coffer at the same time that it would procure his pardon.[29] Remarkably, that deep conviction and Ralegh's massive gamble were based on one man's word, Laurence Keymis's, that he had seen the fabled mines. Greenblatt tells us that Ralegh never doubted this account, not because Keymis possessed the reputation for being a reliable witness, but because he himself never lost his romantic vision of recovering paradise on earth.[30] For Sir Walter Ralegh, the Eden of the colonial imagination was not the stuff of fiction, but reality itself. On one level, then, Ralegh may be viewed as a monumental dreamer locked tragically into an outmoded frame of reference, clinging on to old fantasies about gaining access to cities of gold. The symbolic forms expressed in Elizabeth's fabulous and golden reign encouraged such flights of fancy. But if Ralegh's transaction with James I for permission to make a second trip to Guiana appears to reveal he had not divested himself of a mindset shaped by Elizabethan mythmaking, it can also indicate the culmination of a dark cynicism that came at the end of having spent thirteen years in the Tower for treason. And if it was, in fact, such a cynicism that led Ralegh to embark on an enterprise that any reasonable man knows will most probably end in failure, then the voyage to Guiana was, as it were, a project undertaken with a suicidal impulse.

The second voyage to Guiana failed and Ralegh returned to England to his execution. One question persists in this narrative of Ralegh's tragic end: Why did he return to England when the experience of his earlier buccaneering activities must surely have equipped him with the knowledge and means to survive on his own outside of England? In a letter addressed to James I on 24 September 1618, Ralegh made it clear to the king that his return to England after the incident at San Thomé was a voluntary choice. Outside of England, he was the "master of [his] life"; if he had decided to sell his ships and goods, he would immediately have "put five or six thousand pounds in [his] purse."[31] Ralegh's letter also indicates that he made the choice of returning to England, so that the king would not be misunderstood for having "given libertie and trust to a man whose ende was but the recovery of his libertie, and whoe had betrayed [his] Majesties trust": the interests of the monarch are privileged over his own.[32] Furthermore, Ralegh celebrates James's "wisdome and goodnes"[33] and registers his trust in the monarch to ensure that justice is carried out. And this justice, if it is enacted, will certainly ensure that Ralegh is not held responsible for the outbreak of hostility between the English and the Spanish at San Thomé. Not only had he always, Ralegh elaborates, exercised great restraint in dealing with the Spanish, he did not direct the attack on the Spanish settlement.

In writing to James I that he chose to become "poore" when he was in reality "rich" is to fashion for himself an identity in which he is the declared master of his own political destiny, controlling his relationship with the king.[34] Ralegh portrays his return to England not only as a choice made by a man who possessed the power to exercise absolute control over his life, but also as a form of self-sacrifice. If James is a just and noble king, as Ralegh's letter describes, then any decision of his to realize Ralegh's execution necessarily negates those attributes. Endorsing Ralegh's death would reveal the monarch's true identity as a tyrant who exercises his authority and power arbitrarily and unscrupulously. Ralegh wants to contest James's belief that the exercise of power is the prince's prerogative, sanctioned by God. The Stuart monarch had written in his *True Lawe of Free Monarchies* that kings are appointed by God and not by law; in James's formulation, monarchs obey the law not by compulsion, but by choice. James's *True Lawe of Free Monarchies* argues that God confers absolute authority on kings. Given this divine mandate, subjects have no choice, but to endure the worst form of tyranny rather than rebel. The absolute power of the prince and the complete helplessness of the subject are vividly dramatized in the death sentence meted out to Ralegh on the conviction of high treason in 1603, a sentence that would not be carried out until much later, in 1618. Richard Wilson argues that this commutation of Ralegh's death sentence amounts to a "tragical comedy" of sorts, staged by James to enact the intervening hand of mercy. But mercy's intervention, in this case, does not translate into liberty for the condemned Ralegh; what it does instead is replace "the spectacle of the scaffold" with an economy of "surveillance and confinement."[35] Wilson reads this literal and symbolic commutation in terms of a paradigm shift, in which Jacobean justice—as embodied in the regal body of the prince—elected to break Ralegh's spirit rather than his body.[36] The carceral economy, in Foucault's terms, consti-

tutes a far more technically refined and effective means of exercising control over the individual and social body, partly because it removes citizen reprisals in reaction to atrocities committed in the name of the monarch and the state. Ralegh's body can be read as the symbolic site that James I, the new monarch, chose to demonstrate the absolute power he exercised over a man recognized to be "the proudest of the Elizabethans,"[37] and also a pawn in the larger political relationship between the English monarch and Spain. James had really no desire to jeopardize the friendly relations he had worked so hard to establish with England's traditional enemy, and Ralegh was a convenient and necessary sacrifice for guaranteeing political stability.

Ralegh might also have found it necessary to return to England and to certain execution because he adhered implicitly to the codes of chivalry that defined much of the interactions taking place between monarch and subject in Elizabeth's reign. Honor holds an important place in the articulation of these codes. It is possible that Ralegh functioned with a distinct understanding of honor when he returned to England after the failure of his second Guiana expedition, enacting in real life an adherence to the very codes of chivalry that shape Antony's raison d'être as portrayed in Shakespeare's *Antony and Cleopatra*. In this play, the politically astute Augustus knows full well the limits within which the recalcitrant Roman can function. Antony works with the codes of chivalry and not with the Machiavellian expediency that defines the political space of Rome's pragmatic present. Significantly, as Jonathan Goldberg reminds us in *James I and the Politics of Literature*, the first Stuart monarch defined his reign symbolically with reference to Augustus Caesar's pragmatic rule.[38] Ralegh was fully aware of this new Stuart mythmaking, but he did not divest himself of an identity forged in many ways by the Elizabethan symbolic order. Perhaps the decision not to transact with the codes of Jacobean absolutism is itself a critique and gesture of resistance. The act of returning to an England and monarch demanding his head for treason could constitute an interrogation of the tyranny that marked the rules of kings. Ralegh's death subjected James to critique by implication.

Mary Fuller has also contextualized for us James I's response to Ralegh's failure to bring back the gold he promised from Guiana. The king's response is registered in a document, *Declaration of the Demeanor and Cariage of Sir Walter Raleigh*, produced James's behest after Ralegh's execution.[39] The ostensible but convincing reason given for James's displeasure is that Ral

undertook the second voyage to Guiana to "procure his libertie, and then to make new fortunes for himselfe, casting abroad onely this tale of the Mine as a lure to get aduenturers and followers; hauing in his eye the *Mexico* Fleete, the sacking and spoyle of Townes planted with Spaniards, the depredation of Ships, and such other purchase."[40] But the *Declaration,* Fuller elaborates, then appears to proceed to *charge* Ralegh with what amounts to "neglecting a 'labor' of 'nourishing' and 'maintaining' belief—belief that 'he meant to make his voyage upon the profite of the Mine'."[41] The "belief" referred to here is the understood purpose of tapping to the full the wealth of Guiana, of positing through performance the reality of its material existence. James I, according to the *Declaration,* is not interested in yet another narratological performance of conviction, like the one attempted in the earlier *The Discoverie of Guiana.* To undertake the second voyage to Guiana in order to "substantiate his own language with material proof—a token of reliability to generate further credit" did not coincide with the reason underwriting the king's commissioning and funding of the project.[42] James, Fuller tells us, "expected payment in full": in other words, nothing short of being brought and given the gold mines of Guiana that Ralegh had insured with his life.[43] Ralegh was finally accused of fabrication and misrepresentation, of narrativizing that which is not as that which is. The disjunction between the rhetorical performance of conviction and the production of material proof, and between an empire nowhere and an empire somewhere, is read as a form of deceit by James. The very same accusations of fabrication and misrepresentation tainted the earlier 1596 reception of *The Discoverie of Guiana.* But their repetition in Jacobean England some two decades later signifies in a radically different symbolic and political context. In 1596 Ralegh was able, even with the insignificant "proof" of the mine that his powerful and romantic imagination conjured to be out there, to win back a modicum of the queen's pleasure. The "proof" that moved Elizabeth I was not the materiality of Guiana's gold, but its symbolic crystallization of the "painefull pilgrimage" (*DG* 10 : 340) highlighted in Ralegh's dedicatory preface to Charles Howard and Robert Cecil. Ralegh had announced quite explicitly that his expedition in the Orinoco basin was undertaken as a kind of penitential ritual with the hopes of gaining restoration into royal favor. His negligible ocular and material "proof" could still hope to obtain a meaning in the Elizabethan symbolic economy; the Virgin Queen might have scrambled the

codes defining how the game of courtly love was played, but she continued to have the ability to play.

In *A Relation of the Second Voyage to Guiana*, Laurence Keymis rouses his readers to shame for their timidity and absence of conviction, giving Ralegh the recognition that readers of *The Discoverie* refused to give. *A Relation* functions as an intervening text striving to break the deadlock of unsympathetic response. A great deal of the blame is placed on the reader and passive observer: "concerning Guiana, . . . nothing is begun, before all be ended" because of general apathy and lack of support.[44] Keymis tells his reader that he is writing "to remove all fig-leaves from our unbeliefe, that either it may have cause to shake off the colourable pretences of ignorance: or if we will not be perswaded; that our selfe-will may rest inexcusable."[45] After material *evidentia* fails to validate the language of performance, *The Discoverie of Guiana* and *A Relation of the Second Voyage to Guiana* trace Guiana's immateriality not to the lack or absence of substantive performance, but to the prejudices of the skeptical and apathetic reader.

Prefixed to Laurence Keymis's *A Relation of the Second Voyage to Guiana*, George Chapman's "De Guiana, Carmen Epicum" evokes the motifs of Ralegh's *The Discoverie of Guiana*: gold and the importance of expanding England's political and colonial body to the Americas. In *The Discoverie of Guiana*, Ralegh bases his case for the imperative of England's colonization of Guiana on the nation's need to propel itself to the forefront of the international political arena, to move from marginality to centrality. Guiana's gold is indispensable for the coffers of the nation, and it facilitates negotiations and transactions with other European nations from a position of inherent privilege. Ralegh's *The Discoverie of Guiana* attempts to rest its claims on a recognition of pragmatic considerations. In George Chapman's poem, "De Guiana," Guiana is still gilded and there continues to be a call for England to extend and expand itself into the New World. But Chapman's Guiana is not the passive and virginal female body awaiting ravishment, but sister to and the daughter of England:

> *Riches,* and *Conquest,* and *Renowme* I sing,
> *Riches* with honour, *Conquest* without bloud,
> Enough to seat the Monarchie of earth,
> Like to *Ioues* Eagle, on *Elizas* hand.
> *Guiana,* whose rich feet are mines of golde,
> Whose forehead knockes against the roofe of Starres,
> Stands on her tip-toes at faire *England* looking,

Kissing her hand, bowing her mightie breast,
And euery signe of all submission making,
To be her sister, and the daughter both
Of our most sacred Maide: whose barrennesse
Is the true fruite of vertue, that may get,
Beare and bring foorth anew in all perfection,
What heretofore sauage corruption held
In barbarous *Chaos;* and in this affaire
Become her father, mother, and her heire.

(lines 14–29)[46]

In the logic of Chapman's metaphor, England is female, a figuration consonant with the iconic identity of its presiding genius, Elizabeth I, whose virginity is fertile and procreative. England is also both Guiana's sibling and her mother. Biological filiation marks their relationship, precluding any politics of rape like that imagined by Ralegh. Furthermore, Guiana's materiality, linked to literal geographical land, opens outward and upward: her "rich feet are mines of golde" and her "forehead knockes against the roofe of Starres." Ralegh's narrative of pilgrimage and questing, bound to the horizonal axis of experience, is expanded in Chapman's poem into a vertical rise in which the very stars of heaven are reached by Guiana's expanding body. Metaphorical expansions of Chapman's kind communicate the sense of epic dimensions. If *The Discoverie of Guiana* is based on a powerful literalism as Ralegh negotiates the harshness and treachery of the topography of the Orinoco, "De Guiana" is centered on metaphor, making it what Jeffrey Knapp calls "oddly spiritual."[47] Knapp offers an incisive meditation on the tensions present in the quest for gold in the writings of the English Renaissance. Gold is an important end to be sought after in the material ambitions of self and nation, but it must at the same time be divorced from the moral contaminations of greed and lust. The reputation of the Spaniard's rapacious greed for gold is one that the English can do very well without in conceptualizing their own colonial agenda. As Knapp also observes of Chapman, "Enticed by Guiana's gold from a Prospero-like contemplative isolation, antimaterialists like Chapman will in turn transform that gold from an end in itself to an earthly manifestation of spiritual power":[48] "Sit till you see a woonder, *Vertue* rich: / Till *Honour* hauing golde, rob golde of honour" (lines 74–75). Chapman may be "immaterial" or "spiritual" in his poetic emphasis when compared to Ralegh in *The Discoverie of Guiana,* but he is just as deeply caught up in the dreams of territorial expansion. "De Guiana" gives to the object of gold an otherworldliness in a narrative that argues the importance of its material acquisition: the lines, "Golde is our Fate, / Which all our actes doeth fashion and create" (lines 146–47), carry both materialist and antimaterialist resonances.

"De Guiana" indeed beseeches the queen:

> let your breath
> Goe foorth vpon the waters, and create
> A golden worlde in this our yron age,
> And be the prosperous forewind to a Fleet,
> That seconding your last, may goe before it
> In all successe of profite and renowme.
>
> (lines 30–35)

Elizabeth I is asked to engage in an act that repeats the creation of the universe when the spirit of God hovered over the face of the waters and gave it form. The queen is creative and procreative principle, and the form that emerges out of her constructive and constitutive power is "A golden worlde," the expanse of empire. The breath gives form by generating the impetus propelling ocean travel: "be the prosperous forewind to a Fleet," the poet exhorts England's Virgin Queen. Following this encomiastic praise of Elizabeth I, Chapman proceeds to exhort the queen to exert a force that is not momentary and violent, but sustained and extensive:

> Then be not like a rough and violent wind,
> That in the morning rends the Forrestes downe,
> Shoues vp the seas to heauen, makes earth to tremble,
> And toombes his wastfull brauerie in the Euen:
> But as a riuer from a mountaine running,
> The further he extends, the greater growes,
> And by his thriftie race strengthens his streame,
> Euen to ioyne battale with th'imperious sea
> Disdaining his repulse, and in despight
> Of his proud furie, mixeth with his maine,
> Taking on him his titles and commandes:
> So let thy soueraigne Empire be encreast.
>
> (lines 52–63)

Associated with the forces of the natural world, Elizabeth will extend her symbolic body across and into the medium of water connecting England to the larger world. It is in the seas that Elizabeth must wrestle with *Iberian Neptune* (line 64), Chapman's name for King Philip II of Spain. Command of the seas is needed for England to launch its own epic ventures, to send her own Argonauts in search of the golden fleece in Guiana. The Armada is never far from Chapman's epic imagination.

Where Sir Walter Ralegh persuades the queen to colonize Guiana by impressing upon her the materiality of the land in the face of immaterial proof, Chapman amplifies immateriality—love, honor, nobility, glory—to generate support for getting at the material. Chapman does not ground his call for English expansionism on material verifiability, but on eliciting an emotive response to the sense of England's epic capability.

Toward the conclusion of "De Guiana," Chapman sees Queen Elizabeth "rise from her throne, / Her eares and thoughtes in steepe amaze erected, / At the most rare endeuour of her power" (lines 149–51). This image of emergence coincides with the provision of the force—both figurative and literal—needed for Ralegh to fulfill his dreams of the colonization of Guiana: "And now she blesseth with her woonted Graces / Th' industrious Knight, the soule of this exploit, / Dismissing him to conuoy of his starres" (lines 152–54). Ralegh is celebrated:

> And now for loue and honour of his woorth,
> Our twise-borne Nobles bring him Bridegroome-like,
> That is espousde for vertue to his loue
> With feastes and musicke, rauishing the aire,
> To his *Argolian* Fleet, where round about
> His bating Colours English valure swarmes
> In haste, as if *Guianian Orenoque*
> With his Fell waters fell vpon our shore.
>
> (lines 155–62)

Espoused to his love who is England's Virgin Queen as well as the object of his desire that is Guiana, Ralegh is brought in "proper Virginian fashion" as a bridegroom to his fleet.[49] At this moment, the distance of the seas separating England from Guiana is annihilated for "*Guianian Orenoque*" appears to have lapped the English shore; and likewise, even before anything is begun, the wind that is supposed to give push to the English fleet bound for Guiana "Sets [the Englishmen's] glad feet on smooth *Guianas* breast" (line 164). The poem ends with the prophetic vision of an English imperialistic *fait accompli:*

> And there do Pallaces and temples rise
> Out of the earth, and kisse th'enamored skies,
> Where new *Britania*, humblie kneeles to heauen,

The world to her, and both at her blest feete,
In whom the Circles of all Empire meet.

(lines 180–85)

If as Louis Montrose says, Ralegh's *The Discoverie of Guiana* registers "the embarrassment of England's cultural and imperial *belatedness*" in its "anxious and impatient patriotism,"[50] then we can say that Chapman's "De Guiana" writes with much greater confidence of England's epic capabilities as a colonial power. Chapman's prophetic vision occupies its proper place at the beginning of Keymis's *A Relation of the Second Voyage to Guiana,* written to reinforce Ralegh's aim to obtain royal endorsement and support for his desire to undertake the colonization of Guiana. Where Ralegh attempts to do so through a narrative that impresses the materiality of Guiana's wealth, Chapman does so more through the immateriality of a prophetic vision whose hold on the reader depends on its epic force.

2

"Let Us Possess One World": John Donne, Rationalizing Theology, and the Discourse of Virginia

WHEN WE TALK ABOUT THE DISCOURSE OF COLONIALISM AND IMPE-
rialism in Tudor and Stuart England, we need to identify the
conditions and forces that push a nation toward expanding its
territory beyond the seas. Obviously the political and economic
factors of having to engage in contestation with other European
nations for prestige and a place in the world of international
commerce are compelling ones. The presence of imperial Spain
and the threat it poses furnishes the English with an identifiable
political entity open to rhetorical demonization and textual containment. But there are other factors less tangible, but no less
urgent. These include the rapid growth in projects associated with
scientific discovery and endeavor, and new knowledge obtained
about the universe in which the earth has its place. With the
growth in scientific awareness comes the realization that time and
nature must somehow be harnessed effectively and efficiently. We
find this cognizance evident in a play like Shakespeare's *The Tempest,* where the compulsive necessity to observe time is needed for
projects and systems to remain intact. And even as the Ptolemaic
universe loses its credibility before the revolution inaugurated by
Copernicus and resurrected by Galileo, poets and dramatists respond with the terrifying sense that things are getting out of
control.

In Renaissance England, expansion of the epistemological and
geographical domains leads to the construction of a self and subjectivity riddled through with exhilaration and terror. A sense of
relentless urgency predominates, expressed through the terrifying need to outstrip time and the fracturing of existing societal
and theological structures. Unsettling expansions of this kind also
lead to the crystallization of new metaphors used to describe and

64

construct subjectivity. One poet in the English Renaissance who effects this memorably is John Donne. For Donne gives to the reader a self launched excitingly into space and time. His love lyrics thrive on *agon*, in which the relationship between the man and his mistress is articulated through rhetorical contestation and dialectic. In the deep ironies of the love lyrics, the woman is given opportunities to contest and resist the advances made or the rhetorical logic given by the man, but she is always finally contained, even if precariously, by the controlling voice and stance of the male. Donne's male narrator offers rhetorical concessions to the woman in order to facilitate his agonistic discourse, one needed for the construction of subjectivity. I will elaborate on Donne's portrayal of the relationship between the male speaker and the woman later on in this chapter with reference to Renaissance England's colonial concerns.

One of the central metaphors used by Donne to situate the identity of the narrator is that of sea and travel. The medium of water through which Renaissance England makes contact with the larger international community becomes the metaphor through which Donne can poeticize the painful experience of parting and through which he can also effect the resolution of union. The navigational images and metaphors cannot be separated from Donne's fascination with maps and cartography. For Donne, ocean travel can be evoked in the play of metaphor, but it also points to a preoccupation with scrutiny and inspection. In "Hymn to God my God, in my Sickness," the physicians poring over the sick body of Donne the patient are specifically said to be examining and scrutinizing a map of the world, a cartographic parchment that figures the process of translation from death to life in heaven and that also points to a new technology that permits accommodating geographical configurations at a glance. The analogy of man as the microcosmic unit of a macrocosmic universe now gets articulated with compulsive reference to cartographical and navigational metaphors that are central tropes in the discourse of colonialism. In Donne's love lyrics, bodies are constantly being made subject to scrutiny. Donne is examined by his physicians just as the lady in "Elegy 19: To His Mistress Going to Bed" is scrutinized by the desiring male; similarly, the metaphorical map of the world is subjected to Donne's gaze as the real artifact is pored over by men in early modern England possessing a desire to travel to and explore new worlds.

Maps and cartography constitute important signifiers of Renaissance England's emerging colonial ambitions. In *Forms of Na-*

tionhood, Richard Helgerson tells us that the maps and atlases produced in Elizabethan England by such various figures as Christopher Saxton, William Camden, and Michael Drayton helped to strengthen a people's sense of both local and national identity. Cartographies and chorographies create this sense of identity by forging affiliations between people and the area of land represented on the map. When people begin identifying themselves with a parcel of land, say a county seat represented on a map, it does not take long for that identification to expand into the larger dimensions of a patriotic experience. In the largest possible cartographic context, the geographical entity called the British Isles becomes not simply a geographical reality but a political and ideological one. A people's sense of nationalism, fed in part by its affiliative and emotive connections with land, is a necessary component in the rise of a colonial consciousness. Helgerson also points out that even as the English people began identifying themselves with the particularities of specific geographical areas offered by maps, the side effect is produced of displacing absolutist ideology by relegating the regal insignia found in maps to the literal and symbolic margins of a piece of cartographic parchment. If the body of the monarch can be symbolically tied to the land as head of the political entity that is England, that body can also be displaced when maps channel people's allegiance to literal land itself. What results is an emerging interest in property; and if England itself offers no adequate promise for satisfying a people's need and desire for property, then there are, of course, geographical spaces existing overseas that can become transformed into objects of desire. Ortelius's revolutionary world atlas, the *Theatrum Orbis Terrarum* (1570), for example, opens up the possibilities of a larger world existing outside the boundaries of England.[1]

When writers of the English Renaissance show themselves to be particularly fascinated by the existence of maps, even if the maps portrayed are largely metaphorical, they point to the emerging importance of cartography to the English cultural and literary imagination. If lands represented by maps once obtained significance in relation to the literal and symbolic body of the monarch, they now function to express individual needs and desires. The human body, locus of individual desire, becomes interchangeable with maps. Interestingly but predictably enough, when this human body gets translated figuratively into a piece of cartographic parchment, it becomes strangely disembodied. Essence gets demystified and the self begins to obtain its identity with reference to an increasingly technical discourse: the reading of maps cannot be separated from an interpretation of technical details intrinsic to the science of cartography. As individual identity gets defined in this new technical framework, it may find itself, like the male narrator in Donne's love lyrics, hurtling into the dimensions of a new space. Improvisations of the self then begin also to be articulated in spatial terms.

Donne's use of the metaphor of cartographers scrutinizing a map of the world to describe a situation of physicians examining the sick body of a patient in "Hymn to God my God, in my Sickness," offers one example of a conception of the self figured in spatial terms. The yoking together of heterogeneous ideas through lexical and figurative violence in this instance points to a culture's preoccupation with maps and, by extension, ocean travel. At the same time, it also draws self-referential attention to the poet's anxieties about a world that is far from cohesive and ordered. The agonistic relationship set up between the narrator and the woman that is a common feature of Donne's love lyrics attests to the presence of these anxieties. The general sense that the resolution arrived at in the conclusion of the individual love lyric is precarious and tenuous is enforced by the repetition of this agon and strained resolution in the other poems in the corpus. Michael Schoenfeldt would place the kind of linguistic violence found in Donne's poetry within a rhetorical economy in which "the cultivation of lyric obscurity" cannot be separated from "the achievement of poetic authority"; for Schoenfeldt, Donne is "one of the most intentionally opaque of Renaissance poets."[2] I wish to add to Schoenfeldt's observation by specifying that the opacity characteristic of Donne's poetry constitutes a vivid register of the poet's terrified sense that the world is not as stable as it is made out to be. The frailty of a decaying world is powerfully communicated in "An Anatomy of the World: The First Anniversary," a poem on the death of one Elizabeth, the daughter of Sir Robert Drury, Donne's patron and friend. In this poem, the elegiac strain is palpable in Donne's portrayal of a world that has lost an important figure of influence: Elizabeth. As a result, it is now dead and decayed:

> And new philosophy calls all in doubt,
> The element of fire is quite put out;
> The sun is lost, and th' earth, and no man's wit
> Can well direct him where to look for it.
> And freely men confess that this world's spent,
> When in the planets, and the firmament

They seek so many new; they see that this
Is crumbled out again to his atomies.
'Tis all in pieces, all coherence gone.

(lines 205–13)

The reality of a decayed world that can never be renewed is then linked directly to the theological ruin of humankind, beginning with Adam and Eve whose first marriage "was our funeral" (line 105). The poet's anatomy of the sad state of the world cannot separate itself from a consideration of theological dogma explaining the fall of the human race. "An Anatomy of the World" concludes with an otherworldly consolation of Elizabeth Drury's "second birth" (line 450) in heaven, but not before it registers Donne's resonating anxieties about the condition of a world that appears to be divorced from any affirmative understanding of order and harmony.

But in Donne's love lyrics, anxieties intertwine with and are accommodated, or at least partially diffused, by the expansion of creative energies embedded in the proliferation of linguistic and representational violence. Or they are channeled into imagining new and exciting ventures, like going out and colonizing new worlds. That is why Donne's lyrics with their distinctive violence are also poems of desire: lusting after the body of the woman with its interrelated motif of lusting after foreign lands. Whereas in "Elegy 19: To His Mistress Going to Bed," the male speaker figures the body of the woman as the New World to be discovered and appropriated, in "Elegy 18: Love's Progress," he depicts the journey to arrive at "that part / Which thou dost seek" (lines 74–75) by evoking metaphors linked to the activities of English merchandising and ocean travel. References are made to "the Islands Fortunate" (line 51), an old name for the Canary Islands, "her India" (line 65), and "fair Atlantic" (line 66), all linked in this poem to different parts of the female anatomy. The male speaker makes use of these references to demonstrate how difficult it is to arrive at "the centric part" (line 36) of the woman's genitalia if you begin from the face, the usual starting point for celebrating female beauty. There are simply too many obstacles to overcome. A rest from the long sea voyage of discovery needs to be made at "her fair Atlantic navel" (line 66), but even after that, the journey is not going to be smooth: "Yet ere thou be where thou wouldst be embayed, / Thou shalt upon another forest set, / Where many shipwreck, and no further get" (lines 68–70). The treacherous journey across the ocean is inseparable from the destructive nature of feminine beauty and its charms. After having highlighted in detail the treacherous terrain of the female body, the male speaker proceeds to offer a more direct route to "the centric part," beginning this time with the lower extremities.

Anatomized for the masculine gaze and controlled by the description given by the male speaker, the body of the woman in "Elegy 18: Love's Progress" constitutes the discursive site of a poet's "general critique of the cult of female beauty with its prescribed forms of hyperbolic praise."[3] This critique, as Arthur Marotti argues, is embedded in the elegy's "satiric debasement of women."[4] The poem can be said to invert the tradition and technique of the blazon by working to elicit a response from the man that deviates from the usual one, which is to be excited by the prospect of setting forth to discover new lands. The effect of arousal, which is the primary aim of an erotic poetics, is undermined by the text's figuration of the woman as a treacherous object. The poem suggests that the woman's genitalia—metaphorically linked to the wealth of India—is the goal of a misplaced masculine desire.

If "Elegy 18: Love's Progress" appears, on the surface, to be about masculine desire seeking fulfillment, it is also a poem that inscribes what Marotti refers to as an "antifeminist brutality."[5] Achsah Guibbory agrees with Marotti's view that underwriting Donne's need to assert male control over the woman in poetic representation are cultural anxieties generated by the reign of a female monarch.[6] Where the conventions of courtly love poetry are evoked in the *Elegies,* they are done so as to invert and interrogate the idealization of the mistress figure in an effort to reinstall the controlling voice of the man as producer and generator of discourse and narrative. Frequently in Donne's poetry—and this includes "Elegy 18: Love's Progress"—the desire to exert mastery over the body and identity of the woman through anatomy and itemization is expressed through metaphors obtained from English activities in the New World and its oceanic trading voyages. When the male speaker in Donne's love lyrics gets the opportunity to express his deep-felt emotions at having to leave to pursue business concerns abroad, he relishes the occasion afforded him to transform the experience into an intellectual exercise. The comfort he attempts to bring his mistress is couched in a rhetoric replete with imagistic and metaphorical violence, ironizing any ostensible display of genuine emotions.

Figuring a foreign and alien land as the body of a woman is a familiar rhetorical gesture in writings that aim to propagate the

politics of expansionism; it depends on an imagination of spatial
dimensions and sizes, in which different parts of the female anatomy become metaphors and metonymies for actual geographical
locations. The land as geographical Other is also the desiring
woman awaiting the arrival and embrace of the male lover. As
Samuel Purchas vividly describes the status of Virginia in "Virginias Verger: Or A Discourse shewing the benefits which may grow
to this Kingdome from American English Plantations, and spe-
cially those of Virginia and Summer Ilands":

> But looke upon Virginia; view her lovely lookes (howsoever like a
> modest Virgin she is now vailed with wild Coverts and shadie Woods,
> expecting rather ravishment then Mariage from her Native Savages)
> survay her Heavens, Elements, Situation; her divisions by armes
> of Bayes and Rivers into so goodly and well proportioned limmes and
> members; her Virgin portion nothing empaired, nay not yet improo-
> ved, in Natures best Legacies; the neighbouring Regions and Seas
> so commodious and obsequious; her opportunities for offence and
> defence; and in all these you shall see, that she is worth the wooing
> and loves of the best Husband. (*VV* 19:242)[7]

Ralegh's figuration of England as colonial ravisher in *The Discoverie of Guiana* becomes Purchas's figuration of the nation as
"the best Husband" in an analogy of courtship. The tradition of
the blazon underwrites Purchas's dilation of the different aspects
of a feminized Virginia to England's masculine gaze.

We recall also the famous lines in Donne's "Elegy 19: To His
Mistress Going to Bed":

> Licence my roving hands, and let them go
> Before, behind, between, above, below.
> O my America, my new found land,
> My kingdom, safeliest when with one man manned,
> My mine of precious stones, my empery,
> How blessed am I in this discovering thee!
> To enter in these bonds, is to be free;
> Then where my hand is set, my seal shall be.
>
> (lines 25–32)[8]

The thrill and ecstasy experienced in this poem are linked to the
privilege of naming: "O my America, my new found land, / My
kingdom." We hear echoes of this apostrophe in Columbus's exu-
berant effort to collate the discovery of new land with his geographical knowledge when he identified Haiti to the Pope in

1502: "This island is Tarsis, is Cythia, is Ophir and Ophaz and Cipanga, and we have named it Española" ("Esta isla es Tarsis, es Cethia, es Ofir y Ophaz é Cipanga, y nos la habemos llamado Española").[9] When Virginia—England's plantation in the New World—is, as Purchas puts it, "violently ravished by her owne ruder Natives" (VV 19:229), the land as site of individual and cultural desire, assumes different symbolic aspects as eager colonists dream to effect a final appropriation.

When we talk about figurations of the New World as the female body awaiting rape and conquest, we want to remember that legitimized violation is also attended by anxieties concerning the erotic appeal of the wilderness and the Other. If we find Ralegh imaging Guiana as a chaste maiden, other English colonists respond to the Virginia colony in ways not always consistent because of the enigmatic figure of the Amerindian. One very important figure in early English contacts with the Amerindian is Pocahontas, daughter of Powhatan and the princess referred to by Hart Crane some three hundred years later as "the mythological nature-symbol chosen [in The Bridge] to represent the physical body of the continent or the soil."[10] Both heathen native and woman, Pocahontas inscribes in her fabled and symbolic body all the ambivalences embedded in the figure who bridges two cultures: Algonquian and English. Pocahontas is as such many things to different peoples: she is the legendary savior of Captain John Smith, convert to the true faith, traitor to the Algonquian, intermediary between English and Amerindian, eroticized daughter who is both desirer and object of desire, the wanton woman. Leslie Fiedler offers a cogent account of the Pocahontas myth and meanings generated by its cultural appropriations in The Return of the Vanishing American. One thing that is noticeable in the hybrid figure—Pocahontas is one such, intermingling the European and Indian worlds, herself object of Otherness and assimilation—is its inevitable associations with the traitor. By warning her white lover's community of an impending attack by her father's people, Pocahontas is what Fiedler describes as "Our first celebrated traitor to her own race."[11] For both Ann Kibbey and Leslie Fiedler, the Amerindian and the woman are linked in the cultural imagination of the male colonists.[12] Both have to be taken in, as both have something the men need. But both are dangerous: Other, whether sexy or de-eroticized, they are figures that attract but must be contained because of the destructive potential inhering in their difference. Stephen Greenblatt tells us that after initially responding with unabated excitement to the life and culture of

the Other because of the exoticism of difference, the European
brings to that encounter a reflexively generated violence instilled
and shaped by a theology that identifies difference and Otherness
as pagan and ultimately demonic. Greenblatt, for example, reads
Guyon's violent destruction of the Bower of Bliss as a Christianized response to the alluring hold and charms of the exotic, and
finds in Spenser's representation a paradigm for describing European encounters with Otherness and cultural difference.[13]

European desire to rape the land cannot be extricated from
European anxieties about being raped: by the traitor, the hybrid,
the erotic American native. It is significant that in *The Tempest*,
the European colonist finds himself threatened with the rape of
his daughter by the native. The cultural anxiety registered in
Shakespeare's portrayal of the libidinal savage is tied to the tremendous fear and distrust of intermingling. And we remember
that in *Othello*, Brabantio and Iago look upon Desdemona as a
traitor to her own race. Considerations of where to place, or how
to respond to, the hybrid/traitor are present in *Othello* and
Spenser's *A View of the Present State of Ireland*, and will pervade
American literature from Cooper through Ralph Ellison and beyond. This chapter will consider two early English responses to
the figure of the Amerindian as Other, responses shaped by and
mediated through a theological framework that engages a culture's dreams of territorial expansion: one by John Donne, poet
and dean of St. Paul's; the other by the reverend Samuel Purchas,
chaplain to the archbishop of Canterbury. The New World occupies a central place in the creative imagination and theological
understanding of Donne; and it also exerts a fascination for Purchas who finds himself articulating a theological discourse that
cannot be separated from the economic considerations of
amassing great wealth.

John Donne, Samuel Purchas, and Theological Imperialism

In 1622, an event took place that shook the Virginia Company
and the people of England familiar with English colonial activities
taking place in the New World. In that year, the Indians massacred
three to four hundred English settlers in Virginia, an event that
further complicated the running of affairs in the colony. The
council of the Virginia Company in London faced internal political divisions, and there were religious factions as well as accusa-

tions of corruption in the field. Compounding these already existing problems and complications, the 1622 massacre caused much consternation and ratified the views of those English men and women who began with the belief that the American Indian was locked in his/her condition of innate savagism. Because there was no place for such an aberration in both nature and the civilized world, extermination and annihilation appeared to present a logical response. That was, of course, the governor and captain-general of Virginia, Sir George Yeardley's reaction to the massacre when he issued a commission to wage war against the Indians. The horror of the Indian massacre of the Virginia colonists also provoked a response from Christopher Brooke, Donne's friend, who wrote "A Poem on the Late Massacre in Virginia." In this poem, Brooke describes the Indians as creatures without any character of God or goodness in them; Indians are "Soules drown'd in flesh and blood," "Errors of Nature," and "The very dregs, garbage, and spawne of Earth." Brooke calls for the complete destruction of the Indians so that not one of them will be left to restore "such shame of Men, and Nature."[14] William Shakespeare had already provided a plethora of epithets receiving their impact from literatures that represent Indians as savages who have no souls, as lesser than human creatures, as children of the devil, and as beasts: in *The Tempest*, Caliban is "A freckled whelp hag-born" (1.2.283), "disproportion'd in his manners / As in his shape" (5.1.290–91), "got by the devil himself / Upon [his] wicked dam" (1.2.321–22), "earth" (1.2.316), and "This thing of darkness" (5.1.275).[15] In *A Counter-Blaste to Tobacco*, James I himself depicted Indians as dispossessed beasts caught irrevocably in their inherent depravity. Unable to assess value and worth because they desire only useless trifles and artifacts, the Indians are also devil worshippers spurned by God and excluded from his salvific plan for human history.[16]

How did John Donne, who also had full knowledge of the Indian massacre of the Virginia colonists, respond to the topics of extermination and dispossession heatedly debated by members of the Virginia Company? Donne's response is shaped by his understanding of Scripture and influenced by his vocational calling as the dean of St. Paul's. On 13 November 1622, he specifically preached a sermon to members and friends of the Virginia Company, stressing the important need to bring the gospel to the natives of the New World. In this sermon, he frames his support for the English project in Virginia in terms of the evangelical mandate given in Acts 1:8, where the disciples are instructed to become Christ's witnesses throughout the world. Donne exhorts: "bee you a light to the *Gentiles,* that sit in darkenesse; be you content to carry him over these *Seas,* who dryed up one *Red Sea* for his first people, and hath powred out another *red Sea,* his owne bloud, for them and us."[17] Donne's interest in the sea controls the polemic thrust of his sermon. He refers to God as a *"Shipwright"* who gives to man the model of a ship, which is the ark; this ship is given by God solely in order "to passe from *Nation* to *Nation"*: so *"God* taught us to make Ships, not to transport our selves, but to transport him."[18]

Donne's missionizing motif is a commonplace feature in the travel writings of Elizabethan and Stuart England. Giving an account of the geopolitical situation of the 1580s, Richard Hakluyt's *A Discourse of Western Planting* (1584) starts off its first chapter by reinforcing the missionizing mandate:

> it remayneth to be thoroughly weyed and considered by what meanes and by whome this moste godly and Christian work may be performed of inlarginge the glorious gospell of Christe, and reducinge of infinite multitudes of these simple people that are in errour into the righte and perfecte way of their saluation. . . . Then it is necessary for the salvation of those poore people which have sitten so longe in darkenes and in the shadowe of deathe, that preachers should be sent unto them. But by whome shoulde these preachers be sente? By them no doubte which have taken upon them the protection and defence of the Christian faithe. Nowe the Kinges and Queenes of England have the name of Defendours of the Faithe.[19]

Because God is the archetypal shipbuilder, the sea-going vessel is not designed to transport man's mercenary and profiteering ambitions, but to spread the good news of the gospel. Donne's use of the shipping metaphor and analogy is especially relevant to a sermon directed at people who are involved in setting up the Virginia plantation. The colonization of the New World must not be thought of in terms of satisfying the temporal interests of obtaining riches and commodities. England must not aim at expanding an earthly and literal empire in America, but at disseminating the Good News. He warns the Virginia Company against acting like kings and living with *"Libertie* and *independency, and Supremacie,"*[20] for these are caught up in the temporal and fallen desire to obtain wealth the shortest possible way.

Donne's familiarity with the seas and ocean travel did not come only from the rich reservoir of images and metaphors yielded by England's increasing experience with navigation in the late sixteenth and early seventeenth centuries. It owed also to his early experience of sailing with the English fleet that surprised and routed the Spanish ships anchored at Cadiz harbor in 1596. Donne's spectacular introduction to warfare in 1596 led him to volunteer to sail with another expedition organized to attack the Spanish fleet at Ferrol the following year. In this second expedition of 1597, Donne found himself landing in Plymouth after a terrible storm had forced the fleet of the "Islands Expedition" there for refitting. It was probably from Plymouth that he sent his poem, "The Storm," to Christopher Brooke.[21]

In another verse letter, "To Mr R.W.," Donne expressed his support for Essex and Ralegh's desire and eagerness to attack the Spanish colonies across the Atlantic. Both Essex and Ralegh had gone personally to London to persuade Queen Elizabeth to grant them permission to attack the Spanish colonies. The queen refused, disappointing not only the two men, but also Donne, who wrote:

> All news I think sooner reach thee than me;
> Havens are heavens, and ships winged angels be,
> The which both gospel, and stern threatenings bring;
> Guiana's harvest is nipped in the spring,
> I fear; and with us (methinks) Fate deals so
> As with the Jews' guide God did; he did show
> Him the rich land, but barred his entry in:
> Oh, slowness is our punishment and sin.
> Perchance, these Spanish business being done,
> Which as the earth between the moon and sun
> Eclipse the light which Guiana would give,
> Our discontinued hopes we shall retrieve:
> But if (as all th' all must) hopes smoke away,
> Is not almighty virtue an India?
> If men be worlds, there is in every one
> Something to answer in some proportion
> All the world's riches: and in good men, this
> Virtue, our form's form and our soul's soul, is.
>
> (lines 15–32)

In his verse letter, Donne translates the conceit of man as a little world into an argument for possession. If man is a world unto himself, then the wealth of that world also belongs to him. But as far as Donne is concerned, this wealth belongs to the English and not to everyone else on the globe. The queen's refusal to allow the English fleet to attack the Spanish colonies is then viewed by Donne as a disruption of Christ's divine mandate to spread the

Good News to the entire world. Elizabeth I had prevented English ships from becoming "winged angels" that brought "stern threatenings" to the Spaniards and the "gospel" to the natives. For this reason, "Guiana's harvest is nipped in the spring," prevented from enjoying full bloom. Donne's poem proceeds to offer a response to the queen's lack of support for the building of colonies by asserting that "Virtue" is an equal and compensating wealth. Virtue is a colony ("an India") in itself.

Donne's interest in the New World and England's Atlantic activities is inscribed in his later sermons and religious writings, where metaphors of travel and navigation frequently appear. In his *Essays in Divinity* (published posthumously in 1651), for example, he expresses the primacy of faith over reason with reference to the analogy of ocean travel. According to Donne, people who seek out God through reason are like mariners who sailed the seas before the invention of the compass. Because there is no sure guiding principle in such ventures, the mariner is unwilling to leave the sight of land. Faith, Donne elaborates, is the opposite of reason:

> But as by the use of the Compass, men safely dispatch *Ulysses* dangerous ten years travell in so many dayes, and have found out a new world richer then the old; so doth Faith, as soon as our hearts are touched with it, direct and inform us in that great search of the discovery of Gods Essence, and the new *Hierusalem,* which Reason durst not attempt. And though the faithfullest heart is not ever directly, and constantly upon God, but that it sometimes descends also to Reason; yet it is <not> thereby so departed from him, but that it still looks towards him, though not fully to him: as the Compass is ever Northward, though it decline, and have often variations towards East, and West.[22]

Unlike reason, which is inadequate because it is linked to a knowledge that can only be acquired by degrees, faith has the power to comprehend God.

Similarly, preaching on joy in his Second Prebend Sermon, Donne again uses his favorite conceit of the map:

> If you looke upon this world in a Map, you find two Hemisphears, two half worlds. If you crush heaven into a Map, you may find two Hemisphears too, two half heavens; Halfe will be Joy, and halfe will be Glory; for in these two, the joy of heaven, and the glory of heaven, is all heaven often represented unto us. And as of those two Hemisphears of the world, the first hath been knowne long before, but the

other, (that of America, which is the richer in treasure) God reserved for later Discoveries; So though he reserve that Hemisphear of heaven, which is the Glory thereof, to the Resurrection, yet the other Hemisphear, the Joy of heaven, God opens to our Discovery, and delivers for our habitation even whilst we dwell in this world.[23]

Donne is especially fascinated by the ability of maps and compasses to connect England to the larger world. There remains the powerful sense that contemporary England exists at a privileged moment because it possesses a highly sophisticated level of cartographical and navigational knowledge. Donne's use of the word "discovery" in his explication of the relationship between faith and reason in finding God also resonates with topical significance. The "discovery of Gods Essence" that only faith can accomplish is intertwined metaphorically with "a new world richer then the old." No mention of the "new world" in the English Renaissance failed to evoke the context of the Americas, of Columbus's discovery, and of England's own emerging contestation with Spain for the building of empire. Appropriating a commonplace trope, Donne figures America as a land rich in treasures, ensured by God's own special dispensation. America exists not only as a metaphor by which Donne can communicate the essence of faith, it is also literal land that needs the Church's intervention to bring it from a wild to civilized condition. The New World still exists in inchoate form and needs the transforming powers of faith to give it shape. And according to Donne, England occupies a very important place in the divine scheme of things because it is the starting point from which religion can be transmitted and disseminated to the New World.

Even though England is an island, its role in providential history is not linked to its geographical confines. That is why, in his sermon to the Virginia Company, Donne writes about the evangelical mandate in these terms:

Those amongst you, that are old now, shall passe out of this world with this great comfort, that you contributed to the beginning of that Common Wealth, and of that Church, though they live not to see the groath thereof to perfection: *Apollos* watred, but *Paul* planted; hee that begun the worke, was the greater man. And you that are young now, may live to see the Enemy as much empeach'd by that place, and your friends, yea Children, aswell accommodated in that place, as any other. You shall have made this *Iland*, which is but as the *Suburbs* of the old world, a Bridge, a Gallery to the new; to joyne all to that world that shall never grow old, the Kingdome of heaven, You shall add persons to this Kingdome, and to the Kingdome of heaven, and adde names to the Bookes of our Chronicles, and to the Booke of Life.[24]

A bridge is extended from the island of the Old England to the New. This figure of colonial expansion is not restricted to Donne. In Milton's *Paradise Lost,* Satan's success in destroying Eden is followed by the construction of a bridge across Chaos by Sin and Death—this bridge gives hell access to its newly colonized dominion.

In invoking the missionizing mandate to extend English authority and territory into the New World, Donne also makes use of an understanding in medieval concepts of Natural Law, where uninhabited territories become the possession of the first nation to discover them. Because many of these lands when encountered by the Europeans were already inhabited by natives, or when marked out for English imperial designs were previously colonized by the Spanish, a rhetorical strategy often practiced involved transforming the native into *terrae nullius* or the Spanish into demonic and brutal colonizers. Because the native is *terrae nullius,* a savage without the ability to understand and speak, it is the European's prerogative to fill in the sign, in other words, to construct the Other according to a conceptual image one brings or desires. This power to fill in the empty sign means the European can always figure the native as an aberrant of nature to be excised from existence or removed from land.

Appropriation of territory can always find rationalizing and legitimating pretexts: protecting the native from the cruel colonial practices of Spain, helping nature to cancel out an aberrant life form (one thinks here of the Houyhnhnm meditation on possibly obliterating the Yahoo in Swift's *Gulliver's Travels*), enriching the national coffer by taking possession of the treasures of a foreign land, sharing one's enlightened civilization with the savage, giving one's nation that invincible power which comes from possessing a huge empire, fulfilling the dream of creating a master race to be served by the ethnic Other. In colonialist discourse, appropriation of territory—the material manifestation of penetration into the space of the Other—rewrites the ancient Stoic teaching that the mind at birth is a tabula rasa, a blank tablet that obtains the first traces of knowledge by the imprinting of sensory impressions: it says that those impressions can be controlled and determined. It is precisely this ability for control that makes it possible to infuse the blank tablet that is the mind and soul of the American native with specific kinds of impressions and knowledge: the colonial imperative Miranda obeys reflexively in educating Caliban. So before John Locke offered the first principles of his new empirical psychology grounded in the rejection of innate ideas in *An Essay Concerning Human Understanding,* the concept of tabula rasa had existed as a central trope in European colonial discourse, appearing most often as the metaphor of the virgin land awaiting intervention and redemption. In *A Dedication to Sir Philip Sidney,* Fulke Greville writes, for example, about the Spanish colonial design in these terms: "Spain, managing the popedom by voices and pensions among the cardinals, and having the sword by land and sea in his hand, seemed likewise to have all those western parts of the world laid as a *tabula rasa* before him to write where he pleased *yo el rey.*"[25]

Another rationale often evoked to legitimize the politics of territorial appropriation is the obligation of the (Christian) colonist to make all arable land yield its fruit. This obligation is framed in terms of a theological imperative. God does not desire any land that he has given to humankind to go to waste. That is why it is mandated that a people who do not fulfill their responsibility should be removed and the unused land given to others who have the ability to translate soil into produce, raw material into utility. The understanding that all "empty things," including unoccupied land that falls under this category, remain the common property of all humankind until they are put to some use is based on the Roman Law argument known as *res nullius.*[26] In this legal argument of *res nullius,* the first person to use the land, in other words, make it yield its natural bounty instead of allowing it to go to waste, becomes its owner.[27] Understandably, the word "improving" is central to articulations of the *res nullius* argument.[28] In his 1622 sermon, Donne specifies when a piece of land can be legitimately possessed by an outside people, such as the English:

There is a *Power* rooted in *Nature,* and a *Power* rooted in *Grace;* a power yssuing from the Law of *Nations,* and a power growing out of the *Gospell.* In the Law of *Nature* and *Nations,* A Land never inhabited, by any, or utterly derelicted and immemorially abandoned by the former Inhabitants, becomes theirs that wil posesse it. So also is it, if the inhabitants doe not in some measure fill the Land, so as the Land may bring foorth her increase for the use of men: for as a man does not become proprietary of the Sea, because he hath two or three Boats, fishing in it, so neither does a man become Lord of a maine Continent, because hee hath two or three Cottages in the Skirts thereof. That rule which passes through all *Municipal Lawes* in particular States, *Interest reipublicæ ut quis re sua bene utatur, The State must take*

order, that every man improove that which he hath, for the best advantage of
that State, passes also through the Law of *Nations,* which is to all the
world, as the *Municipall* Law is to a particular State, *Interest mundo, The*
whole world, all Mankinde must take care, that all places be emprov'd, as farre
as may be, to the best advantage of Mankinde in generall. Againe if the
Land be peopled, and cultivated by the people, and that Land produce
in abundance such things, for want whereof their neighbours, or
others (being not enemies) perish, the Law of *Nations* may justifie
some force, in seeking, by permutation of other commodities which
they neede, to come to some of theirs. Many cases may be put, when
not onely *Commerce,* and *Trade,* but *Plantations* in lands, not formerly
our owne, may be lawfull. And for that, *Accepistis potestatem,* you have
your *Commission,* your *Patents,* your *Charters,* your *Seales* from *him,*
upon whose acts, any private Subject, in Civill matters, may safely
rely.[29]

A land that belongs to no one in particular is up for grabs; also,
a land that is not fully occupied by its native inhabitants can be
taken over by England because the potential of this land to yield
fruit and profit is not realized responsibly. In the English Renaissance, Donne's reference to the Law of Nature and Law of Nations
to justify the colonial enterprise would assume extra theological
and political implications. One play in the English Renaissance
that comes to mind invoking the "law of nature and of nations"
(2.4.80) to validate the English monarch's claim to the French
throne is *Henry V* (1599).[30] This history play of the second tetral-
ogy offers an interesting gloss on how concepts instrumental in
creating legitimating pretexts for theological imperialism and territorial expansionism also enable historical and political claims
for waging war against another nation. In *Henry V,* Shakespeare
specifically describes the Law of Nature and the Law of Nations
as a "gift of heaven" (2.4.79). King Henry is told by the clergy
that his claim to the French throne is legitimized by God's law
encoded in nature ("The blood and courage that renowned them /
Runs in your veins" [1.2.118–19]) and by extension in society.
What we find expressed in this play is a policy of foreign aggression rationalized with reference to divine legitimation.

In Puritan discourse, especially in the first half of the seventeenth century, the Law of Nature is taken to refer to the law of
God written in the fleshly tables of men's hearts, a law that has
authoritative jurisdiction over all human laws and constitutions.
The Law of Nations, on the other hand, refers to that Law that
ensures the preservation of men in society, even at those moments
when the persons to whom authority belongs fail to procure the

good of the people. It is this Law of Nations that teaches that the end of the state is the good of the people. Given the political contexts in which the Law of Nature and the Law of Nations are often invoked, Donne's allusion to these two laws in his sermon is significant. Donne asserts that God has inscribed in the fleshly tables of the hearts of his Englishmen the legitimate enterprise of taking over land where there is obvious neglect in ensuring that arable land is made to produce good harvest and yield its natural goodness. This utilitarian principle is shared by all civilized nations—as suggested in the concept of the Law of Nations—that are given the mandate to protect land from going to waste. Recognition of this mandate is made possible through right reason, upheld by the Law of Nature.

The secular analogy of the theological understanding that it is a divinely mandated duty to make arable land yield its natural bounty can be found in the efforts of a colonist like John Smith planting the Jamestown colony, efforts that reveal a disjuncture between enjoying the idea of plantation and the harsh actualities of settling a colony. The difficulties encountered are, in addition to having to engage the natives of the land, created and compounded by the English colonists themselves, a large number of whom came from the poorest elements of society: disbanded soldiers, single men, unemployed youths, even convicted felons. Lack of discipline found among the settlers in Virginia, combined with their subjection to a draconian law, led to insubordination, desertions to join the Indian tribes, mutinies, and insurrections. Desertion of many Englishmen to the Indians led to loss of weapons and tools from the fort. In *The Proceedings of the English Colony in Virginia,* we learn about a destructive mutiny that took place immediately following the arrival of the much-awaited support contingent led by Gates and Somers: "It would bee too tedious, too strange, and almost incredible, should I particularly relate the infinite dangers, plots, and practices, [John Smith] daily escaped amongst this factious crue, the chiefe whereof he quickly laid by the heeles, til his leisure better served to doe them justice."[31]

One of the ways in which the leaders of the early settlement in Virginia attempted to impose some form of order and control to create Eden out of the wilderness was to emphasize the indispensable importance of work. John Smith is especially harsh when criticizing the idle gentlemen of the Virginia colony who will gladly trade in objects of value for food, and all because they are simply too idle to produce their own. He links these men who are unable to distinguish between things of value and mere trifles, to the Indians who will exchange commodities of worth for the trifles of beads, baubles, and trinkets. Smith's attack on idleness registers the crucial point that survival in the Virginia colony can only be assured, apart from the help of the Indians themselves, through the expansion of labor and fruits of hard work. He betrays an anxious desire to translate work into a discipline that may, hopefully, facilitate governance and control in the colony.[32]

The discourse of work occupies an important place in Thomas Hariot's *A Briefe and True Report of the New Found Land of Virginia* (1588), John Smith's *A Map of Virginia* (1612), and *Proceedings of the English Colonie in Virginia* (1612). These texts interweave the conditions of living on the land with a theological apprehension with respect to creating a viable Eden in the New World. I am not suggesting that Hariot and Smith emphasized the Puritan motif of work by envisioning the creation of a city on a hill: they did not. The Puritans had their own ideological agenda, in which work figured as a special kind of discipline, requisite to forming godly character and shaping social order and coherence. Rather, what Hariot and Smith shared with the Puritans was a metaphor for understanding the taming of the implacable wilderness.

When the vagrant, disbanded soldier or felon disrupts the fragile order of the Virginia colony, he is chastised and made subject to a brutal martial law. And he is also contained discursively, enclosed in that space reserved in the English colonial imagination for the demonized Other that is the native of the New World. It is significant that the body of the recalcitrant who is English is figured in terms similar to the body of the American native. In *A Counter-Blaste to Tobacco,* for example, James I specifically links those Englishmen addicted to the evils of tobacco smoking to the uncivilized and pagan natives of the New World through analogy, one that also transforms the body of the recalcitrant English into the space and site of the Other:

> And now good Countrey men let us (I pray you) consider, what honour or policie can moove us to imitate the barbarous and beastly maners of the wilde, godlesse, and slavish *Indians,* especially in so vile and stinking a custome? Shall wee disdaine to imitate the maners of our neighbour *France* (having the stile of the first Christian Kingdom) and that cannot endure the spirit of the Spaniards (their King now being comparable in largenes of Dominions to the great Emperor of *Turkie*).

James's exhortation to the English not to follow in a servile manner "the barbarous and beastly maners" of the Amerindians is predicated on the superiority of English ways and customs. England is not a nation that follows after the ways of another. It has spurned even the manners of France and repudiated the spirit of Spain. If England possesses the ability to affirm its own specific national and cultural identity over and against other European states, it must surely possess the capacity not to subscribe to the ways of the Amerindian, a figure linked to the worship of the devil. The entire passage is framed as a series of questions, the forceable "shall wee" functioning as an eye-opening refrain:

> Shall wee, I say, that have bene so long civill and wealthy in Peace, famous and invincible in Warre, fortunate in both, we that have bene ever able to aide any of our neighbours (but never deafed any of their eares with any of our supplications for assistance) shall we, I say, without blushing, abase our selves so farre, as to imitate these beastly *Indians*, slaves to the *Spaniards*, refuse to the world, and as yet aliens to the holy Covenant of God? Why doe we not as well imitate them in walking naked as they doe? in preferring glasses, feathers, and such toyes, to golde and precious stones, as they do? yea why do we not denie God and adore the Devill, as they doe?[33]

For civil order to prevail, the space of the Other must always be subjected to strict scrutiny and brought under emphatic control. Control over the self, an act resonating with theological implications, finds an analogy in the control of the savage inhabiting the space of the New World. And just as it is necessary to contain recalcitrance and rebellion in the camp of one's own people, it is imperative to subdue the violence of savagism unless one, like John Donne, happens to advocate a theological imperialism based on disseminating God's Word without the compulsion of the sword.

To summarize, then: In his sermons, the anxieties Donne registers rhetorically in the love lyrics are present but framed by the affirmations of faith that constitute the lexicon of the preacher, communicating and explicating God's Word to a congregation. As a public persuasive mode, the sermon by definition cannot obfuscate truth (ideally) in lexical and rhetorical opacity. Displays of stylistic virtuosity are means to effecting change in the hearts of the listeners or impressing a doctrinal point on the congregation. As such, the importance of the missionizing mandate must be conveyed in a homiletic discourse that possesses the ability to convince its auditor of the imperative of disseminating the good news to the world. Where Donne's poems ground a voice and identity through agon and rhetorical violence, where the figures of seas and cartography aim to furnish consolation to the self and mistress as well as to revel in one's ability to engage in celerity of thought, the sermons strive to create conviction. When Donne gives his sermon to members of the Virginia Company, he is addressing a constituency that at one time he had hoped to be a part of in a secretarial capacity. For these members, Donne articulates a missionizing project that involves moving into and converting the natives of Virginia: a vision of theological imperialism that, despite its ostensible disavowal of physical violence, nevertheless uses the language of transformation and cultural appropriation. In Donne's sermon of 1622, ocean travel functions not only as a metaphor, but also as concrete reality since it offers a clear and viable way for materializing the evangelical mandate given by Christ. Even as we look at Donne's sermons in relation to his poetry, we find that the preoccupation with maps and ocean travel does much more than direct attention to the overseas activities of Renaissance England. It reveals a poetic consciousness that always thinks of expanding the geographical and political boundaries of England into the New World, albeit via the pretext of converting the native.

We find that the more Donne attempts to come to grips with individual and cultural anxieties, the more forcefully he inscribes the allusive presence of America in his writings. The poet-as-physician anatomizing the world also opens up in its figurative economy the interrelated activities of itemizing, compartmentalizing, and scrutinizing, activities that Foucault sees as central to the exercise of power and control of the individual and social body. Probably without recognizing the political implications of his metaphor, Donne, who imagines physicians poring over the body of the patient as a piece of cartographic parchment, speaks in the language of a technology of control. The anatomist-as-cartographer possesses an omniscience that is the attribute of deity. This fantasy of being in control of the world, figured in the activity of scrutinizing a cartographic parchment, cannot ultimately be separated from the economy of desire: of setting forth to bring under control the wild space of the New World and the metonymized body of the woman. It is a short step from here to the figure of Marlowe's Tamburlaine. Tamburlaine embodies the appetitive machine whose life involves consuming geographical space. Tamburlaine would have gone on satisfying his appetite by further conquests had he not succumbed to an illness, a biological intervention that stands for the reality principle disrupting fantasies of immortality. And just before he dies, Tamburlaine looks

significantly at a map and specifically at those spaces he has yet to
fill with the literal body of his consuming and colonizing presence.

The discourse of evangelism is never fully comfortable with the
figure of man as appetitive machine, because of its implicit emphasis on inordinate human ambition. And so, one way out of the
ethical dilemma is to allow scriptural injunctions themselves to
occupy the space of desire. For the desire of deity is law and
truth—incontrovertible and inexorable. In relation to this truth,
individual desire then translates into obedience to God's will; and
going into the land of the Other and converting or eliminating
the native then enjoy the sanction of divinity. In tandem with
the demands of this theological economy, the blazon then gets
rewritten as the exotic experience of the Song of Solomon, read
sometimes as an Old Testament type of the New Testament vision
of Christ's marriage to the Church when the salvific plan finally
obtains culmination and closure. In typology, the Church that is
the bride for whom Christ died and the one that he will come to
claim as his own must be pure. If the Church is the body of
believers, then the individuals making up the community must all
be made clean through the blood of the lamb: saved by grace
through faith. It is the duty of the believer to spread the good
news of the gospel to make sure that this Church remains strong
and viable. Donne's understanding of the evangelical mandate
feeds directly into this conception of Christian duty. Virginia has
also been figured as the bride awaiting her bridegroom. In "Virginias Verger," Samuel Purchas uses the metaphor of the bridegroom to refer to both Christ and England, and of Virginia to
both Church and land in the New World. Here apocalyptic language gets charged with contemporary and typological resonances. Later on, in the antiprelatical tracts of the early 1640s,
John Milton also appropriates the language of evangelical expansionism when he writes that the faster you can bring about Reformation in England, the sooner you can then proceed to bring
true faith to Europe and the world. The urgency with which England should fulfill its role in the divine scheme of things stems
from Milton's millenarian belief that Christ's coming is just
around the corner. What is needed is for England to hasten the
process by first demolishing the prelatical system of church
government.

Donne's exhortation to the English to engage in the conversion
of the native does not bristle with the urgency of Milton's millenarian tenor, forged by the conviction that the believer has the
ability to help hasten Christ's second coming. His explicatory

mode communicates one understanding of the Christian's relation to a lost heathen world—that the native is to be converted
through the power of the Word rather than the coercive and
violent pressures of the sword—even as it defines a conception of
property that contributes directly to England's emerging discourse of territorial appropriation. Once you say that a land that
is left to waste must be corrected because God does not counte-
nance poor stewardship, then it is easy enough to move from there
to assert that a group of people or a tribe has been remiss in
fulfilling its divinely-mandated duty. Underwriting Donne's reading of the Virginia colony as text is an implicit recognition of
the importance of economic profits: Donne's understanding of
property, framed by theological language, is nonetheless an understanding of material yield. The discourse of commercialization
is inextricably intertwined with the discourse of evangelism. In
delivering his sermon, Donne understands that he is explicating
and communicating God's Word, guided and empowered by the
Holy Spirit: this understanding is a Reformation one. He is God's
ambassador, very much like Milton's Raphael in *Paradise Lost:*
reaching out, explaining, warning, teaching, instructing. Donne
explicates God's Word in relation to his inscription in absolutist
ideology. If as Jonathan Goldberg tells us, for Donne, "the court
is the center and the only reality of society; not to be there is to
be nowhere,"[34] then we may add that not to be God's minister is
also to be nowhere. In Goldberg's reading, James as analogy of
God sustains, leads, reclaims, and makes Donne—he is the "cre-
ator" of the poet and his identity. To expand the kingdom of God
in this world is also to enlarge James's dominion, for the king is
God's regent and representative in time. And to bring the heathen
nations under the banner of the true faith is to reinforce the
absolutist authority of the Christian God and James I, who is his
earthly representative and anointed.

Three years after the Virginia massacre, in 1625, Samuel Purchas published "Virginias Verger," the document I mentioned
earlier in this chapter, as a response to the infamous event. Like
Donne and many other writers of the period, Purchas found himself evoking the politically resonant pair of labels—Natural Law
and Law of Nations—to argue for displacing the Amerindians
from their land. "Virginias Verger" constitutes an important contribution to the discourse of theological imperialism because it
provides legal reasons—legitimized by God's own deterministic
scheme for the world and relations between peoples—for displacing the Amerindians from their land and for Christianizing Vir-

ginia. In this particular text, Purchas explains how the Law of Nations gives England the right to trade freely and settle on un-peopled lands, but does not extend that privilege automatically to usurping and appropriating lands belonging to others. The 1622 massacre gives him the necessary pretext for articulating the conditions under which such appropriation is legitimate, an articulation that grounds itself in nothing less than God's very own divine sanction:

> The Barbarians themselves by light of nature saw this, and gave Ours kind entertainment in mutuall cohabitation and commerce: and they having not the Law were a Law to themselves, practically acknowledg-ing this Law of Nature written by him, which is Natura naturans, in their hearts: from which if they since have declined, they have lost their owne Naturall, and given us another Nationall right; their trans-gression of the Law of Nature, which tieth Men to Men in the rights of Natures commons, exposing them (as a forfeited bond) to the chas-tisement of that common Law of mankind; and also on our parts to the severitie of the Law of Nations, which tyeth Nation to Nation. And if they bee not worthy of the name of a Nation, being wilde and Savage: yet as Slaves, bordering rebells, excommunicates and out-lawes are lyable to the punishments of Law, and not to the priviledges; So is it with these Barbarians, Borderers and Out-lawes of Humanity. Arma tenenti, Omnia dat qui justa negat, If the Armes bee just, as in this case of vindicating unnaturall, inhumane wrongs to a loving and profitable Nation, entertained voluntarily, in time of greatest pre-tended amity. (VV 19:224)

Purchas argues that atrocious acts of violence like the kind perpe-trated by the Indians constitute an infringement of Natural Law; through these acts, the Algonquians have divorced themselves for-ever from the land.

In "Virginias Verger," the land of the New World and the bodies of English men, women, and children become interchangeable terms. Purchas does not hedge in his reasoning that the 1622 massacre sanctions the passing of the Virginia colony by theologi-cal and legal logic into English hands. Referring to the slain colo-nists, he writes:

> if the Savages dealt perfidiously with them (as Powhatan confessed to Cap. Smith, that hee had beene at their slaughter, and had divers utensills of theirs to shew) their carkasses, the dispersed bones of their and their Countrey mens since murthered carkasses, have taken a mortall immortall possession, and being dead, speake, proclaime and

cry, This our earth is truly English, and therefore this Land is justly yours O English. (*VV* 19:228)

The massacre, also referred to by Purchas as "disloyall treason" (*VV* 19:229), has miraculously transformed the Algonquians into "unnaturall Naturalls" (*VV* 19:229) who forfeit whatever rights they once possessed under the Law of Nature, *natura naturans*. This forfeit "made both them and their Countrey wholly English" (*VV* 19:229). The English, not the Algonquian, is now the "natural" inhabitant of the land. Peter Hulme tells us that the legal and theological reasoning employed by Purchas finds its way into different colonial discourses in their efforts to dispossess the American natives from their land. He cites the example of John Winthrop who argues that the Indians had "natural" but not "civil" rights over the land; the legal argument of *vacuum domicilium* denied the Indians "civil" rights over the land because they had not "subdued" it.[35] In "Virginias Verger," Purchas writes without embarrassment that only Christians "have and hold the world and the things thereof in another tenure, whereof Hypocrites and Heathens are not capable" (*VV* 19:219). Once a statement like this is uttered, any number of pretexts can be found to dispossess another people from land that one desires to appropriate for oneself. For colonialism obtains its sanction from none other than the triune God himself, as Purchas's text makes abundantly clear.

"Virginias Verger" offers one of the most succinct expressions of the inseparable relationship between theological imperialism and territorial appropriation in the literature of the English Renaissance:

> The end of a thing is the beginning, being first in intention though last in execution: the end which Christians ought to ayme at is God, Doing all things in the name of our Lord Jesus Christ, to the glory of God the Father, by the gracious guide and assistance of the Holy Ghost. Glory is, Frequens de aliquo fama cum laude, And heereby is our Father glorified, sayeth Christ, if yee bring forth much fruite, and so shall yee be my Disciples. Loe here the scope of Christians Plantations, to plant Christianity, to produce and multiply Christians, by our words and works to further the knowledge of God in his Word and Workes. . . .
>
> God is a Glorious Circle, whose Center is every where, his circumference no where: himselfe to himselfe is Circle and Circumference, the Ocean of Entitie, that very ubique, from whom, to whom (the Centre of unitie) all diversified lines of varietie issue and returne. And

although we every where feele his present Deitie, yet the difference of heavenly climate and influence, causing such discording concord of dayes, nights, seasons; such varietie of meteors, elements, aliments; such noveltie in Beasts, Fishes, Fowles; such luxuriant plentie and admirable raritie of Trees, Shrubs, Hearbs: such fertilitie of soyle, insinuation of Seas, multiplicitie of Rivers, safetie of Ports, health-fulnesse of ayre, opportunities of habitation, materialls for action, objects for contemplation, haps in present, hopes of future, worlds of varietie in that diversified world; doe quicken our mindes to apprehend, whet our tongues to declare, and fill both with arguments of divine praise. On the other side considering so good a Countrey, so bad people, having little of Humanitie but shape, ignorant of Civilitie, of Arts, of Religion; more brutish then the beasts they hunt, more wild and unmanly then that unmanned wild Countrey, which they range rather then inhabite; captivated also to Satans tyranny in foolish pieties, mad impieties, wicked idlenesse, busie and bloudy wickednesse: hence have wee fit objects of zeale and pitie, to deliver from the power of darknesse, that where it was said, Yee are not my people, they may bee called the children of the living God: that Justice may so proceed in rooting out those murtherers, that yet in judgement (imitating Gods dealing with us) wee may remember Mercy to such as their owne innocence shall protect, and Hope shall in Charitie judge capable of Christian Faith. And let men know that hee which converteth a sinner from the errour of his way, shall save a soule from death, and shall hide a multitude of sinnes. And Saviours shall thus come on Mount Zion to judge the Mount of Esau, and the Kingdome (of Virginia) shall be Lord. Thus shall wee at once overcome both Men and Devills, and espouse Virginia to one husband, presenting her as a chast Virgin to Christ. If the eye of Adventurers were thus single, how soone and all the body should be light? But the loving our selves more then God, hath detained so great blessings from us to Virginia, and from Virginia to us. Godlinesse hath the promises of this life, and that which is to come. And if wee be carefull to doe Gods will, he will be ready to doe ours.

All the rich endowments of Virginia, her Virgin-portion from the creation nothing lessened, are wages for all this worke: God in wisedome having enriched the Savage Countries, that those riches might be attractives for Christian suters, which there may sowe spirituals and reape temporals. (*VV* 19:230–32)

Purchas begins by describing the ineffable God through the metaphor of the circle, the signifier of perfection. This God who "to himselfe is Circle and Circumference" is the center as well as occupier of all space. In order not to limit and confine this God, Purchas proceeds to elaborate on the diversity of the divine unity, a Renaissance version of Hopkins's "Pied Beauty." The diversity of the natural world fills the rapturous beholder with "arguments of divine praise." At a moment when the text's celebration of diversity appears to move in the direction of embracing difference, perhaps also in people, a gap opens up between those who are in possession of culture and give praise to God and the "so bad people, having little of Humanitie but shape, ignorant of Civilitie, of Arts, of Religion." Enjoying diversity in the natural world is completely different from appreciating diversity in people.

"Virginias Verger" separates the inhabitants from the land: the Algonquians "range rather then inhabite." The massacre of the Virginia colonists has transformed them into the children of Satan, a demonization that renders them "more wild and unmanly then that unmanned wild Countrey." In fact, Purchas offers an explanation for the 1622 massacre in terms of the actions of the devil. The treachery and brutality of the Algonquians stem from the envy of the devil who wants to disrupt "the very prosperity and pregnant hopes of that Plantation" (VV 19:246) for the English. Purchas's use of the term "range" to describe the dispossession of the Algonquian from his land is a familiar one in the discursive alienation of the American native from his or her land. Earlier on in 1609, Robert Gray invoked the analogy of wild beasts in the forest to describe the relationship of the Indians to their land in A Good Speed to Virginia. Gray contended that the American Indian had no individual titles to the land "but onely a generall residencie there."[36] In "Virginias Verger," Purchas also evokes the nomadic existence of the American native to emphasize the absence of a natural rootedness to land. Gray argues for the native's alienation from the land because there is no such thing as "law or government" in tribal life.[37] For him, the absence of law and government means the absence of a legal framework to interpret even the basic politics of dispossession. Even if the American Indian possesses such a legal framework, he/she cannot fight for right to land because his/her existence is no different from that of the beasts: "if the whole lande should be taken from them, there is not a man that can complaine of any particular wrong done unto him."[38]

The excerpt I have cited from "Virginias Verger" concludes with a fascinating vision of judgment, where "Saviours shall thus come on Mount Zion to judge the Mount of Esau, and the Kingdome (of Virginia) shall be Lord." What is interesting here is that the pluralization of "Saviour" removes its identification with Christ; and without a clear subject antecedent, we can only hazard a guess as to its referential meaning. My reading is that "Saviours" refers here to the English colonists who act in accordance with the divine will either in dispensing justice or mercy. In "Virginias Verger," Purchas finds himself having to accommodate scriptural injunction and the Law of Nations making it unlawful for Christians "to usurpe the goods and lands of Heathens" (*VV* 19:220), and at the same time opening up these theological and legal restrictions to reinterpretation. In responding to the 1622 Indian massacre of the Virginia colonists, Purchas recognizes that there is a need for the exercise of justice. The slaughtered colonists, like so many Abels, cry out "for just vengeance of rooting out the authors and actors of so prodigious injustice" (*VV* 19:225).

The text's emphasis on the unnatural acts of the natives and the demand for divine justice and retribution registers Purchas's deep-seated desire for the use of the sword to deal with the Algonquian's savage conduct; except that this desire is inscribed in a text whose need to include a vision of Christian conversion of the heathen is also impelled by a moral obligation to accommodate the claims of mercy. But in any debate taking place between justice and mercy in the colonial rhetoric of Purchas's text—and Purchas must, I said, include a recognition (more a platitude) that God's mercy should also be made available to the Indians—the operative word is "overcome." You do not overcome the self so much as you overcome "both Men and Devills." The result of successfully enacting this "overcoming" is the espousal of "Virginia to one husband, presenting her as a chast Virgin to Christ." On the one hand, the "husband" in this line refers to "Christ," the symmetrical and referential logic of the syntax supporting this. On the other hand, "husband" can just as easily refer to the English colonist and his extension in the English nation. The excerpt ends in a note of urgency. The entire "body" that "should be light" has not become so. Something is wrong. But what is it? Purchas identifies it as "loving our selves more than God"; in the context of the immediate concerns of "Virginias Verger," it almost certainly means the lack of concerted action and unity in settling Virginia well. Proper settlement involves dispossessing the American Indians from the land. Purchas's politics of dispossession subsumes any uneasy relationship between the desire to punish the savage natives and an obligation to practice mercy. There is, according to the logic of Purchas's text, no need for further argument because the demands of justice have been met: "I follow the hand of God, which have given England so many rights in Virginia, right naturall, right nationall, right by first discovery, by accepted trade, by possession surrendred voluntarily, continued constantly,

right by gift, by birth, by bargaine and sale, by cession, by forfei-
ture in that late damnable trechery and massacre, and the fatal
possession taken by so many murthered English" (VV 19:266).
Because justice has already been meted out in the discursive logic
of dispossession, the English colonists now have the liberty to "remember mercy" (VV 19:266). Because the duty of settling the
colony well has not been recognized by the English colonists, the
"so great blessings" that should logically flow "from us to Virginia,
and from Virginia to us" have been detained. Purchas then makes
the remarkable statement that "Godlinesse hath the promises of
this life, and that which is to come. And if wee bee carefull to doe
Gods will, he will be ready to doe ours."

It is important, when considering the ways in which the New
World is represented in the writings of the English Renaissance,
Purchas's "Virginias Verger" presenting a good example, to emphasize that narratives of America are constructed from England's vantage point. The blazon itself can be read, for example,
as a discursive construction: making geographical space available
for scrutiny and consumption. The point is that the geographical
space and the woman, standing in for each other as metonymies
or enjoying a synecdochic relationship, are excluded from having
a say in this discursive construction. Excluding the woman or the
native of the New World from the construction of narratives is
necessary for the expansionist and colonialist project. This principle of necessary exclusion also extends into the domain of hermeneutics and interpretations of scriptural significance. We know
that every time the New World is described as a bride awaiting
her beloved, the bridegroom, we are dealing with the language
of typology and Apocalypse, and also with the Old Testament
Song of Solomon. In the erotic expressions and proclamations of
love between Solomon and his "black" bride can be found, in
typological exegesis, a secularized version as well as prefiguration
of Christ's marriage to his Church.[39] But even the language of
typology is far from straightforward, and exegetical readings of
the larger spiritual significance of the Song of Solomon cannot
be extricated from the embedded prejudices of reader response
and gender considerations. The seventeenth-century Puritan
John Cotton's exegesis of the Song of Solomon offers a cogent
example of the influence of such prejudices in the interpretation
of sacred truth. Ann Kibbey summarizes succinctly Cotton's particular exegesis, shaped by his understanding that historical events
fulfill figures, and not historical events, of the Old Testament.
According to Kibbey, John Cotton's Solomon is

the counterpart of the cleric, the speaker of sacred tropes. Cotton emphasizes Solomon as prophetic visionary in contradistinction to the bride, who has no spiritual vision whatsoever. She is constrained within the poetic genre, for Cotton implies that she herself is unaware that the words seemingly meant for her are not addressed to her. . . . In Cotton's view, the author-bridegroom is aware of a double level of meaning but the bride is not, an interpretation reflected further in the interpretation of the groom, but not the bride, as a type. . . . By contrast, the bride's marriage only underscores her exclusion from the prophetic vision. . . . The form of the poem as a dialogue is also treated as a poetic figure that must be reordered to the spiritual sense. As Solomon's prophetic vision alone, Canticles becomes a dramatic monologue, a poem delivered at the "marriage feast" in the presence of a bride who is a silent audience despite her literary appearance of speech in the poetry. In the presence of Solomon, the originator of the sacred words of the poem, the bride is similar to a loaf of bread, an object whose material presence is all that is religiously necessary. . . . The duplicity of allegorical meaning that makes Solomon's words significant is overtly denied to the bride. Or rather, it is acknowledged only metonymically.[40]

I cite in some detail Kibbey's rendition of Cotton's particular interpretation because it reveals a hermeneutic that depends on an understanding that the male reader is in complete control of narrative and its meanings. In relation to the discourse of the New World, this male reader is the one who packages the complexities of new lands and new peoples for easy consumption by appealing to the desire for eroticized experiences and for sexual conquests central to a tradition like the blazon. Like Cotton's bride, who is excluded from language—or from what Jacques Lacan would call the symbolic order—the geographical land and the woman who are the objects of representation are appropriated, discursively constructed, and rhetorically contained. They are objects of representation because they cannot represent themselves; excluded from language and the symbolic order, they cannot signify.

In "Virginias Verger," the language of typology implicit in Purchas's description of Virginia as a bride awaiting her bridegroom is nonetheless suffused with considerations of economic profit. There is really no space given in Purchas's text to an otherworldliness that is the reward of living a life of Christian humility and suffering. For holiness, what Purchas calls "godlinesse," has its promises in this life; and by "promises," he means the wealth of the New World. Purchas sets up a relationship between the Christian colonist and his God based on the reciprocal exchange of

favors: "if we bee carefull to doe Gods will, he will be ready to
doe ours," and if we undertake the divinely mandated task of
settling the colony in Virginia, God will readily yield us its wealth.
Purchas's is fundamentally a theology of materialism, and Scripture exists to validate it. This can be read as a version of what
Max Weber calls "the spirit of capitalism." Kim Hall has commented that for Purchas, conversion, "one of the more persist-
ently articulated motives for colonialism, works to support
cultural hegemony and the economic imperatives of imperial
trade."[41] Equating conversion with economic gain, Purchas em-
braces a conception of English trade that "rather than fostering
a mixing of cultures, will eradicate religious as well as cultural
and gender differences under one patriarchal God."[42] Purchas's
statement toward the end of "Virginias Verger"—"I seeke the
good and not the goods of England and Virginia" (*VV* 19:266)—
is pure rhetoric and a concession to the Pauline idea that one
cannot worship God and Mammon. Much of "Virginias Verger"
provides a drawn-out account of the natural wealth of the plantation, an account elaborated through itemizations of all the bounties that the land is capable of yielding. In fact, there is a purpose
for the very presence of the American natives on the human
scene: "All the rich endowments of Virginia, her Virgin-portion
from the creation nothing lessoned, are wages for all this worke:
God in wisdome having enriched the Savage Countries, that those
riches might be attractives for Christian suters, which there may
sowe spirituals and reape temporals." The theological underpin-
nings of this statement are staggering. God's created order is a
Calvinistic one, in which in his infinite wisdom, "Savage Countries" were preordained from time immemorial to line the coffers
of the English colonists. By extension, the 1622 massacre of the
Virginia colonists by the Algonquian is a predetermined event
and significantly so. Purchas's God is not only the God of creation
and eternity, but indeed the "Alpha and Omega . . . of the Virginian Plantation" (*VV* 19:230).

Toward the end of the seventeenth century, the medieval concept of Natural Law, appropriated and recontextualized while re-
taining its core colonial message in Donne's sermon and Purchas's
document, obtains philosophical valorization in a text like John
Locke's *Second Treatise of Government*. After the appearance of
Donne's sermons, a few decades remained for this medieval apprehension of Natural Law and the Renaissance understanding of
"property" to be given the legitimating signature of philosophical
discourse. In the *Second Treatise*, Locke's definition of *property* ex-

plicitly supports the rationale that all land must be put to use and bear fruit, ratifying and validating the central pretext of most colonial enterprises. The Lockean concept of "property" as materialized by "labor" is central to interpreting not only Donne's rationale for involvement in Virginia, but also the conflicting views of land held by the colonists in and natives of America. In *The Poetics of Imperialism,* Eric Cheyfitz comments on how "property" as a concept understood by the European does not exist in the conceptual universe of the native American. Because of this, any interaction transpiring between the European colonist and New World native involves "translation" of language and signs for and between parties; the difficulty or impossibility of "translation" ensures inevitable breakdown in "cross-cultural" communication. When the Algonquians negotiated to share their land with the English, for instance, they did so in "terms not alienable in individualized places that could be traded in a market economy."[43] Unlike the European who conceived of land-as-property, linked to the idea of possession, the Indian held an unmarked, unbounded, and unfenced conception of land. For the Indian, land is directly related to use, not possession.[44]

In his *Second Treatise of Government,* Locke begins his chapter, "Of Property," by premising that because the earth belongs to humankind in general for the purposes of enhancing convenience and giving advantage to life, it belongs "in common" to everyone; he equates this divinely ordained condition with the state of nature. "Labor" is defined as the work of a person's hand that gives him/her a "title" to anything that such work acts upon; the expansion of "labor" that bestows "title" and ownership, creates "property":

> The same *measures* governed the *possession of land* too: whatsoever he tilled and reaped, laid up and made use of, before it spoiled, that was his peculiar right; whatsoever he enclosed, and could feed, and make use of, the cattle and product was also his. But if either the grass of his inclosure rotted on the ground, or the fruit of his planting perished without gathering, and laying up, this part of the earth, notwithstanding his inclosure, was still to be looked on as waste, and might be the possession of any other. Thus, at the beginning, *Cain* might take as much ground as he could till, and make it his own land, and yet leave enough to *Abel*'s sheep to feed on; a few acres would serve for both their possessions. But as families increased, and industry inlarged their stocks, their *possessions inlarged* with the need of them; but yet it was commonly *without any fixed property in the ground* they made use of, till they incorporated, settled themselves together, and

built cities; and then, by consent, they came in time, to set out the
bounds of their distinct territories, and agree on limits between them and
their neighbours; and by laws within themselves, settled the *properties*
of those of the same society.[45]

Subscribing to the Roman Law argument of *res nullius,* both
Donne and Locke agree that "labor" must be harnessed to cultivate and improve land otherwise "left to nature" and neglect.[46]
Locke's political philosophy of possessive individualism not only
maintains that it goes against natural law for land to remain idle,
but stresses that it is necessary to translate it into utility. Implicit
in his definition of property is the view that there are people
incapable of transforming land into utility and others who must
intervene to correct this. When the people of England make it
their responsibility to ensure that the resources of the natural
world are not left unharnessed, they are not doing so simply with
the ethically questionable purpose of garnering for themselves
the wealth of a foreign land. They are doing so in conjunction
with a divinely mandated responsibility, one inseparable from the
understanding that the world of nature is present for the profit
and sustenance of humankind. It is impossible to divorce obtaining the earth's riches from obeying what is believed to be God's
injunction on human responsibility. That responsibility extends to
proselytizing the savages of the New World, or even exterminating
them in order to re-create versions of paradise, actions undertaken always with the motive of territorial and material appropriation deeply inscribed. Anthony Pagden tells us that according to
the terms of Locke's argument, the establishment of a settlement
and property rights—"the *dominium* exercised over things"—also
means that henceforth, any attempt made by the native to regain
lands that have been appropriated involves violating nature's laws
and might.[47] In such a situation, the native is to "be destroyed as
a lion or tiger, one of those savage wild beasts."[48]

ANALOGY AND DIFFERENCE:
PURITANISM AND RATIONALIZING THEOLOGY

We know that the Virginia Company stressed the responsibility
of disseminating faith to the dark regions of America as one important reason for settling the Virginia colony. The Charter of
the Virginia Company in 1609 expressly states as its purpose the
"propagating of Christian religion to such people, as yet live in

darkness and miserable ignorance of the true knowledge and worship of God, and may in time bring the infidels and salvages living in these parts to humane civility and to a settled and quiet government."[49] This does not necessarily mean, however, that the evangelical impulse remained the crucial impetus for early English activities in Jamestown. Evocations of the evangelical mandate often amounted to nothing more than rhetoric. The Virginia Company had no qualm about appropriating the religious motif to legitimize activities carried out in the New World colony. It must be remembered that activities in Jamestown did not meet with unequivocal approval. There were those who saw the invasion of Virginia as an immoral act. To such critics, the formulation of an idealistic religious mission by the Virginia Company could always be depended upon to offer a counter critique.[50]

In his sermon on Virginia, preached before a group of adventurers and planters on 25 April 1609, William Symonds invoked God's call to Abraham to leave his home as a type of his call to Englishmen to leave their beloved England and journey to Virginia.[51] In another sermon delivered in the same year before Lord De La Warr's departure to Virginia, William Crashaw specifically invoked the examples of Nehemiah and David to show how Virginia can, with God's blessings, start off from humble beginnings and develop to become a great settlement.[52] What sermons like Symonds's and Crashaw's perform is to enforce God's design for England to move from the old world to the new by evoking a typological vision of history. In the Book of Genesis, God is said to have called Abraham to leave his native homeland in the Chaldees and proceed to a new land that will be shown to him in time. The point of Abraham's departure is that he figures significantly in God's divine plan to make him, after the test of his faith, the patriarch of a great nation. The Englishman journeying to Virginia is placed in an analogous position with Abraham, and by virtue of that analogy, also enjoys God's protection and blessing. Underwriting typological rhetoric of this kind is the understanding that England figures in the divine scheme of things as a second Israel. By providing a religious cast to the undertakings in Virginia and furnishing spiritual comfort in the anticipated experience of difficulties, typology gave legitimation to the efforts made to settle the Jamestown colony. These efforts aimed specifically at producing lucrative profits by locating gold mines and a water route through the continent to the legendary East Indies. Crashaw's and Symonds's sermons were delivered to members of a joint-stock corporation whose primary motivation was profit making.

The language of typology is also prominent in "Virginias Verger." Purchas evokes God's promise in the Old Testament to lead Israel to the promised land in order to confer on Virginia the status of the Canaan of old. Canaan, the promised land flowing with milk and honey, is read as a type of the Virginia colony:

> But let us consult with the wisest Councellour. Canaan, Abrahams promise, Israels inheritance, type of heaven, and joy of the earth! What were her riches? were they not the Grapes of Eshcol, the balme of Gilead, the Cedary neighbourhood of Libanus, the pastury vale of Jericho, the dewes of heaven, fertility of soile, temper of climat, the flowing (not with Golden Sands, but) with Milke and Hony (necessaries, and pleasures of life, not bottomelesse gulfes of lust) the commodious scituation for two Seas, and other things like (in how many inferiour?) to this of Virginia. (VV 19:233)

Purchas's typological emphasis enables him to show the reader not only the analogy of the tremendous bounty that God gave to Israel in the land of promise, but that he also gives the same and more to England in Virginia: "God goeth before us in making this designe honorable to Religion, to Humanity, to our Ancestors, to our King, to our Kingdome. God goeth before us, and hath given Virginia so rich a portion, to allure and assure our loves" (VV 19:266). The signs of providential guidance and control are unmistakeable for Purchas. And "Virginias Verger" concludes by locating this emphasis on God's leading in the analogy of the Exodus of Israel out of Egypt. Where in the Old Testament the triune God leads through "miraculous fire and cloudy pillars" (VV 19:267), in Purchas's contemporary England, he leads "in the light of reason" (VV 19:267). And when Purchas exhorts God to "come into us and fill us with the spirit of wisedome and understanding, the spirit of counsell and of fortitude, the spirit of knowledge, and the feare of the Lord" (VV 19:267), it is so that "he may vouchsafe to goe with us, and we with him, and after him to Virginia" (VV 19:267). "Be thou the Alpha and Omega of Englands Plantation in Virginia O GOD" (19:267)," he concludes.

The typological discourse we find present in Symonds, Crashaw, and Purchas would be used, but for different purposes, in the ideological expressions of the Puritans who settled in the areas around Plymouth, Massachusetts Bay, Connecticut, and Rhode Island. As Virginians expanded their settlements along the river banks that opened on the Chesapeake, an even more momentous enterprise led by the Puritans was taking place some five hundred miles to the north. Like the Jamestown colonists, the Puritans who migrated from the Old to the New England also had to confront the fact of the implacable wilderness and the hostility of the natives. Accounts given of their experience resemble very much the narratives produced by the colonists in Virginia. In William Bradford's *Of Plymouth Plantation,* for example, we are given an account of how, upon first arriving at Cape Cod, the Pilgrims encountered the savagery and brutality of the natives, who attacked with awful war cries and a barrage of arrows.[53] In this early encounter, the Indians were defeated, a sure sign of God's providential control over the men and women he had led from the Old World to found and create the New. From then on, *Of Plymouth Plantation* is liberally sprinkled with the stories of Indian savagery and hostility, of trade deals transacted between natives and colonists, of violent wars breaking out between rival tribes like the Pequots and the Narragansetts, of God passing judgment on large numbers of Indians by killing them off in the most horrible ways through disease epidemics like smallpox, and even of Indians who died proclaiming their desire to "go to the Englishmen's God in Heaven."[54] God does not only pass judgment on the Amerindians encountered by the Puritans by killing them off through disease, he sometimes expects his chosen people to act as his agents in cleansing the land of evil and idolatry.

For the Puritans who journeyed to America to realize the destiny that God had preordained for them as the founders of New England, the iconoclastic temper that was one of their dominant characteristics got rechanneled to the task of building a garden in the wilderness. Before time even began, God already had a special plan for New England to serve as a light to the nations. To (re)create Eden in the New World in coordination with this plan entailed hard work, part of which involved fighting the Amerindian, whose body is read as a metonymy for the forces of evil that inhabit the American wilderness. To carve a garden out of the wilderness involved eliminating the material of evil—the Amerindian—in its midst. In an important study, *The Interpretation of Material Shapes in Puritanism,* Ann Kibbey traces Puritan "prejudice" against the Other—and this includes the native of the New World—to specific expressions and understanding of iconoclasm in Reformation theology, especially as mediated by John Calvin. Because of a sacramental theology built upon the trope of metonymy, false idols are perceived as having the ability to simulate life, just as living people are responded to as material shapes. What results is the development of a worldview structured on the contestation between competing icons: the elect "who are the true *figurae* of Protestant religion" and the reprobate, who is the living image of opposition to God's living image of grace (in this case, the Puritan).[55] Viewing themselves as living icons, the Puritans perpetrated sacred violence against the body of the Amerindian, whose destruction is the logical outcome of a habit of mind that literalizes figurative language. The literalization of language that leads to the genocidal extermination of native American tribes involves transforming the imagery of fire central to the apocalyptic vision in the book of Revelation—which has all the force of a figurative resonance because of its placement in Scripture as an event in the future—into an actual burning of human bodies in the present. The specific incident referred to by Kibbey, in which a massive bonfire is built out of tortured human bodies, was the violent extermination by the Puritans of Pequot men, women, and children in what is now Mystic, Connecticut, in May 1637. When the Puritans undertook the genocidal massacre of the Pequots, they believed themselves to be working in concert with God's express will to expunge the name of this tribe from history and human memory.

To summarize: Despite the presence of shared motifs in the narratives of both the Pilgrim Fathers and the Virginia colonists, however, the articulation of the religious signification of their respective enterprises is radically different. When the Puritans found themselves taming the implacable wilderness and waging war against the Amerindians, who were viewed as children of the devil, they understood that they were working in concert with God to realize their manifest destiny. The crux of this ideological conception of the New World is cogently encapsulated in a little poem written by Andrew Marvell entitled "Bermudas."[56]

In "Bermudas," the central motifs of the Puritan migration to the New World are presented in microcosm: the flight from Laudian tyranny and persecution into a haven outside of England, the discovery of a *locus amoenus* that has been prepared by divine providence to receive the refugees, the special provision made by God to ensure the comfort of the faithful ones taking refuge. In Marvell's "remote *Bermudas*" (line 1), God has given the sojourners an "eternal Spring" (line 13), removed from the postlapsarian setting of seasonal changes. Divine providence ensures that wants are met through service offered by nature: fowls visit, figs descend, melons drop—all to provide nourishment for the sojourner in his new-found haven. The escape from tyranny that

Marvell celebrates is an escape into a version of paradise. But more importantly, the significance of this place of refuge lies in its removal from the factors of human agency, the efforts of expanded labor made by the refugees, and its situation in the omnipotent control of deity. It is God who protects the refugees from harm, and one important sign of that protection is the generous bestowing of natural providence and sustenance. The refugees do not need to look for food and provision. Bermuda is saturated with natural bounty.

Marvell's psalmic and lyric celebration of deliverance cannot be separated from a conception of power in which the experiences of a group of people enjoy divine protection and sanction. The same rocks that "did frame / A Temple" (lines 31–32) for the refugees are also the locale for articulating power figured in terms of obtaining tribute and provision without the intervention and expansion of labor and effort. When Marvell reifies Bermudan ideality by annihilating the necessary place of labor in the production of goods, he works with a discourse that, in a different political context, enables the exploitation of another's backbreaking work to satisfy one's wants. In Ben Jonson's "To Penshurst," for example, the bounty of the natural world makes itself readily available to serve the noble and aristocratic inhabitants of Penshurst: birds eagerly wait to be killed, fishes leap on land, and fruits ripen before their time. The privileges of aristocracy overlap with those serving the interests of colonialism. The Bermuda pamphlets significantly describe how the earliest visitors could rely on birds to settle on them and then decide upon the heaviest bird to be cooked for food.

In "To the Virginian Voyage," inspired by preparations for the expedition that sailed in December of 1606, Michael Drayton also imagines a condition similar to the one represented by Marvell:

> Virginia,
> Earth's only paradise,
>
> Where Nature hath in store
> Fowl, venison, and fish,
>   And the fruitful'st soil
>   Without your toil
> Three harvests more,
> All greater than your wish.
>
> (lines 23–30)[57]

Considering once again our reading of Marvell's "Bermudas,"
legitimation of the favor enjoyed by the refugees in God's sight is
expressed through a narrative that embeds a conception of power.
If the free and easy delivery of provisions by nature is a sign of
authentication, then the poem implicitly encodes a critique of the
tyrannical order from which the refugees of Laudian England
are fleeing. Ironically, as we know, the history of English colonization of the New World and settlement of New England inscribes
and enacts its own political and theological tyranny, one experienced devastatingly by the dispossessed natives of the land.

In the final analysis, the example of Marvell's "Bermudas"
shows how a disenfranchised and persecuted social group translate their experience of defeat into a narrative of victory. This
reconstituted narrative posits the powerful presence of the Judeo-
Christian God, the transcendental signified in relation to which
all experiences of suffering obtain their focal point and ultimate
meaning. God is in control of time and history, and the gift of
Bermuda existing to offer a safe haven and rest provides ample
proof of his continuing care and control. Underwriting narratives
of the kind we find in Marvell's poem is the premise of a (pre)de-
terministic universe—a haven had been set apart to receive God's
persecuted elect before time and history even began. Calvin's pre-
destinarian emphasis does more than provide comfort to the elect
who are sure of their salvation; it is also used in specific ways to
legitimate self and social identity.

How, for example, does one know that one is elected to salvation? An important measure adopted by English and American
Puritanism is the status of a person's position in society and the
success with which a living is made: the work ethic and the spirit
of capitalism have their roots in this conception. That is why the
hard-working Puritan who makes a decent living for himself can
immediately recognize the signs of his election: the favor of the
Lord is manifest in his life. The vagrant and the beggar, on the
other hand, have all the marks of the predestined reprobate. Calvinistic predestinarianism gets worked into and expressed in
terms of a particular sociology. What we find surfacing is a politics
of self and group validation, one that necessarily creates a space
to absorb the reprobate and demonic Other. The Pilgrim Fathers
who sailed across the Atlantic to escape persecution in Laudian
England brought with them a similar theological framework and
understanding. New England was preordained before the foundation of the world was laid to be the true and proper home of
God's Puritan elect. When the Puritans made their way to the

New World in the 1600s, they were simply working in tandem with the divine plan to fulfill their predestined mission: and nothing must stand in the way of the progress of the saints in the materialization of their manifest destiny.[58] The Manichean characteristic of Puritan engagement with the demonic wilderness shows once again the inscription of a social group in a particular discourse of legitimation. Self and social identity are built by positing the existence of the demonic Other, whether a piece of land or a person. When this Other is tamed, converted, or annihilated, God's protection and workings in the affairs of the elect become evident.[59] In order to accentuate this evidence, the role of human agency in shaping historical events needs to be effaced. Reifying the incontrovertible workings of divine providence independent of human agency is essential to the politics of self-validation. Such a politics, as we have seen, is colonial at its core.

3

"More Faire Than Black": *Othello* and the Discourse of Race Relations in Elizabethan England

In 1614 a fascinating marriage took place between a colonist by the name of John Rolfe and Pocahontas, the daughter of a powerful Algonquian chief. This example of miscegenation in the Jamestown colony attracted much attention at the time because John Rolfe was an Englishman and Pocahontas an American Indian princess. The circumstances leading up to Rolfe's encounter with his heathen bride-to-be were filled with intrigue and political finaglings. Pocahontas was abducted by one Samuel Argall in 1613 and used by the Jamestown colonists as a token of peace with the Indians.[1] Immediately after her abduction, she was placed under the care of a clergyman of Puritan bent by the name of Alexander Whitaker. Within a year she had met the colonist John Rolfe, become his wife, and converted to the Christian faith.[2] Rolfe found himself strangely attracted to this Indian woman, but he had to interpret his feelings for her in terms of the Judeo-Christian discourse of exclusivism.[3] The experience of this famous historical marriage between English colonist and American Indian daughter could not be extricated from the discursive constructions of self and Otherness inhering in European responses to the text of the New World.

Desperately questioning the possibility that love could transpire between a Christian and the heathen Other constitutes the core substance of a letter that John Rolfe wrote to Sir Thomas Dale, then deputy-governor of the Jamestown colony. Underlying Rolfe's scripting of the epistle was the implicit purpose of obtaining Dale's official sanctioning of his intended marriage to Pocahontas. Rolfe discovered that he must respond to any affection that he felt toward Pocahontas as work perpetrated by the devil or as a demonic assault. His letter was suffused with anxiety, largely because he was unable to extricate himself from his Calvinistic convictions and from a cultural reflex that identified Otherness with heathenism and its associations with the demonic. That is why Rolfe's letter foregrounded the missionizing motif in his desperate bid to seek official legitimation for what he himself apparently treated as miscegenation. The following extract from that letter reveals vividly the tremendous tensions Rolfe found himself experiencing as he struggled to find a sound reason for marrying Pocahontas other than love:

> Let therefore this my well advised protestation, which here I make betweene God and my own conscience, be a sufficient witnesse, at the dreadfull day of judgement (when the secret of all mens harts shall be opened) to condemne me herein, if my chiefest intent and purpose be not, to strive with all my power of body and minde, in the undertaking of so mightie a matter, no way led (so farre forth as mans weakenesse may permit) with the unbridled desire of carnall affection: but for the good of this plantation, for the honour of our countrie, for the glory of God, for my owne salvation, and for the converting to the true knowledge of God and Jesus Christ, an unbeleeving creature, namely Pokahuntas.[4]

Rolfe wanted to deflect any suspicion that he was attracted to Pocahontas through eros, or what he called "carnall affection." His intention to marry an Amerindian princess was strictly motivated (or so he claimed) by ambitions larger and nobler than the love of a man for a woman. By marrying Pocahontas, Rolfe believed that he could bring honor and glory to his plantation, his country, and his God. This was to be achieved through the important role he would play in enabling the conversion of the heathen princess to the true faith.

Indeed, as Rolfe's epistle proceeded, the necessity of fulfilling the missionizing mandate got expressed in even more emphatic terms. Pocahontas's very existence as the heathen Other forced an obligation upon him to undertake the task of bringing her to the knowledge of the true faith. Rolfe would carry on the eternal lessons—those leading to the salvation of the soul—imparted by Alexander Whitaker at Henrico. And even though Pocahontas was "blind," "hungrie," and "naked," she also possessed attributes that promised openness to assimilating God's saving Word; there was even the suggestion that Pocahontas had indeed been touched by prevenient grace.[5] Toward the end of his epistle, a classic Puritan document in its emphasis, Rolfe made it a point to emphasize that he planned to marry an Algonquian princess not because he was in a desperate state, devoid of friends, or unable to find a woman from among the English, but because God had impressed upon him its necessity by "perturbations and godly motions."[6] An important emphasis in Rolfe's epistle was that the mandate for marrying Pocahontas came not from himself but God. What God had done was to free him from the confusion that was the "laborinth" of his relationship with Pocahontas. Evidently, Rolfe needed to justify his desire to marry a foreign woman in the face of culture and society.

For the Jamestown colonists, Pocahontas represented an Algonquian, a savage Other, who had been touched by grace and availed herself of the means of salvation. But Pocahontas's conversion to the Christian faith was the exception rather than the rule. Very few of the American natives encountered by the early Virginia colonists converted. Besides being treated as a token of the heathen Other who responded to the saving knowledge of the true faith, Pocahontas also functioned as a useful cross-cultural figure in the political transactions between Algonquian and English. When Samuel Argall first abducted Pocahontas, he sent word to Powhatan, her father, asking for a return of those Englishmen that the Algonquian chief had detained in slavery, and of the arms and tools that the Indians had stolen. He also included the very important item of corn in the list of things required in exchange for Pocahontas. After events turned out differently, and Pocahontas apparently ended up feeling quite at home in the colony, Powhatan said that he would leave his daughter behind with the colonists as a child of Sir Thomas Dale.

In an incisive reading of Pocahontas's relationship to John Smith and John Rolfe in *Colonial Encounters*, Peter Hulme tells us that the role played by the American Indian princess as she passes from her Algonquian culture to an English one cannot be divorced from the anthropological fact that native American cultures interacted with one another according to what has been called the norms of reciprocity.[7] Because native American cultures were undivided or pre-state societies, the operation of a complex system of exchanges was necessary for their functioning and survival. In European cultures or divided societies, by contrast, the state was the guarantor of political and social coherence and cohesiveness.[8] If Pocahontas enabled peace to be established between the Algonquian and the English colonist in the early spring of 1614 because of her function as an object of exchange between the two sides, the different cultural frames of reference ensured that the English always remained one step ahead in the game of political negotiations. Powhatan might have "exchanged" his daughter for the reciprocal gift of harmonious relations, but the English were influenced in their action by having set themselves the task of settling a colony. At a fundamental level, the Algonquian did not want his or her life disrupted; while the English colonist wanted to tap the resources of the New World, he also dreamt of gaining access to the fabled wealth of the Orient. What this meant was that even though, at one level, Pocahontas appeared to have assimilated with some degree of ease the culture of the English colonist, we can never be completely certain about this: for virtually everything recorded of the princess's thoughts and views is communicated through the mediated accounts of English colonists like John Smith. That John Rolfe could experience so much anxiety in his desire to marry Pocahontas stemmed directly from his inscription in a discourse that established a clear division between civilization and savagery, between the city on the hill and the wilderness in which unregenerate forces could be found. The ideology is Puritan. Even though Pocahontas showed herself sympathetic toward the Judeo-Christian tradition to which the English colonist belonged, Rolfe himself found it extremely difficult to view her apart from her heathen background and concomitant barbaric nature. Even as Rolfe found himself caught in painful ambivalences in 1614 in the Virginia colony, due to his deep inscription in culture, William Shakespeare, approximately ten years earlier in England, dramatized the marriage between a black Moor and a white woman.

In Shakespeare's play *Othello,* the same elements we discover in Rolfe's experience—acceptance or rejection of the community, the place of the Christian faith in marrying the Other, and the consequent psychological fractures—are all present, but with a difference. In *Othello,* the black Moor readily and self-consciously assimilates the Judeo-Christian ethic of the dominant culture, but he is unable to extricate himself from deeply embedded anxieties generated by his own insecurities and the prejudices of Venetian society. If John Rolfe tells his own story as a man from the dominant culture coming to grips with the assimilation of the Other into his world, Shakespeare dramatizes the story of a man from the marginalized culture negotiating the problematics of assimilation.

OTHERNESS AND THE COMPOSITIONS OF ANXIETY

In *Othello,* Shakespeare refers to his tragic protagonist as the Moor of Venice.[9] This designation makes it hardly possible for a reader or audience of the play to mistake Othello's ethnic and cultural identity. In the eyes of Shakespeare's contemporary audience, the Moor would stand for somebody who has his origins somewhere in Africa, possesses associative links with the Arabs, and is, most significantly, a Moslem. The Moor signifies the threat posed by the infidel to the stability of the Christian world; he is the pagan Other who must be limited and contained if Christian Europe is to protect itself from the onslaught of the Islamic Orient. The O.E.D. gives the following definition of "Moor": "In *Ancient History,* a native of *Mauretania,* a region of North Africa corresponding to parts of Morocco and Algeria. In later times, one belonging to the people of mixed Berber and Arab race, Muslim in religion, who constitute the bulk of the population of North-western Africa, and who in the eighth century conquered Spain. In the Middle Ages, and as late as the seventeenth century, the Moors were commonly supposed to be mostly black or very swarthy (though the existence of 'white Moors' was recognized), and hence the word was often used for 'Negro'." In *Othello's Countrymen,* Eldred Jones argues that Shakespeare made use of available information on the character of Moors to delineate Othello. To Jones, there is little possibility that Shakespeare could be confused about the difference in color between Moors and Blacks.[10] What I find especially interesting about Shakespeare's portrayal of Othello is that, even though he gives his tragic protagonist the express identity of a Moor, he also emphasizes the blackness of his skin. The emphasis on Othello's blackness, complete with all its symbolic significations, complicates the primary emphasis usually given to the identity of the Moor as the Moslem infidel. Kim Hall also notes that in early modern England, "Moor" functioned as a designation that stood alternatively for many categories: Muslims, Native Americans, Indians, white North Africans, and Jews. It served at that period as a general term to describe the ethnically, culturally, and religiously "strange."[11] There is another term— "blackamoor"—whose designation comes much closer to the person Elizabeth I refers to as the "negar." The O.E.D. defines the "blackamoor" as "A black-skinned African, an Ethiopian, a Negro; any very dark person." When reading *Othello,* it becomes clear that Shakespeare is much less interested in providing any consistent portrait of the Moor or the "blackamoor" than he is in delineating a tragic protagonist defined by his ethnic Otherness and cultural difference.

Othello is not Shakespeare's only play in which the figure of the black Moor is given considerable attention. In his earlier and experimental *Titus Andronicus* (first performed in 1594), Aaron the Moor is made the locus and center of the evil responsible for disrupting Rome's political and social harmony.[12] Aaron, the secret lover of Tamora (the Queen of the Goths, who is made captive by Titus and is later married to Saturninus) is the agent through whom the vengeful Tamora is able to bring about Bassianus's murder and the execution of Titus's two sons. Aaron's significance as the source of Rome's tumult, figured through the gruesome images and metaphors of dismemberment, is highlighted with reference to the color of his skin. Coming across Tamora and Aaron in their secret meeting in the woods, Bassianus and Lavinia react by invoking the discourse of color and race relations.

> Bassianus:
> Believe me, queen, your swart Cimmerian
> Doth make your honour of his body's hue,
> Spotted, detested, and abominable.
> Why are you sequest'red from all your train,
> Dismounted from your snow-white goodly steed,
> And wand'red hither to an obscure plot,
> Accompanied but with a barbarous Moor,
> If foul desire had not conducted you?
> Lavinia:
> And, being intercepted in your sport,
> Great reason that my noble lord be rated
> For sauciness. I pray you, let us hence,
> And let her joy her raven-coloured love;
> This valley fits the purpose passing well.
>
> (2.3.72–84)

Titus Andronicus elaborates on the symbolic relationship between Aaron's blackness and individual as well as communal evil. Aaron himself says, "Let fools do good, and fair men call for grace, / Aaron will have his soul black like his face" (3.1.204–05); and when explaining to Titus Andronicus why he killed a fly, Marcus says, "Pardon me, sir; it was a black ill-favour'd fly / Like to the empress' Moor; therefore I kill'd him" (3.2.66–67). When Tamora bears Aaron a son, she wants him killed, relaying the following message to her clandestine lover through the Nurse:

> A joyless, dismal, black, and sorrowful issue.
> Here is the babe, as loathsome as a toad
> Amongst the fair-fac'd breeders of our clime;

The empress sends it thee, thy stamp, thy seal,
And bids thee christen it with thy dagger's point.

                                        (4.2.66–70)

Represented in one-dimensional terms, Shakespeare's Aaron symbolizes all of Rome's evil and destructive energies because of the
blackness of his skin. Toward the end of the play, the enormities
committed by Saturninus and Tamora are displaced onto the figure of the "coal-black Moor" (3.2.78): Marcus refers, for example,
to Aaron as "an irreligious Moor, / Chief architect and plotter of
these woes" (5.3.121–22). Where, in *Titus Andronicus,* Shakespeare
plays up the relationship between the color of one's skin and the
economy of social evil, in *Othello* that relationship is complicated
because the source of evil is locatable in a white society and the
black protagonist is the victim of white malice. Between the production of *Titus Andronicus* and *Othello,* a period of some ten years,
there appears to be a development in Shakespeare's dramatization
of the politics of race relations. The question that this chapter
proposes to explore is whether the complication of color significations and its symbolic economy leads to any radical reappraisal
of race relations for Shakespeare.

Shakespeare's *Othello* is first and foremost a tragedy about
power played out at the level of ethnic relationships. It explores
what it means for a black man to live in a dominantly white society,
and asks whether he can really belong to that society. To come up
with some answers, Shakespeare makes Othello the great general
and protector of Venice, has him marry a senator's daughter, introduces a disgruntled ensign, and comes up with some amazing
results. The black general is completely deceived by his ensign
and murders his innocent wife. Because Desdemona is innocent
and Othello is made completely incapacitated by Iago's murderous design, the audience is given the burden of judging the wisdom and viability of an interracial marriage. Does the play
suggest, at any point, that Othello's vulnerability and susceptibility
may be traced in some way to his ethnicity? Is Desdemona solely
culpable for the tragic mistake of deciding to go her own way and
marry a black man in secret, disregarding her father's fears and
admonitions? Are the Venetians who always had apprehensions
about Othello finally vindicated in their assessment of his
character?

I would like to begin by considering the response of Desdemona's father to the subject of miscegenation. Brabantio's perceptions of Othello's place in Venetian society introduce, at the very start, the play's preoccupation with the relationship between rank and status on the one hand, and utility and service on the other. As far as Brabantio is concerned, Othello is significant only so long as he fulfills his duties as an employee of the state. He has known Othello only in that official capacity and the secret marriage of his daughter to the Moor comes as a violent shock. Brabantio responds with a profuse and prejudicial invective to the news broken by Iago and Roderigo. He reacts to his daughter's secret marriage by invoking the importance of maintaining purity of race; an intermarriage between a black man and a white woman contaminates this purity. To entertain a Moor as an important officer of the state is different from having to regard him as a daughter's suitor.

Othello understands service differently from Brabantio. He tries to believe that fulfilling his duties as the protector of Venice marks his loyalty to, and confirms his intrinsic place in, the state. Othello believes that as a member of Venetian society, it is his duty to direct its defence. Underwriting that conviction is, however, an anxious need to be accepted by the Venetians. There is a constant need for Othello to affirm for himself his rightful place in Venetian society, and Iago knows this. That is why much of what Iago says to Othello is designed to arouse and heighten his innate anxieties. Iago reminds Othello that he is black and therefore different. The clearest indication of this difference is evidenced, Iago insinuates, in the attraction Desdemona feels toward the handsome Cassio; furthermore, Iago implies, to be attracted to a man like Cassio is to reveal a dangerous sexual incontinence. The relentless cultural logic that a white woman should and would necessarily desire a white man is not only endorsed by Iago, but reinforced by Brabantio:

> Damn'd as thou art, thou hast enchanted her,
> For I'll refer me to all things of sense,
> (If she in chains of magic were not bound)
> Whether a maid, so tender, fair, and happy,
> So opposite to marriage, that she shunn'd
> The wealthy curled darlings of our nation,
> Would ever have (to incur a general mock)
> Run from her guardage to the sooty bosom
> Of such a thing as thou? to fear, not to delight.
>
> (1.2.63–71)

Iago appeals to nature as the central determinant of ethnic and racial affinities and segregations. Nature is the binding force that always brings men and women of one race together. From Braban-tio's and Iago's points of view, Desdemona has undermined a basic law of nature when she enters into marriage with a black man; indeed, her desire to do so is deemed unnatural. Iago tells Roder-igo that after Desdemona has satisfied her lust and "the blood . . . made dull with the act of sport, . . . *very nature* will instruct her to it, and compel her to some second choice" (2.1.225–34; italics mine). He had earlier said: "It cannot be that Desdemona should long continue her love unto the Moor, . . . When she is sated with his body, she will find the error of her choice; she must have change, she must" (1.3.342–53). What Iago really means is that because Desdemona's love for the Moor is unnatural, it cannot be sustained for long and a purgative function will operate as a mat-ter of course; Desdemona, who will give her affections to another man after satisfying her lust for Othello, is following the instincts of her *nature* as a whore. But more than that, she is a woman whose sexual incontinence constitutes a dangerous excess and imbalance.

Othello depicts a social order in which the hierarchy separating master from servant, whites from blacks, and employer from em-ployee is both deeply entrenched and inviolable. A relationship between implied equals, as signified by the marriage of Desde-mona and Othello, must not be permitted to go on; so Iago begins his design of disrupting this relationship by reminding Othello that blackness is the literal and symbolic register of all things unnatural and inferior. Othello reacts to the insinuations about how unnatural it is for a black man to marry a white woman by plunging into emotional chaos. That Iago finds it easy to under-mine the Moor's emotional stability reveals that Othello can never fully obliterate his African self when he fabricates his Venetian/ white identity. If Othello desires to set himself up as a tabula rasa that will inscribe all the values of Venetian culture, his tormented reactions to Iago's insinuations point to the impossibility of fash-ioning an entirely new identity that obliterates cultural barriers. When he accepts Iago's underlying message that a black man can never compete with a white man for the love of a white woman, he reveals not only his anxieties about his own African identity, but registers this anxiety as a subscription to colonial fiction. Othello ultimately makes sense of his tragedy in terms of the proscriptive strictures offered by the dominant culture. By referring to him-self as "a malignant and a turban'd Turk" (5.2.354) to describe his own situation at the end, Othello reveals he is unable to divorce himself from the basic Venetian construction of social and cultural identity. The Turk that he perceives to be distinct and separate from himself is inscribed indelibly in his identity as Venice's cultural and ethnic Other. Othello is what Jonathan Dollimore calls "a domesticated foreigner,"[13] a man who can never ground his identity in a white society.

When Othello finally invokes the metaphor of the Turk who "Beat a Venetian" (5.2.355) to conclude his definition of his own identity, he appropriates the language of cultural relations he knows best. He recognizes that he is defined by language and the identity language bestows. At the end, Othello's literal and symbolic body incorporates both the Turk and the Venetian. According to the logic of the analogy he sets up and the metaphor he invokes, Othello the cultural Other kills the Venetian, who happens also to be himself. The convergence of the Venetian and the Turk in the person of Othello points to the dual and contradictory twists of identity in which he is caught up inexorably and defined tragically.

It is possible to argue that the ease with which Othello becomes befuddled can be traced to anxieties he always had, but suppressed, concerning his place and position in Venetian society. A sign of this anxiety is seen in the way Othello does all he can to live as a Venetian by embracing its cultural values. Venice is an identifiably Christian society, something Shakespeare goes to great lengths to foreground in the play. Othello significantly responds to the orchestrated altercation between Cassio, Roderigo, and Montano by asking angrily, "Are we turn'd Turks, and to ourselves do that / Which heaven has forbid the Ottomites?" (2.3.161–62). He reads the situation in terms of a fundamental conflict between the Christian world of order and "propriety" (2.3.167) and a pagan world of disorder and chaos. When he wins the battle against the Turks at Cyprus, Othello embodies the strength and stability of Christian Venice.

Shakespeare's representation of Christian Venice reverses the emphasis found in many writings of the period, where Christian soldiers lack discipline in contrast to the organized infidels. The disciplined Turk finds his identity in the discourse of those Europeans who had travelled in Turkey and concluded that these infidels appreciated learning, the arts, and civilized comforts. Their discipline and serious approach to their religion had much to teach the flabby and generally uncommitted Christian.[14] In *Othello*, Shakespeare invokes instead the other tradition that defines the identities of the European and pagan armies in terms of the opposition set up between the disciplined Christian soldier and the barbarous and disorderly Turk. In this tradition, the forces of the infidel are defined by all the values antagonistic to and abhorred by the European: they are chaotic, undisciplined, treacherous, barbaric, even cowardly. The emphasis given in *Othello* to Christian order and pagan disorder belongs to the metaphorical framework of a play defined by a distinct and explicit politics of domination and control. Preserving the Venetian way of life depends on the very strict defense and maintenance of this order. Any action or ethos perceived as running counter to and threatening the Christian world of order and coherence must be opposed and annihilated. So Othello fights against the Turks who belong to the margins of culture and civilization to keep intact the world of Venetian order and also to affirm his identity as the custodian of the values of a dominant white culture. But he discovers he can never belong to the society for which he would gladly have laid down his life as its military general.

In defending the values and standards of Venetian society, Othello enacts and ratifies its prejudices. One of the most obvious involves the perception that women are treacherous, willful, and sexually promiscuous. From the very start, Brabantio had already interpreted his daughter's actions in terms of deceit: "Look to her, Moor, have a quick eye to see: / She has deceiv'd her father, may do thee" (1.3.292–93). But women are not only deceitful but willful, and willfulness is always responded to with tremendous anxieties by fathers in Shakespearean drama.[15] King Lear responds to what he perceives to be Cordelia's willfulness in not acceding to his demands for protestations of love by disowning her. Brabantio responds to the willful Desdemona by effectively doing the same. Furthermore, it does not really take much for willfulness to be confused with deceit—these two aspects are blurred into one in Brabantio's and, later, Othello's minds. The anxieties the father expresses concerning his daughter's exercise of her will moves beyond the threat this expression of the will poses to the father's authority in the domestic economy, and by symbolic extension, to the health of the larger commonwealth; they belong to a larger discursive universe in Renaissance England where the willful and assertive female is apprehended in "unnatural" categories: as demons, whores, witches, or beasts. Where the father may disown a daughter whose will is appetitive, a brother may drive his sister insane and get her killed off for presuming to thwart the life he has planned and shaped for her. This second example of the murderous brother is the subject of Webster's *Duchess of Malfi,* a tragedy based on a familiar theme in English

Renaissance drama—the inevitable friction generated when female desire collides with patriarchal authority. It is interesting that in the desperate need to procure the compliance of their daughters' will, fathers like Lear and Brabantio lose sight of the necessary reconstitution of the filial relationship in the light of their children's entry into the new marriage economy. Cordelia and Desdemona recognize that marriage requires them to prioritize the conjugal over the filial relationship. In *King Lear* and *Othello*, the fathers are unable to come to terms with this change, preferring instead to interpret the shift from obedience to parental wishes to affection for the husband as a transgression, with irreparable consequences.[16]

In *Othello*, the treacherous female body is not only Iago's phobia, but the discursive construct of Venice's larger patriarchal system. This body is associated with the secrets of the dark continent, secrets that must be uncovered and exposed to the gaze of the audience. Patricia Parker has commented on the centrality of the trope of discovery to colonialist discourse, one that crosses over easily to patriarchalism.[17] Like the writers of travel narratives (assuming the roles of explorers and more insidiously of informers) who open up the interior of Africa to the European gaze, Iago proceeds to "discover," stage by stage, for Othello, the monstrous nature of Desdemona's uncontrolled sexuality. Ironically, the *evidentia* needed for this discovery of the secrets of the woman's sexual excess is supplied by Othello's own imagination and anxiety. The idea of the monstrous in this play is complicatedly the discursive construct of an anxiety-riddled patriarchy as well as a colonialist-minded one.

As a patriarchalist construction responding to the female body which it cannot control, the conferral of the category of the monstrous reveals male anxiety at recuperating the grounds of its once assumed but now eroded power. Strident efforts made to contain the errant woman are powerfully enacted at various moments in the play. In act 3, scene 3, for example, Iago alludes to Brabantio's admonition that Othello should always keep in mind Desdemona's deceitful nature. Brabantio, we recall, had earlier encountered tremendous difficulties when forced to come to terms with a daughter who possessed the unexpected ability to exert her own independent will. Iago uses repetition to revive a latent memory, activating it through reinforcement and recontextualization. For Brabantio, Desdemona's decision to marry a black man fractures the ideality of a child's filial link to the father; but more than that, the ability of the child to exert her will becomes an incomprehensible phenomenon when it is situated in relation to the established premises upon which members of a particular culture and system function and operate. It is unnatural, as far as Brabantio is concerned, for a white woman—in this case unfortunately his daughter—to love and marry a black man. Brabantio's sense of the unnaturalness of miscegenation is experienced by Othello himself in act 3, scene 3: "And yet how nature erring from itself—" (line 231). His iteration of Iago and Brabantio's motifs registers his own innate anxieties concerning ethnic interactions. Iago happily elaborates upon and reiterates these motifs after Othello:

> Ay, there's the point: as, to be bold with you,
> Not to affect many proposed matches,
> Of her own clime, complexion, and degree,
> Whereto we see in all things nature tends;
> Fie, we may smell in such a will most rank,
> Foul disproportion; thoughts unnatural.
>
> (3.3.232–37)

Iago also evokes another important motif—that of witchcraft—to demonize Desdemona in Othello's eyes. He stresses the supernatural power Desdemona possesses and exercises when she blinds Brabantio: "She that so young could give out such a seeming, / To seal her father's eyes up, close as oak, / He thought 'twas witchcraft" (3.3.213–15). Implicitly, if she had been successful in the past, what is to prevent her from pulling off a similar stunt in the present? Desdemona's choice in loving Othello gets rewritten in Iago's text as a narrative of deceit and manipulation. Even worse, she eludes comprehension because she dabbles in the occult. In *Othello*, witchcraft is the label given to an experience that resists straightforward interpretation; it is also the sign of the incomprehensible culture and identity of the Other. When Iago tells Othello that Brabantio "thought 'twas witchcraft," his direct reference is to the senator's response to the occultic workings of the Moor. But if "witchcraft" is the word used by Iago to describe the black magic that Brabantio accuses Othello of practicing, it also defines what Desdemona is about. The status of demonic Otherness gets transferred in this equivocation from Brabantio's Othello to Iago's Desdemona.

Othello's response to the threat posed by the maternal body is tied to his inability to ground his identity in a particular social world because he cannot negotiate the political complexities of being married to a white woman, defending Venice against the alien Turks, and guarding the cultural values of his adopted country. The harder Othello tries to entrench himself in Venetian society, the more rigidly he consolidates his identity as Venice's ethnic Other. Likewise, the more relentlessly he defends the values of Venetian culture, the deeper appears to be the confusion into which he loses himself. Ironically, this need to be fully Venetian gives to Othello those cultural codes that, stretched to its perverse extreme, render the killing of Desdemona legitimate. The shared anxieties Othello and Iago have about the nature of women appear to have their roots in certain expressions within the Judeo-Christian tradition, one Shakespeare identifies as constituting the basis of Venice's cultural system. The play specifically foregrounds the literal as well as symbolic antagonisms transpiring between Christian Venice and the pagan Turks. Significantly, Othello fights on the Christian side. But Shakespeare's evocation of a Christianized Venetian culture is not confined to the wars waged between the Christian and the Turk; it also appears in the portrayal of Othello's and Desdemona's marriage.

In *Renaissance Self-Fashioning*, Stephen Greenblatt situates Othello's and Desdemona's responses to love and passion against the vast backdrop of commentaries and exegeses on marriage produced by and defining Christian orthodoxy. A central theme in these commentaries is the general distrust of eroticism and a need to ensure that the wife occupies a position of secondariness in the conjugal economy. According to Greenblatt, Othello defines his relationship with Desdemona by subscribing to the codes of authority and submission shaped by "the colonial power of Christian doctrine over sexuality."[18] The Moor is tragically caught between the joys of fulfilled sexual desire and anxieties generated by the understanding that such desires are linked to fallen human passions. Fueling Othello's anxieties, then, is an underlying theological system that defines physical nature as radically evil and the *damnosa hereditas* of the fall. When Iago conjures up, for Othello, Desdemona's sexual incontinence, he also gives to him the portrait of a woman who subverts the order of gendered hierarchy as institutionalized in Christian orthodoxy. Othello's tortured response to Iago's insinuations betrays a need to preserve the sanctity of the conjugal bed, conditioned and influenced by doctrinal views stressing the sacredness of marriage and evils of adultery. In seventeenth-century England, these views found ample expression in the Puritan idealization of marriage; linked directly to this idealization was the rigid legislation of sexual behavior in those places where the Puritan ethic gained cultural dominance. In Renaissance England, this Puritan conception of marriage led to the enactment of a law in 1650, in which adultery constituted a crime punishable by death. In drama, Desdemona had already been made subject to that law, albeit unjustly.

The Christianity that Greenblatt describes as "the alienating yet constitutive force in Othello's identity"[19] is a system that the Moor is willing to defend with his life, for it represents for him the central values of the Venetian world. But the play shows that even as Othello subscribes to identifiable Christian norms and practices (or those expressed in particular ways in Puritanism), it also reveals how their absorption can produce disastrous results. In desiring to protect at all costs values that he deems important because linked to the state, Othello loses his perspective and the ability to make judgments. It is significant that, in Shakespeare's portrayal of the fracturing of the marital relationship, Othello is shown to permit his identity as a high-ranking official of the state—his public self—to determine the functionings of the private and domestic space to which conjugal love belongs. When Othello explains that Desdemona needs to die to protect the interests of men in society, he figures himself as a defender of the male community, a metonymy in his vocabulary for Venice itself. He does not limit the interests to be served by his premeditated murder of Desdemona to the desires of the self, but opens these up to embrace an entire society (of men). In the play's symbolic economy, the defense of the male is inseparable from the defense of Venetian society; definitions of identity in the public sphere cross over into the domestic, so even Iago can successfully make Othello "read" Desdemona as a form of threat to social security, one that needs removal by the soldier. It appears that in absorbing the Christian roots of the culture he lives in, Othello also assimilates its ethics of marginalization and exclusion. By fighting, for example, against the Turk as the cultural Other, and by punishing Desdemona as the transgressing whore, Othello accepts implicitly an ethical system founded on exclusivity, a system that operates theologically as well as socially by defining a cultural center set over and against the existence of the (un)*ethical* Other. In order to preserve and protect the sanctity and inviolability of this system, Othello resorts to violence: he routs the Turks and murders Desdemona.

Set against this male world of the soldier and the misogynist—as represented by Othello and Iago respectively—is a community of women bonding together on the basis of their (mis)treatment by the men. Michael Cassio laughs at Bianca and treats her as a trifle, but Bianca continues to care for him despite his callousness.

Even though Emilia lives up to what is expected of her as Iago's wife—the subservient woman who performs the will of the husband—she knows enough of the world to recognize that it is the men who do not "use [their women] well" (4.3.102) and sufficiently revolted to speak out against her husband at the end. Wives get alienated from their husbands and gravitate toward one another in sympathy. The creation of the symbolic space occupied by women calls attention to the larger patriarchal world threatening its existence. At the end of the play, this space is destroyed with the deaths of Desdemona and Emilia, but not before it calls attention to the tyranny and violence of the patriarchal order.

Victim or Villain?

The relationship between victimization and complicity in the tragedy is expressed through the shared frames of reference, narrative doublings, and symbolic mirrorings that Shakespeare employs to portray Othello and Iago. Iago and Othello, for example, both invoke the Turk as a metaphor for the alien Other who represents all the values antithetical to Christian Venice. Because both Othello and Iago are identified with the Turk within the symbolic and ethical economies of the play, who the "real" Other might be becomes a complicated question. When Iago says to Roderigo, "Were I the Moor, I would not be Iago," (1.1.57) he appears to be saying that if he were Othello, he would want to be removed as far as possible from the Venetian heart of darkness. He also suggests that if he were in the Moor's position, he would have no reason to execute these dark designs because he would be in possession of Desdemona and a powerful military position. Later in the play, Iago's statement to Othello—"I am your own forever" (3.3.486)—resonates with the suggestion that Othello is himself complicit in enabling Iago's dark designs; Othello is implicated in the evil embodied in Iago because he takes the initiative to make Iago his own. The definition of his "real" identity plagues Othello throughout the play. When Lodovico enters to apprehend Desdemona's murderer, and demands "Where is this rash and most unfortunate man?" (5.2.284), Othello responds: "That's he that was Othello; here I am" (5.2.285). Othello separates the Moor who was Venice's trusted general from the heathen Other who had just committed a hideous murder. The Othello who stands accused of his wife's murder embodies the darkest fears that characters like Brabantio and Iago have of the black man.

The sinister conflation of Othello's and Iago's identities is bound up with the effects of assimilation. The price Othello pays for assimilation into white culture is his transformation into the agency through which the patriarchal and colonial values of Venetian culture get enacted and materialized. Patriarchy demands punishment for the transgressing whore, the name it bestows on the woman who trespasses beyond the confines defined for her by men, and colonialism wages war against the Turk as the ethnic and cultural Other. And this is the violent irony of Othello's need to be assimilated into Venetian society. Fashioning a Venetian identity by striving to obliterate, if possible, the African self relegates originary identity to the Place of the Other. That Othello does not want to recognize himself in this place of the Other does not mean that this Other does not exist. Even as Othello works diligently to fulfill his duties and legitimize his social identity as Venetian general, he finds that the discourse of the Other emerges at deep moments of stress, getting entangled with the discourse of the dominant culture he has assimilated.

Shakespeare highlights Othello's dilemma of being caught between two cultural systems in the stories that he tells. When Othello recounts "the story of [his] life" (1.3.129) at Brabantio's request, he also includes "with it all [his] travel's history" (1.3.139):

> Wherein of antres vast, and deserts idle,
> Rough quarries, rocks and hills, whose heads touch heaven,
> It was my hint to speak, such was the process:
> And of the Cannibals, that each other eat;
> The Anthropophagi, and men whose heads
> Do grow beneath their shoulders: this to hear
> Would Desdemona seriously incline.
>
> (1.3.140–46)

The reference to the chronicle of his life as "my travel's history" positions Othello as a narrator who produces for an auditor his experiences in distant and exotic lands. As such a narrator, he engages in the activity of "bringing to light"[20] for Brabantio and Desdemona the secrets of places and peoples living beyond Venice. But as the narrator of a "travel's history," Othello necessarily finds himself ironically situated, because the genre of the travel or discovery narrative belongs typically to the European traveler or compiler; this irony is further accentuated by the portrayal of the Moor venturing among races to which his origins can be traced (in literature and travel narratives) by virtue of his blackness and difference. (Othello's stories of slavery and adventure, for example, rehearse in abbreviated form the legends and myths of black Africa found in such popular works as Mandeville's *Travels,* reprinted in the Latin text in the first edition of Hakluyt's *Principal Navigations* [1589].) Desdemona responds to Othello's "story" (1.3.165) by "devour[ing] up [his] discourse" (1.3.150), registering her rapacious appetite for the narrative that he uncovers. She tells him that his ability to unfold a "story" is what attracts her to him; the "pilgrimage" (1.3.153) which Othello "dilate[s]" (1.3.153) is filled with such "strange" (1.3.160) occurrences and revelations of courage as to elicit from Desdemona "pity" (1.3.168) and awe. Underwriting Desdemona's response to Othello's dilation and (dis)covering is a sense of wonder at beholding a whole new world that has been "brought to light" for her through his powers of narration. She relates not only to the exoticism inscribed in the Moor's narrative but in his very person; the man who had experienced exotic lands that Desdemona cannot even begin to imagine, inscribes in his literal and symbolic body the difference and Otherness toward which she feels irresistibly drawn.

Travel and discovery narratives are often designed to evoke the reader's sense of wonder in order to inspire colonial ambitions. By giving a foretaste of what is out there in the larger world through representations of "fabulous" and "fantastic" peoples and places, a writer or compiler of such narratives is in the business of energizing a culture's latent colonial desire. If we turn to a colonizing text like *The Discoverie of Guiana,* for instance, we find that Ralegh tells his reader that there is no reason to disbelieve accounts given of the nation of people who lived along the Caora—the Ewaipanoma who had heads growing beneath their shoulders, eyes in their shoulders, and mouths in the middle of their breasts. He has never seen this nation, but professes to accept the verifiability of verbal reports. Like Shakespeare's account of Othello's "travel's history," Ralegh's rendition of the existence of such as the Ewaipanoma owes directly to stories of the exotic and the "fantastic" found in Mandeville's travel narratives. To a colonial explorer like Ralegh, the ability to intersperse imaginary narratives in a text designed to underwrite Europe's colonial ambitions is an implicit privilege enjoyed by the author of travel literature. If representations of the "fantastic" in travel narratives are designed to excite the reader, they are also often recognized for their fictionalizations. So if there are readers who turn to such literature in order to have foreign lands and peoples dilated and (dis)covered for them, there are others who reject it as lies and untruths. (In chapter 1, I have shown how James I sent Ralegh to his death with the immediate charge that he engaged in lies and untruths concerning his voyage to Guiana.)

Iago belongs to the latter group that reads accounts of the "fabulous" in travel narratives as untruths. Specifically, he tells Roderigo that the Moor is given to "bragging, and telling . . . fantastical lies" (2.1.222). Iago's response draws attention to the whole complex issue of veracity that attends receptions of travel narratives in early modern England; as I said, not all readers accept without questioning accounts of the exotic afforded them in this literature. In addition to the narration of his "traveler's history," another important moment in the play in which Othello offers a "fantastic" narrative is when he reveals to Desdemona the magic inhering in the missing handkerchief. Sewn by a sybil and given to Othello's mother by an Egyptian charmer who possessed the ability to read the thoughts of people, the handkerchief must never be lost. Its absence will inevitably lead to a substitution of affections. Here Othello delivers a cautionary tale and a parabolic narrative when he transforms an ordinary object into the guardian of the woman's moral state of being. It is clear that the awesome powers of the handkerchief find their source in the need of the male to police and legislate the domain of female sexuality.

When Desdemona first finds herself responding to Othello's rendition of the magical status of the handkerchief, she can only say that if the case were so, she wishes that she had never laid eyes on it; her answer constitutes a basic reaction to her husband's inexplicable and totally unreasonable reaction to a trifling incident. But the response is also made in a desperate bid to seek a rational explanation for Othello's anger. Through his narrative, Othello has specifically defined himself as the radical Other whose selfhood cannot be extricated from an exotic history signified by the "fantastical" handkerchief: he foregrounds his identity as the cultural Other in a defensive as well as offensive reaction against the woman whom he believes to have been unfaithful to the marriage bed. There appears to be no language capable of mediating between Desdemona's perplexity and Othello's fury. Where Othello earlier on unfolded a "fantastic" narrative to woo Desdemona, he now reveals that he also reacts to anxiety by spinning "fabulous" narratives, a trait that Iago recognizes can be manipulated to full advantage. To Iago, Othello's difference from Venetian society can be highlighted by distinguishing between the "fantastic" discourse of the Other—which he identifies as steeped in lies—and the down-to-earth discourse of the Venetian. Iago, in a word, portrays himself as a skeptic in relation to the reception of travel narratives; not only does he profess his distrust of them, he translates the genre of the "fantastic" into an index of its author's Otherness, his radical difference from mainstream Venetian culture. Iago is insidious: he assists Othello in (dis)covering, and "bringing to light," the secrets of a female sexuality constituted as monstrous—a point I raised earlier in this chapter—only to dilate for the gaze of the audience the Moor's deeply vulnerable self. Iago cannot extricate himself from the colonial activity of writing the body of the African Other as a text for the reading of his audience.

In reading *Othello*, one notices the ubiquitous presence of motifs and metaphors that draw attention to the distinct rhetoric of colonialism, found in numerous travel and discovery narratives compiled in the early modern period. I have pointed out a number of these motifs and metaphors: Othello journeying among people who owe their currency to Mandeville's travel narratives; both Othello and Iago "bringing to light" the secrets of the monstrous Other; Desdemona responding with wonder to the dilation of Othello's "fabulous" narrative; Iago responding to the "free and open nature" (1.3.397) of the Moor as a condition for exploitation. Embedded in a dramatic narrative centered on the experience of miscegenation, they link the play's concerns to the social phenomenon of English colonial activities. Or to put it in another way, awareness of these activities yields important motifs and figures with which Shakespeare is able to represent the structures of domination and submission across the categorical domains of gender and race. The domination that one person exercises over another is figured and interpreted with reference to the working out of colonial relations. The analogies and thematic associations that link narrative moments in the play to the rhetoric of colonialism do not necessarily imply that Shakespeare is making some statement about the politics of expansionism; rather what it shows is that, as in the case of John Donne discussed in chapter 2, awareness of English colonial ambitions provides the poet with a rich and suggestive pool of available metaphors for producing literature. But in using these metaphors, the poet also engages with, and consequently contributes to, the formation of a discourse; literary representation embeds perspectives that interact with others in a larger cultural preoccupation with the dreams of expansionism. So the very presence of colonial tropes in a play like *Othello* means that any grandeur possessed by the tragic protagonist by virtue of his titanic passions and monumental suffering—requisites for classical tragedy—cannot be appreciated apart from a consideration of his connections with the spectacle of blackness, travel narratives, and even the slave trade. Such tragic grandeur may, in relation to these motifs, intervene to rewrite popular conceptions of the African Other; or it may ratify popular prejudices and misconceptions.

TEXTUAL AND SOCIAL ANALOGIES

Othello is a play that dramatizes the implications and ramifications of making prejudgments. Brabantio's and Iago's responses to Othello reveal that they relate to him on the basis of images of the black man inherited as prejudices in their white male culture. Do Brabantio's and Iago's views of the black man actually get confirmed by Othello's actions in the tragedy? Gratiano, for example, says that Brabantio is fortunate to have died because "did he live now, / This sight would make him do a desperate turn" (5.2.207–8) and Emilia refers to Othello as "the blacker devil" (5.2.132). But even as the audience finds itself responding to the pathos generated by Othello's actions, it never forgets that the source and center of evil in Venetian society is Iago, a white man. This tragedy is constructed out of the intersection of two discourses: one positing the destructive anxieties harbored by the ethnic alien, the other locating the white man as the center of a culture's destructive prejudices. The play is therefore radically unstable in its representation of mixed relationships, an instability that calls into question cultural prejudices while endorsing them. *Othello* cannot be interpreted apart from cultural perceptions of ethnic difference.

Brabantio and Iago are not the only ones who have difficulties responding to the marriage between Othello and Desdemona. Later readers of the play too have reacted to Shakespeare's portrayal of Othello and Desdemona with ambivalence. Karen Newman cites the responses of Thomas Rymer and Samuel Taylor Coleridge as examples of such ambivalence, responses I wish to recapitulate here for the purposes of our discussion.[21] In "A Short View of Tragedy" in 1693, Rymer found that Shakespeare was not racist enough because he gave his protagonist a name, made Othello a general, and allowed him to marry "the Daughter and Heir of some great Lord or Privy-Councellor."[22] Rymer considers the marriage between a blackamoor and a white woman "an improbable lye." In 1818 Samuel Taylor Coleridge reconstructed what he imagined to have been the response of Shakespeare's contemporary audience: "as an English audience was disposed in the beginning of the seventeenth century, it would be something monstrous to conceive this beautiful Venetian girl falling in love with a veritable negro. It would argue a disproportionateness, a want of balance, in Desdemona, which Shakspere does not appear to have in the least contemplated."[23] To Coleridge, Othello could only have been a Moor (as opposed to a blackamoor) because aesthetic wholeness was fractured had Shakespeare dramatized the union as between a black man and a beautiful Venetian woman. A *Moor,* for Coleridge, was lighter in color than the *Negro,* and therefore more acceptable.

Both Rymer's and Coleridge's responses to Shakespeare's representation of Othello point to a deep ambivalence inscribed at the center of this drama of race relations. In *Othello,* Shakespeare made use of his audience's awareness of Blacks in England to create dramatic interest. By staging a man defined by his black skin as the protagonist of tragedy, Shakespeare produced a play that foregrounded his central character as a spectacle of difference: Othello crystallizes all the ambiguities of a man of different ethnic origin. Shakespeare's audience lived in an age in which knowledge of Blacks was made available through direct encounters, travel literatures, and myth. These sources indicate that at the time Shakespeare produced Othello, Blacks were already marginalized in various ways—through deportation, transformation into symbolic currencies of exchange, and stereotyping.

Turning to English history for a moment, we learn that a solitary black magician had been employed in the courts of Henry VII and Henry VIII. In 1555 a group of black Africans was brought to England by John Lok, the son of a prominent London merchant and alderman; although these five Africans were referred to as slaves, they were clearly borrowed and not bought. The year 1555 was also the year in which Richard Eden published, along with his translation of Peter Martyr's *Decades,* the first two accounts of English voyages to Africa: Thomas Windham's voyage to Guinea in 1553, and John Lok's voyage to Mina in 1554–1555.[24] It was in 1562–63 that John Hawkins acquired at least three hundred inhabitants off the Guinea coast. Hawkins was the first Englishman to traffic in black slaves for profit. In fact, he set up a company for the purpose of catching Negroes in order to sell them in Santo Domingo. Lord Pemberley, the Earl of Leicester, and Queen Elizabeth I herself invested by purchasing shares in the company.[25] Hawkins's voyages obtained the support of Lon-

doners who thought the slave trade would yield high rates of
profit. The reality was that the size of the market for slaves was
overestimated, and in two of the three subsequent voyages following Hawkins's first venture of 1562–63, the English failed to sell
all their slaves. Londoners withdrew their support for Caribbean
venturing after 1568.[26] If Elizabeth revealed a prejudicial view of
Blacks in her royal edict of 1601, that attitude can be traced all
the way back to the early days of her reign. Elizabeth had lent
Hawkins the use of a six-hundred-ton vessel, the *Jesus of Lubeck*,
for his second slave-hunting voyage of 1564–65. In an account of
his voyage on the *Jesus of Lubeck* to the Guinea coast and West
Indies, Hawkins describes how Negroes were traded and provides
details of the bargaining between the English and the Spaniards.
The trafficking with the Spaniards adds an interesting dimension
to their political rivalry. It was possible for members of the two
sides to submerge religious and ideological conflicts momentarily
for the purposes of trade and profit. Hawkins provides instances
of such transactions in his encounters with the Spaniards.[27] Despite skirmishes, and the authority of the king of Spain's injunction to not have anything to do with the English, trading of
Negroes between the two sides took place.[28]

References and allusions to the traffic in human bodies abound
in the writings of Renaissance England. Sir Walter Ralegh offers
the following account, for example, in his *Discoverie of Guiana:*

> Wee were very desirous to finde this towne, hoping of a feast, because
> wee made but a short breakefast aboord the galley in the morning
> and it was now eight a clocke at night, and our stomacks began to
> gnawe apace: but whether it was best to returne or goe on, we beganne
> to doubt, suspecting treason in the pilot more and more: but the
> poore olde Indian ever assured us that it was but a little further, but
> this one turning and that turning: and at the last about one a clocke
> after midnight wee saw a light; and rowing towards it, wee heard the
> dogs of the village. When we landed wee found few people; for the
> lord of that place was gone with divers canoas above foure hundred
> miles off, upon a journey towardes the head of Orenoque to trade
> for golde, and to buy women of the Canibals. . . . In his house we had
> good store of bread, fish, hennes, and Indian drinke, and so rested
> that night, and in the morning after we had traded with such of his
> people as came downe, we returned towards our gally, and brought
> with us some quantity of bread, fish, and hennes. (*DG* 10:387)

Trafficking in gold and human bodies went hand in hand. In
another account in the same text, Ralegh comments on the Spanish slave trade:

Among many other trades, those Spaniards used canoas to passe to the rivers of Barema, Pawroma, & Dissequebe, which are on the south side of the mouth of Orenoque, and there buy women and children from the Canibals, which are of that barbarous nature, as they will for three or foure hatchets sell the sonnes and daughters of their owne brethren and sisters, and for somewhat more, even their owne daughters. Hereof the Spaniards make great profit: for buying a maid of twelve or thirteene yeres for three or foure hatchets, they sell them againe at Margarita in the West Indies for fifty and an hundred pezos, which is so many crownes.

The master of my shippe, John Dowglas, tooke one of the canoas which came laden from thence with people to be solde, and the most of them escaped; yet of those he brought, there was one as well favoured, and as well shaped as ever I saw any in England, and afterward I saw many of them, which but for their tawnie colour may be compared to any of Europe. (*DG* 10: 376)

Although an organized slave trade would only take place some one hundred years after Hawkins's slave-trafficking, early dabblings in the trade had brought African slaves to England from the 1570s onward. And even if no concrete evidence can be found for the buying and selling of black people in England until 1621, it is quite possible that the bartering of human bodies had taken place before then. Black people constituted a recognizable presence in England when Shakespeare wrote *Othello*. Peter Fryer tells us that in the sixteenth century, Blacks served as household servants (the majority), prostitutes or sexual conveniences for well-to-do Englishmen and Dutchmen, and court entertainers in England. Blacks also found themselves inscribed mythically in texts, translated into terms that satisfied a popular craving for the exoticism that defined much travel literature of the period. This textual inscription also led to the construction of images of the cultural Other—natives were depicted as one-eyed Cyclops-like monsters, lusting beasts, and cannibals. Given their "natural" state and condition, it was only logical for the peoples of a "civilized" culture to want to bring nurture, knowledge, and enlightenment to the heathens.[29]

The colonizing frame of mind that Iago embodies differs in practice from the one Prospero represents, for Iago never entertains hopes of civilizing the Other. To Iago, the Moor exists simply to be exploited. Prospero exploits Caliban in *The Tempest* but, unlike Iago, he first attempts to incorporate "this thing of darkness" (5.1.275) into his own European culture. Caliban's inability to absorb and assimilate the language of his master confirms his savage nature and Otherness. The debate between art and nature that is intrinsic to Shakespeare's dramatization of Caliban's resistance to the acculturating effects of language invokes Montaigne's assertion that nature is more infinitely vigorous than art because it is directly tied to life. "It is not reasonable," writes Montaigne in his essay *On Cannibals*, "that art should win the honours from our great and mighty mother nature."[30] In Montaigne's view, the native is untainted and unmarred by the artificial modifications that European culture thrives in. If the native is wild, he is wild like the spontaneous growth found in the natural world. Montaigne's nature is superior to art; the native's wildness is linked directly to nature. If Montaigne distinguishes *natural* man in the native from *artificial* man in the European, and finds the first to be intrinsically and essentially superior, Shakespeare's Iago never questions the cultural status of the non-European Other. If Prospero's colonialism involves first attempting to assimilate the savage into a higher European culture, enacting Montaigne's observation that "we all call barbarians anything that is contrary to our own habits,"[31] Iago's design to destroy Othello as the Other offers no space for attempting any such integration. Iago recognizes instead that Othello can be "tenderly . . . led by the nose" (1.3.399) because of his Otherness; he possesses "a free and open nature" (1.3.397), which translates in Iago's racialist lexicon into the colonial metaphor of a field ripe for exploitation. The discourse of racism constantly crosses over into the discourse of colonialism in this play.

If Iago had problems with ethnic and cultural difference, so did Elizabethan England. John Hale informs us that in 1581, Elizabeth I had endorsed trading relations with Muslim-controlled Constantinople through the Turkey Company, and had also supported its operations in Aleppo. But there were obvious limits to what the queen was capable of endorsing: she showed her displeasure when Edward Barton, her unofficial ambassador, accompanied Mahommed III on his 1593 war against Austria.[32] To Elizabeth, Barton had not only compromised England's political identity by symbolically registering its allegiance to the Islamic camp, he had violated a religious principle. On 11 July 1596, Elizabeth I also sent an open letter to the Lord Mayor of London and his alderman, and to the mayors and sheriffs of other towns, expressing her displeasure at the great numbers of "Negars and blackamoors" that had crept into the realm.[33] Blacks created social embarrassments when they became idle and poor, and when they were in dire need of work. In response to the queen's displeasure, the Privy Council ordered that "the ten blackamoors that were brought in by Sir Thomas Baskerville in his last voyage shall be transported out of the realm."[34] Almost immediately following this order for deportation, the Lord Mayor of London and other public officers were required to assist Mr. Casper van Sanden, a Lubeck merchant, and send away from England "so many blackamoors" in exchange for eighty-nine of the queen's subjects released from imprisonment in Spain and Portugal. Mr. van Sanden had purchased the release of these prisoners "at his own charges."[35] Elizabeth I categorized Blacks as currency that can be transacted for subjects of real value. According to her, "Negars and blackamoors" caused "great annoyance of her own liege people, that want the relief [i.e., food], which those people consume, as also for that the most of them are infidels, having no understanding of Christ or his gospel."[36] The queen's view that Blacks caused great annoyance to her proper and rightful subjects because they were infidels inscribes a discourse of cultural difference in both the social text and the dramatic text.

In addition to the view current in Elizabeth's reign that Blacks caused social embarrassments and that they were expandable commodities, uncertainties about the nature of their difference also produced a literature that attempted to explain the "phenomenon" of blackness. We read in George Best's *Discourse,* reprinted in a substantially cut version in the 1600 edition of Hakluyt's *Principal Navigations,* the following account of blackness, which I cite in some detail for the light it throws on a particular perception of ethnic difference:[37]

Others againe imagine the middle Zone to be extreme hot, because the people of Africa, especially the Ethiopians, are so cole blacke, and their haire like wooll curled short, which blacknesse and curled haire they suppose to come onely by the parching heat of the Sunne, which how it should be possible I cannot see: for even under the Equinoctiall in America, and in the East Indies, and in the Ilands Moluccæ the people are not blacke, but tauney and white, with long haire uncurled as wee have, so that if the Ethiopians blacknesse came by the heat of the Sunne, why should not those Americans and Indians also be as blacke as they, seeing the Sunne is equally distant from them both, they abiding in one Parallel: for the concave and convexe Superficies of the Orbe of the Sunne is concentrike, and equidistant to the earth; except any man should imagine somewhat of Aux Solis, and Oppositum, which indifferently may be applied aswel to the one place as to the other. But the Sunne is thought to give no otherwise heat, but by way of Angle in reflection, and not by his neerenesse to the earth: for throughout all Africa, yea in the middest of the middle Zone, and in all other places upon the tops of mountaines there lyeth continuall snow, which is neerer to the Orbe of the Sunne, then the people are in the valley, by so much as the height of these mountaines amount unto, and yet the Sunne notwithstanding his neerenesse, can not melt the snow for want of convenient place of reflections.

. . .

Therefore to returne againe to the blacke Moores. I my selfe have seene an Ethiopian as blacke as a cole brought into England, who taking a faire English woman to wife, begat a sonne in all respects as blacke as the father was, although England were his native countrey, and an English woman his mother: whereby it seemeth this blacknes proceedeth rather of some natural infection of that man, which was so strong, that neither the nature of the Clime, neither the good complexion of the mother concurring, coulde any thing alter, and therefore, wee cannot impute it to the nature of the Clime.[38]

In his *Discourse*, George Best writes about the responses of different peoples to warm and cold climates, concluding that skin color has no direct correlation to climatic conditions. If proximity to the sun does not affect one's skin color, then there must be another reason for the phenomenon of blackness. For Best, this blackness can be traced to "some natural infection," caused by transgressing divine law:

And the most probable cause to my judgement is, that this blacknesse proceedeth of some naturall infection of the first inhabitants of that Countrey, and so all the whole progenie of them descended, are still polluted with the same blot of infection. Therefore it shall not bee farre from our purpose, to examine the first originall of these blacke men, and howe by a lineall discent they have hitherto continued thus blacke.

It manifestly and plainely appeareth by holy Scripture, that after the generall inundation and overflowing of the earth, there remained no moe men alive but Noe and his three sonnes, Sem, Cham, and Japhet, who onely were left to possesse and inhabite the whole face of the earth: therefore all the sundry discents that until this present day have inhabited the whole earth, must needes come of the off-spring either of Sem, Cham, or Japhet, as the onely sonnes of Noe, who all three being white, and their wives also, by course of nature should have begotten and brought foorth white children. But the envie of our great and continuall enemie the wicked Spirite is such, that as hee coulde not suffer our olde father Adam to live in the felicitie and Angelike state wherein hee was first created, but tempting him, sought and procured his ruine and fall: so againe, finding at this flood none but a father and three sonnes living, hee so caused one of them to transgresse and disobey his fathers commaundement, that after him all his posteritie shoulde bee accursed. The fact of disobedience was this: When Noe at the commandement of God had made the Arke and entred therein, and the floud-gates of heaven were opened, so that the whole face of the earth, every tree and mountaine was covered with abundance of water, hee straitely commaunded his sonnes and their wives, that they should with reverence and feare beholde the justice and mighty power of God, and that during the time of the floud while they remained in the Arke, they should use continencie, and abstaine from carnall copulation with their wives: and many other precepts hee gave unto them, and admonitions touching the justice of God, in revenging sinne, and his mercie in delivering them, who nothing deserved it. Which good instructions and exhortations notwithstanding his wicked sonne Cham disobeyed, and being perswaded that the first childe borne after the flood (by right and Lawe of nature) should inherite and possesse all the dominions of the earth, hee contrary to his fathers commandement while they were yet in the Arke, used company with his wife, and craftily went about thereby to dis-inherite the off-spring of his other two brethren: for the which wicked and detestable fact, as an example for contempt of Almightie God, and disobedience of parents, God would a sonne should bee borne whose name was Chus, who not onely it selfe, but all his posteritie after him should bee so blacke and lothsome, that it might remaine a spectacle of disobedience to all the worlde. And of this blacke and cursed Chus came all these blacke Moores which are in Africa, for after the water was vanished from off the face of the earth, and that the lande was dry, Sem chose that part of the land to inhabite in, which nowe is called Asia, and Japhet had that which now is called Europa, wherein wee dwell, and Africa remained for Cham and his blacke sonne Chus, and was called Chamesis after the fathers name, being perhaps a cursed, dry, sandy, and unfruitfull ground, fit for such a generation to inhabite in.[39]

George Best explains the African's blackness in theological terms. The skin color of the African reveals the transgression of his/her father Cham, whose ambition to have his offsprings dominate the earth violated Noah's injunction to his children not to engage in "carnall copulation" with their wives. Best fuses the Genesis story of man and woman's original transgression with the dominant Hebraic motif that the holy nation of Israel is commanded by Yahweh never to enter into sexual liaisons with the women of foreign and pagan tribes. Cham's disobedience reenacts Adam's and Eve's violation of the Genesis prohibition. In the same way that God cursed the ground for man's sake in Genesis, he made sure that Africa was "a cursed, dry, sandy, and unfruitfull ground." And just as anyone who comes across the fugitive Cain will recognize that he is guilty of fratricide, so anyone who sees

the African will know he is the descendant of a man who disobeyed God. The body of the black African then functions as a
figure inscribing an important cautionary tale; the black African
provides the world with a vivid reminder that disobedience to
God fetches a terrible price. That is why George Best calls his
black African the "spectacle of disobedience." "Thus you see,"
concludes Best, "the cause of the Ethiopians blacknesse is the
curse and naturall infection of blood, and not the distemperature
of the Climate."[40]

I began this chapter by showing how Shakespeare made use of
differences in skin color to dramatize the moral world and political workings of *Titus Andronicus*. In *Titus Andronicus*, the loath-
someness of Aaron and Tamora's illegitimate offspring is such
that the mother even demands its death; and Aaron recognizes
that Roman society can never accommodate his son as a spectacle
of Otherness. Remarkably, Tamora, who is a Goth and therefore
foreign to Roman society, responds to the blackness of her son by
speaking in the language of the dominant culture. In the *Discourse,*
Best recounts how he had come across a very black Ethiopian
married to a fair English woman, and how their son had inherited
the blackness of his father. The fact that this offspring of miscegenation, born in England and of a white mother, still retains the
color of the father reveals, to Best, that climate is irrelevant to the
construction of physical fairness or blackness. Blackness comes
from some general infection in the blood, an infection that was
traced, as we have seen, to a theological transgression. Responses
to climatic conditions constitute a common trope in the rhetorical
and discursive constructions of difference. In Spenser's *View,* for
instance, the anthropologically curious Irenius talks about "the
Moors and Egyptians which are much offended and grieved with
much extreme heat of the sun, do every morning when the same
riseth, fall to cursing and banning of him as their plague and
chief scourge" (*View* 58). This account of what the Moors and
Egyptians practice obtains its significance from a discourse that
reads the cultural practices of peoples different from one's own
as a signature of their barbarism; it is for this reason that Spenser
elaborates on the similarities that he finds between the Scythians
and the Irish in the *View.*

George Best's travel narrative aims at arousing curiosity about
the nature of black Africans, and it does so by playing up the
African as a spectacle of difference. An object of exoticism, the
black African is also the savage Other, marked by his impervi-
ousness to culture and civilization. The African and the American

Indian share similar traits in their savagery. The representation of the savage Other that we have encountered in such diverse texts as English accounts of the Jamestown colony, Shakespeare's *Tempest*, Montaigne's *On Cannibals*, and Best's *Discourse* is also present in epic. One European epic that elaborates at some length the encounter with the Negro is *Os Lusíadas*. We read the following account in Camões's text:

> Then suddenly, looking up, I saw my men returning with a black-skinned stranger in their midst, whom they had taken by force as he was gathering honeycombs on the mountain-side. His face betrayed his alarm at finding himself in such a predicament. A savage more uncouth than Polyphemus, he could not understand us, nor we him. I showed him samples of gold, of silver, of spices: they made no impression on him whatever. Then I bade the men produce baubles of no value, glass beads, tiny tinkling bells, a bright red cap; and it was at once clear from his signs and gestures that these delighted him greatly. I told them to let him have the lot and go free, and he made off for his village, that lay not far away.[41]

This excerpt from the *Lusíadas* shows that European narratives that portray Otherness and difference often share common motifs. Here the Negro, even more uncouth that the Polyphemus who is Homer's prototypical savage Other, does not possess the language that forms the basis of communication and that enables the building of civil society. Together with the inability to engage in intelligible discourse, the Negro also lacks the basic ability to recognize things of value: gold, silver, and spices; he prizes instead objects that are devoid of any material value in the European world. To not possess a linguistic medium is inseparable from not having the ability to have a norm for appreciating things of value. Strategies to give "baubles of no value" in exchange for things of value are central also to the colonialist discourses of figures like John Smith and Thomas Hariot. Peter Hulme tells us that from the European point of view, the native's complete lack of language reveals his inability to forge and form a community, something that condemns him to a life of ceaseless hostility. Generally, colonialist discourse refuses to recognize that another person can possess his own language, his own unique linguistic structures. "At the heart of European recourse to the Law of Nations," Hulme elaborates, "was the grandiose concept of *consortium hominum*, an intellectual version of . . . reciprocity . . . inasmuch as it posited an ideal of exchange of various kinds as the centre of properly human activity. *Consortium* was the seed of many arguments that would be developed at length between the twelfth and eighteenth centuries; and at its core was what Albertus Magnus called *communicatio,* thereby stressing that it was through language that men came to understand that their common purposes could be achieved only through bonding together in civil society."[42]

The truth is that when the European colonialist discovered forms in native societies that indicated the presence of a coherent community, he refuses to recognize them. To him, difference in cultures were never bridged, in order to protect the dreams and interests of colonial expansionism; alien forms that cannot be easily recognized with reference to a European experiential framework are simply defined and discursively constituted as demonic and unnatural. But this poetics of difference, built on the premise of incompatible absolutes, is not the only rhetorical means by which a dominant culture legitimizes its own superior and transcendent identity. *Othello* suggests another way, and one equally destructive of the individual and of his cultural identity as the Other, which relies on portraying the Other as possessing an innate love of all things European. In Shakespeare's tragedy, the experience of wonder originates from the ethnic Other—Othello himself—whose primary desire is to be allowed incorporation into the glorious culture and experience of Venetian society.

In an important essay on the representations of race, gender, and ethnicity in early modern England, Lynda Boose identifies cultural anxieties concerning the potential actualization of lineal descents that inscribe and enable black dominance, specifically in cases where an African man married a white woman.[43] Boose identifies George Best's *Discourse* as an important document that meditated on such an issue. These anxieties also extended to instances in which black women marry white men: there "in the person of the black woman . . . the culture's preexisting fears both about the female sex and about gender dominance are realized."[44] When we consider the nature of these anxieties in Renaissance England, we find at its base a culture responding with tremendous dis-ease to threatened disruptions of the social order. Miscegenation disrupts the cultural logic of family, procreation, and most importantly, community. Elizabeth I made the ideological choice of defining Albion a "white" society. Her reaction toward Africans and Moors cannot be extricated from a larger cultural definition of what constitutes English-ness. Considerations of ethnicity at that time had already been influenced by the links made between skin color and essential identity. Set in place are the discursive and political structures for suppressing and oppressing a people different from ourselves. To prevent racial contamination, laws are set, for example, later on in the British West Indies imposing harsh penalties for miscegenation. If distrust of miscegenation erects a systemic check on the potential of culture and society to disrupt its efforts to define the nation, it can police the efficacy through suppression and containment. It does not take much to cross over from protecting cultural/ethnic purity to colonizing the Other.

The queen's attitude toward Africans and Moors can be said to obtain its significance in relation to what I wish to call the discourse of nascent English nationalism. In *Imagined Communities*, Benedict Anderson makes a couple of observations on the relationship between patriotism, an important experience in the imaginary construction of the nation, and racism, which are of interest here. While the focus of Anderson's concerns is on the heyday of European imperialism in the nineteenth century, and on the origins of nationalism in the twentieth, his commentary can be applied to a reading of the discursive constructions of difference in early modern England. Anderson writes:

> The fact of the matter is that nationalism thinks in terms of historical destinies, while racism dreams of eternal contaminations, transmitted from the origins of time through an endless sequence of loathsome copulations: outside history. Niggers are, thanks to the invisible tarbrush, forever niggers; Jews, the seed of Abraham, forever Jews, no matter what passports they carry or what languages they speak and read.[45]

Anderson's "nigger" is Elizabeth's "blackamoor" and his "Jew" Marlowe's Barabas and Shakespeare's Shylock: identities of Otherness constructed out of the "dreams of eternal contaminations," dreams that go hand in hand with the constitution of a national identity imagined as community. The community imagined by Elizabeth and ratified by her Privy Council was white, industrious, belonging to the land. The name of this land was Albion. It was a fantasy of purity which was needed to propel the patriot of the imagined community to lay down his life for the state: the ultimate sacrifice. The nation, Benedict Anderson also writes, is "a community imagined through language."[46] And this language that enables the imaginary constitution of the nation is also the one that designates Othello or Shylock as the Other. The word "blackamoor," like "slant" (abbreviated from "slant-eyed" used to typify the Oriental), "does not simply express an ordinary political enmity. It erases nation-ness by reducing the adversary to his biological physiognomy."[47] As Lynda Boose reminds us, "Racial identities can be constituted by linguistic myths as well as by myths of origin."[48] The need to erase "nation-ness" means that there is a "nation" from which the Other comes and that is set in contradistinction to one's own. In the rhetoric of colonialism, the "nation" of the Other is merely a term of convenience used to designate a tribe, a conglomerate of people, a social unit that may possess nothing resembling the paradigmatic structures of social organization found in Europe. It does not refer to a legitimate political entity, like Ralegh referring to the "Caora, . . . a nation of people" (*DG* 10: 406) in *The Discoverie of Guiana.*

In Elizabethan England, one very important text that set out to crystallize England's identity as a nation that exercised colonial jurisdiction over a subject state was Edmund Spenser's *A View of the Present State of Ireland.* The purpose of *A View* is to provide Queen Elizabeth with a blueprint for effecting the conclusive colonization of Ireland. One reason which Spenser offers for colonization is the difference of the Irish from everything identifiably English. In the colonial lexicon of *A View,* English-ness and civilization are metonymies for one another. The identity of the Irish as the Other is clearly registered in its system of incomprehensible laws, designating the absence of a coherent legal framework as the basis of organized society. The Irish, Spenser elaborates, are the product of innumerable ethnic interactions. Tracing their ancestry to the Scythians whom Spenser equates with the Scots, the Irish had intermingled with the Spaniards, Gauls, Britons, and Saxons. Because the Irish are racially contaminated and impure, it makes no sense for English families of high station to have assimilated themselves into Irish life and culture. Having adapted Irish culture and ways, these assimilated English families are categorized in *A View* as barbaric. Spenser, like Iago, possesses a distrust of miscegenation, but in his case, the taint of miscegenation is applied to interminglings between two people not separated by the color of their skin. Spenser's *A View of the Present State of Ireland* reveals that fears of miscegenation are often tied to anxieties about the definition and preservation of nationhood that hinges on consolidated political authority. For Spenser, the colonization of Ireland cannot be extricated from a desire to define the English nation as a viable political entity.

Kim Hall reminds us that anxieties about miscegenation and racial intermingling also possess larger political significance, given the fact that Elizabeth I's relationship to the English nation is defined by her status as the Virgin Queen while James I's is grounded in family. The Elizabethan polity, marked by its inward vision and insularity, gives way to the Jacobean one that is much more accommodating toward forging foreign alliances and making connections through economic ties with a larger international community. Significantly, the *semper eadem* that is Elizabeth's motto is replaced by James's conception of himself as *rex pacificus*, "the royal peacemaker."[49] This conception of the king as *rex pacificus* and as England's Solomon is well known. John Williams, Lord Bishop of Lincoln, in his sermon preached at the funeral of James I on 7 May 1625, praised the deceased king as Great Britain's Solomon. According to Williams, "*Salomon* was a *Type* of *Christ* himselfe, and by consequence a *Pattern* for any *Christian*."[50] John Donne's Sermon Number 14, preached at Denmark house, some days before the body of King James was removed for burial, conjoins the image and metaphor of Solomon's "crowns," derived from Canticles 3 : 11, with the crowns of humiliation and victory of Christ: "behold your selves in that first glasse, *Behold King Solomon; Solomon* the sonne of *David,* but not the Son of *Bathsheba,* but of a better mother, the most blessed *Virgin Mary.* For, *Solomon,* in this text, is not a *proper* Name, but an *Appellative;* a significative word: *Solomon* is *pacificus,* the *Peacemaker,* and our peace is made in, and by Christ Jesus: and he is that *Solomon,* whom we are called upon to see here."[51] In the delivery of Donne's sermon with its evocation of James I's identity as the English Solomon, the dead body of the king, Jonathan Goldberg writes, "is an equal authority to the text in which the name of Solomon represents Christ. The authority of the corpse is the authority of the text; both illuminate and represent God, equally instruments and mirrors. Donne, preacher of the word, preaching over the body of the king, gains his authority by looking in these '*two glasses*'."[52]

Texts that link James I typologically and associatively with Solomon also produce the interesting effect of establishing the king's identity as a monarch well known for his interactions with foreigners as well as intermingling with foreign women and contaminating England's national identity and cultural integrity. To recognize that insularity cannot offer immediate and long-term benefits for England does not necessarily obviate or minimize fears concerning mixings and interminglings between the English people and foreigners. A subterranean anxiety relating to plunging into the world of international commerce registers itself in the writings of the period suspicious of the social phenomenon and experience of miscegenation. One of the features Kim Hall notes about the international flavor of James I's court is the

marked presence of Africans there. But as Hall also tells us, the
black presence in James's court does not have much to do with
any "liberal" understanding of equality and happy coexistence:
"Blacks were a common feature in the Scottish court, kept there
as dehumanized alien curiosities, on par with James's pet lion and
his collection of exotic animals."[53]

The politics of race, gender, and national identity in the period
discussed here also defines another very important work, Ben
Jonson's *The Masque of Blackness*, produced after Jonson was ap-
proached by Queen Anne to devise a masque in which Moors
played an important part. The request was made in 1604, the
same year in which *Othello* was first performed. Queen Anne
wanted Jonson's spectacle of Otherness to be mounted for the
year's winter festivities: "it was her Maiesties will, to haue them
Black-mores at first." *The Masque of Blackness* was performed on
Twelfth Night in 1605 at Whitehall.

Jonson's masque tells the story of how Niger, a son of Oceanus,
the king of floods, proudly has twelve black daughters renowned
for their beauty and agelessness.[54] The daughters live happily in
that understanding until they discover there is a larger world existing beyond their own in which very beautiful women can be
found. Distraught by this new knowledge, Niger's twelve daughters go off in search of a land where the air is temperate and the
sun gentle on their skins. Niger later learns that this land is Britania, "which the triple world admires" (line 241). "*A world, diuided
from the world*" (line 248), Britania is ruled by a sun that shines
both day and night, possessing the power to "blanch an ÆTHI-
OPE" (line 255) and to "salue the rude defects of euery creature"
(line 257). England's ability to whitewash the blackness of the
Ethiopian is inseparable in the masque from its privileged position as the moral and spiritual transformer of the entire human
race ("euery creature") that, by virtue of ethnic difference, is always excluded from the center of the world. As a diamond set on
the ring of the world, Britania is identified as the source from
which civilization is brought to the rest of the world. England
enables the fulfillment of desire, one that amounts to nothing
less—as Æthiopia reveals—than becoming English.

In Jonson's *Masque of Blackness*, the quest of Niger's daughters
for fairness is depicted in terms of making a journey to England,
which possesses the power to fulfill their desire, one which assimilates blackness to its own perfect beauty. In the performance of
this masque at Whitehall, Queen Anne and her ladies painted
themselves in black instead of availing themselves of the visors

conventionally worn by courtiers when impersonating black characters. Critics like David Riggs, Lynda Boose, and Kim Hall have
variously noted the destabilizing effects of the queen with a black
"skin," and have also identified at play symbolic political contestations waged by Anne against the king.[55] If the affirmation of
Albion's cultural transcendence is enabled by the performance of
a masque in which the "blackened" queen and her ladies draw
attention to race significations, their subtextual associations with
the elements of the antimasque succeed in generating a certain
unease. David Riggs has suggested that Queen Anne's choice of
the subject of African females and an African queen carried powerful connotations of female autonomy and ethnic diversity. Significantly and disturbingly, *The Masque of Blackness* concludes with
the queen and her retinue, still with a blackened face, setting off
for the sea as to a ritual of purification undertaken by women.
The sanctioning figure of the king and prerogative of masculinist
authority is excluded from this gender-coded symbolism. Even in
its sequel, *The Masque of Beauty,* the person who transforms the
ladies' island into an earthly paradise is not the king but Ethiopia,
their queen.[56] After the disturbing display of blackness in the
masque of that title, the rewhitened bodies of the queen and her
ladies in *The Masque of Beauty* pleased James I tremendously. But,
as Boose tells us, "what nonetheless returns to haunt the King's
response [to the rewhitened bodies of his queen and her women]
is the indigestible excess represented in the original masque by
the pregnant blackamoor queen."[57] If the masque directs a subtextual challenge to the Jacobean myth of male supremacy and
imperial rule, that challenge, inscribed in the symbolics of racial
difference, crosses over into an affirmation of the imperial theme:
for what gets celebrated at the end is Albion's purity and its aristocratic lineages. Blackness needs to be whitewashed in order to
celebrate Albion's glory. We are never made to forget that even in
The Masque of Blackness, Africa's dark daughters seek the beauty of
Albion's whiteness. According to Kim Hall, *The Masque of Blackness*
obtains cultural significance through its situation at a historical
moment coincident with the celebration of empire: for the term
"Great Britain" had just been coined very recently. Hall reminds
us that even though this term was not legally adopted until 1707,
James I expanded much energies to make the term official.[58]

    At the time that Best's *Discourse* appeared, Jonson performed
his *Masque of Blackness,* and Shakespeare produced *Othello,* that is,
during the late sixteenth and early seventeenth century, Blacks
were defined by their exoticism and their mythic roles; as "specta-

cles of strangeness,"[59] they appeared in texts for dramatic and exotic purposes. The dramatic and the exotic, however, cannot be divorced from the ideological. As we have already seen, Elizabeth I's attitude toward Blacks had registered early on the literal and symbolic marginalization of a race because of social and economic realities. "Blackamoors" belonged not only to the representational world of drama, confined to the semiological boundaries of the playhouse; they were inscribed in the text of English society as expandable currency and exotic manifestations. As long as Blacks did not grow into a sizeable group that threatened the economic situations of white working people, they could rest more or less peaceably in the mythic texts in which they were defined and confined. I call these texts *mythic* because knowledge of Africa in sixteenth-century England was derived secondhand from popularized translations of tales of classical writers and contemporary accounts of sailors who had themselves seen Africa.

The proliferation and popularity of literatures on Africa coincide with what Peter Fryer perceives to be the presence and development of hostile attitudes toward Blacks in the latter half of the sixteenth century. A different social scenario is constructed by Karen Newman, who finds that, although there were Blacks who worked as servants in sixteenth- and early seventeenth-century England, there were others who owned property, paid taxes, and went to church. It was only with the establishment of the sugar industry in the Caribbean and the tobacco and cotton industries in America, that the value of Blacks as slave labor was fully recognized and exploited.[60] Maureen Quilligan observes that the slave trade, which started late in England, gathered urgent momentum in the mid-century during the Interregnum because there now existed the sense of a labor shortage; this opposed the prevailing sentiment at the start of the seventeenth century that England enjoyed a surplus of labor. The deportation policy practiced by the government during the Interregnum was apparently influenced in large part by a similar sense that England faced a crucial shortage of labor. Quilligan continues: "This shortage was especially crucial in the New World, specifically in the newly valuable sugar islands such as Barbados (so that "to barbadoe" had become a verb meaning to kidnap someone into slavery). The switch from the cultivation of tobacco to the fantastically more profitable sugar meant the need to put vast amounts of land into cultivation of cane, which required huge capital outlays and a massively increased labor force. It was a convulsive economic need only capable of being met finally by the African slave trade."[61]

In the late years of the Commonwealth, England's trade in human bodies began to get complicated because there were Englishmen themselves who became slaves. A number of them were sent to the Barbados after they chose to become slaves in lieu of paying with their lives for involvement in a rebellion. When Parliament famously debated their case on 25 March 1659, as Maureen Quilligan draws to our attention, it became clear that any discussion of this kind had to consider the issue of slavery in relation to the ethnicity and nationality of the people who were enslaved. Analyzing this particular situation, Quilligan tells us that distinctions were made between slaves who were sold—specifically the Africans—and those who entered into servitude as the result of political defeat. Then slaves who were English also had to be distinguished from the numerous Scotsmen and Irish children shipped to work as slaves in the plantations.[62] Debates on the status of slaves were influenced by the contingencies of economic as well as political interests. By the late seventeenth century, there is no longer any doubt that the English had come to recognize the significance of the slave trade to the British economy and newspapers advertised slaves for sale as well as notices seeking out runaway slaves.[63] In fact, at the close of the century, English sugar planters had brought a quarter of a million Negroes from Africa to their colonies in the West Indies and branded them perpetual bondsmen.[64]

Peter Fryer, Karen Newman, and Maureen Quilligan offer different emphases in their readings of the social positions occupied by Blacks in late sixteenth- and early seventeenth-century England, but they all agree that perceptions of cultural difference that later assumed the form of a systematic slave-trade were present at the time Shakespeare wrote *Othello*. Shakespeare's dramatization of Othello elicits responses to representations of the exotic that are shaded by perceptions of ethnic difference, and by a larger cultural interest in the African and the "blackamoor." As I have shown, this play registers a fascination with individual and social responses to the figure of the Other. *Othello* finally provides no secure answer to the experience of interracial relationships in a white society; it offers instead a dramatization of the motivations, fears, and anxieties that attend any attempt to procure union based on ethnic differences. The play's refusal to ground itself definitively in an identifiable ideological center relates this tragedy to the often complex and highly ambivalent social practices and prejudices that make possible theatrical performances themselves.

4

Figuring Justice: Imperial Ideology and the Discourse of Colonialism in Book 5 of *The Faerie Queene* and *A View of the Present State of Ireland*

In any reading of the relationship between poetic creation and the ambitions of empire-building in Elizabethan England, one immediately calls to mind Edmund Spenser. In *The Faerie Queene*,[1] Spenser refers to English colonial designs in the New World and also to the much-discussed project of subjugating a rebellious Ireland. Because of the presence of these allusions and references, readers of Spenser's writings have been especially keen to determine the scope of the poet's imperialist leanings, how these are expressed, and the extent to which they feed into the theories and practices of Elizabethan and Jacobean colonial ambitions. The result has been some very fine readings of Spenser's use of genres to communicate political and ideological meanings. Much, for example, has been done to interpret the politicization of genres like pastoral and the chivalric romance. Colin's radically unstable relation to the symbolics of the natural world intrinsic to pastoral in *The Shepheardes Calender* inscribes, for instance, an ambiguated conception of England as Eden that is also nowhere, as spiritual/immaterial entity that is at the same time fallen/material polity. Having to grapple psychologically and creatively with a virgin queen, whose (in)significance, when juxtaposed against other European monarchies, compels poetic treatment, Spenser strives to extend the notion of "England" beyond the virginal idea embodied by Elizabeth, all the while hoping to further his own career in the court. The task Spenser sets for himself to translate "trifles" into substance is tied to the project of representing the greatness of an English queen who is viewed by some as only a political "trifle" in the powerful arena of Euro-

142

pean politics.[2] This discursive and rhetorical *translatio* is made cogently manifest in *The Faerie Queene,* where England's greatness is simultaneously here and nowhere, Elizabeth's power immaterially present and materially absent, celebration of private and public virtues embedded in the inconclusive romance meanderings of circles and errors.

Pastoral and romance may embed specific political and ideological codes and conceptions, and while these situate poetic texts in social and material reality, their significance and meanings derive from the mediating perceptions of an historically contemporary audience. Understanding these codes can yield a picture of Spenser engaging in dialogue/dialectic with the discourse of England's nascent colonial ambitions. At the time when Spenser wrote, Ireland, not the New World, was the great Tudor colonial project; it is not insignificant that while a romance epic like *The Faerie Queene* may make references to the New World, its interest in the subject of Ireland is more immediate and palpable. In fact, Spenser's interest in the "Irish question" was such that elsewhere he created a fictive dialogue between two characters centered precisely on the motif of enacting the conquest of Ireland. In this chapter, I will focus my reading of Spenser's place in England's nascent imperialist discourse by examining the references he makes to Ireland in *The Faerie Queene* and relating these to the imperialist program and vision given in the controversial *View of the Present State of Ireland.*

The program Spenser proposes for colonizing Ireland in the *View* provides one of the most sustained imperialist articulations in Elizabethan England. Spenser works out methodically the strategies that can be implemented to bring the rebellious Irish under English sovereignty and domination. While, however, he obviously does not stand alone in holding to such an implacable imperialist policy, his views stand in direct opposition to Elizabeth's own. And it is in Spenser's conflict with the queen concerning the conduct of English foreign policy that we locate a central significance of the *View:* Spenser's imperialist text obtains its symbolic status within a field of contestatory views, and as such cannot be appropriated and read as the paradigm of any larger cultural confidence in a sustained dream of national imperialism. The narrative of the *View* encodes quite cogently the gap separating the colonialist dreams/desires of a poet and the political practices of a monarch extremely reluctant to spend huge sums of money in the conduct of foreign policy. The presence of this gap is palpable in Spenser's anxieties betrayed in the *View*'s textual and ideological negotiations. The *View* tells us that there is no coherent imperialist policy existing in Elizabeth's England, and also that a discourse is available questioning the monarch's actual control of events and effective governance. Spenser's criticism elsewhere of the queen's passive response to the threat posed to the Low Countries by Catholic Spain propels into circulation the idea of an ineffective queen who should do more to fulfill her symbolic identity as protector of the Protestant cause in Europe. The Earl of Essex shared this idea but translated it into the materiality of rebellion when he attempted later on to bring about the queen's overthrow and displace the power of her symbolic/cultic identity with his own masculinist charisma. The interrogation of Elizabeth's political methods Spenser sends into ideological circulation and negotiation is, however, according to his own understanding and practice, an affirmation of the queen's authority. In Spenser's writings, the cautionary narrative is not simply balanced by the celebratory, it validates (at least for the most part) the encomiastic. One could say that Spenser's interrogatory narrative never translates into the language and practice of a subversive politics because Spenser is defined by the absolutist ideology Elizabeth as monarch embodies. When Spenser writes to tell the queen she is tardy in extending protection to beleaguered Protestants in the Low Countries, he does so in the desire to enhance and consolidate Elizabeth's symbolic and material authority. Spenser believes that the practice of imperial expansionism is needed not only to enhance but consolidate Elizabeth's royal identity. Building England's status as a colonial power is finally inseparable from the legitimation of monarchical authority.

Spenserian Romance and the Matter of Spain

Book 5 of *The Faerie Queene* deals with the subject and identity of justice as it originates from and ends in the monarch's authority. Subtitled the "Legend of Justice," this book highlights the workings of justice through the adventures of Artegall and Talus. It also provides a highly symbolic narrative in canto 9, in which Elizabeth I is represented in emblematic terms. Spenser's portrayal of the queen in these terms accentuates Elizabeth's symbolic and iconic identity, one that cannot be separated from the poet's desire to create and produce encomium in book 5. Spenser's praise for the queen is enacted through his highly structured and ritualized representation of the throne that Elizabeth occupies.

Pageantry marks the remarkable trappings of the queen whom
Spenser calls Mercilla:

> All ouer her a cloth of state was spred,
> Not of rich tissew, nor of cloth of gold,
> Nor of ought else, that may be richest red,
> But like a cloud, as likest may be told,
> That her brode spreading wings did wyde vnfold;
> Whose skirts were bordred with bright sunny beams,
> Glistring like gold, amongst the plights enrold,
> And here and there shooting forth siluer streames,
> Mongst which crept litle Angels through the glittering gleames.
>
> (5.9.28)

The naming of Mercilla is self-evidently significant. Mercy is a
central aspect of the monarch's identity. But if mercy remains the
only virtue practiced by the monarch, then the preservation of
social order is in danger of disintegrating. For the demands of
justice must be fulfilled in order that society not degenerate into
the condition of chaos. Spenser's representation of the monarch
as the figure who brings into conjunction the attributes of mercy
and justice reveals his understanding of what should appropriately go into the making of Elizabeth's royal identity. The interesting feature of Spenser's allegorical depiction of the monarch's
authority here is that this representation is strategically situated
in a book in *The Faerie Queene* that draws the reader's attention
to the queen's ineffective exercise of justice. Elizabeth/Mercilla's
symbolic identity becomes, in relation to the larger narrative context of book 5, Spenser's idealized conception of his monarch that
has no basis in reality. Spenser finds that Elizabeth's hesitation in
making sure that the demands of justice are met—both in her
tardiness to defend the Protestant cause abroad and to subdue a
rebellious Ireland—fractures his ideation of her symbolic identity.
It is for this reason that encomium in book 5 cannot be divorced
from Spenser's critique of the queen's "ineffectiveness."

Spenser's preoccupation with the relationship between justice
and mercy as aspects of imperial authority is cogently expressed
in his allegorization of Mercilla's judgment of Duessa, and I would
like to begin my discussion by recapitulating some of the salient
features of this relationship. Spenser's portrayal of the iconic Mercilla is, we said, first and foremost encomiastic: England is described as a "happie land" (5.9.30) that has enjoyed the fruits of
a peaceful reign; in Mercilla's court, "the name of warre" is never
spoken, "ioyous peace and quietnesse" reign, and judgments are

meted out (5.9.24). This *pax anglicana* is, however, threatened by Duessa—Spenser's allegorical portrait for Mary Queen of Scots—whose treachery involves nothing less than attempting to dethrone the monarch and undermine England's ordered realm. A transparent allegory of the trial of Queen Mary, this episode impresses upon its reader that even though Mercilla/Elizabeth embodies the princely virtue of mercy, the demands of justice must be met for the good of the commonwealth to prevail. The monarch must dispense justice to protect the security of the state.

Spenser represents mercy as an important attribute of royal authority not only in book 5 of *The Faerie Queene*, but also in *A View of the Present State of Ireland*. When he invokes Elizabeth as "Her sacred Majesty" who is "by nature full of mercy and clemency" (*View* 105) in *A View*, the reader recalls the Mercilla/Duessa allegory in book 5 we have just considered. In *A View*, the character Irenius provides at length an account of the queen's mercy. He expresses the wish that a general proclamation be made that will enable outlaws to submit themselves to the queen. This submission will procure their safety, because Elizabeth will respond to them with grace and mercy. The extension of these theological principles to enemies of the crown is enabled only through the act of absolute submission to the English monarch. Anything that falls short of this uncompromising obeisance and obedience cannot procure for the outlaws their "life and liberty" (*View* 123).

The reference to Elizabeth's mercy made by Irenius, like Spenser's allegorical representation of Mercilla, is encomiastic. This praise does not, however, exempt Elizabeth from blame in recalling Lord Grey from Ireland because of his harsh regime. Spenser's *View* indeed inscribes an indirect critique in its defense of Lord Grey. Irenius portrays Grey as a gentle and temperate man who resorted to violence in Ireland only because of absolute necessity and the particular demands of circumstance. Lord Grey had no choice but to check the calamity that followed in the wake of the Desmond Rebellion and to punish the Spaniards at Smerwick, described as irresponsible soldiers whose main interest was to seek adventure and fortune.[3]

Another allusion to Elizabeth's recall of Lord Grey de Wilton from Ireland is found in book 5, canto 12, of *The Faerie Queene*. In praising the former governor's role in breaking the force of the rebellious Fitzgeralds of Desmond, Spenser writes about the part played by justice in reforming "that ragged common-weale" (5.12.26) of Ireland. In this last canto of book 5, justice is shown to operate beyond the confines of England. In Ireland, where people "vsed to rob and steale, / Or did rebell gainst lawfull gouernment" (5.12.26), Talus "did inflict most grieuous punishment" (5.12.26). According to Spenser, the punishment meted out for robbery and rebellion is only right and proper. So when Talus who "could reueale / All hidden crimes" (5.12.26) is, together with Artegall, recalled to the court, a critical statement is made by Spenser about the mistake of withdrawing the mechanisms of justice requisite for the maintenance of all social and civic order. And the person responsible for making this mistake is none other than Elizabeth I herself. Spenser allegorizes his understanding and defense of Grey's administration in Ireland by depicting Artegall battling against and killing Grantorto (whose name suggests "great wrong"), freeing Irena from tyranny and imprisonment. But Irena, whose name etymologically means "peace," enjoys only a short lease of joy. Spenser now points to envy to explain the unpopular response to Grey's administration in Ireland. Envy's "nature is to grieue, and grudge at all, / That euer she sees doen prays-worthily" (5.12.31). Like Milton's self-consuming Sin, Spenser's Envy "feedes on her owne maw vnnaturall, / And of her owne foule entrayles makes her meat" (5.12.31). Significantly, Envy's close ally is Detraction, who primarily "weaue[s] false tales and leasings bad, / To throw amongst the good, which others had disprad" (5.12.36). In the logic of Spenser's allegory, Lord Grey is the victim of envy, backbiting, and slander. His task, like Artegall's, is to free peace from the clutches of tyranny. Artegall "sorely punished with heauie payne" (5.12.25) the people who were involved in tyrannizing Irena; and he was preoccupied with the task of dispensing "true Iustice" (5.12.26) and the question of "How to reforme that ragged common-weale" (5.12.26). Unfortunately, that task remains incomplete and the Blatant Beast with "his hundred tongues" (5.12.41), Envy and Detraction's very own pet, significantly survives to escape even Calidore's clutches in book 6 and to roam the world striking terror at the conclusion of Spenser's epic poem.[4] When the mechanisms of colonial administration and justice are withdrawn, anarchy logically ensues.

In portraying Artegall's recall, Spenser reveals his feelings that Grey had been unfairly treated by Elizabeth. In *A View,* he criticizes the people who accuse Grey of being "a bloody man" (*View* 106) and of treating the Irish as "no more than dogs" (*View* 106). This criticism is implicitly aimed at the monarch herself. Strategically placing Eudoxius's account of the criticisms levelled against Grey after the description of the devastation and famine caused by the Desmond Wars, Spenser argues that "the necessity of that present state of things enforced him to that violence" (*View* 106). Spenser shares Ludovick Bryskett's view that Grey's "Iustice is a terror to the wicked, and a comforte vnto the good, whose sinceritie very envie it self cannott touche, and whose wisdome might, in the oppinion of the wysest that consider his proceedinges, governe a whole Empyre."[5] His portrayal of the relationship between justice and the establishment of civil order links book 5 to *A View of the Present State of Ireland.* And in the latter text, bringing about civil order cannot be extricated from the cause of British imperialism. Stanza 26 of book 5, canto 12 shows Talus in Ireland. The force of justice required for the smooth functionings of society also serves to disseminate the immeasurable benefits of culture and civilization to a savage people. In stanza 39 of book 5, canto 11, Spenser refers to Ireland as "the saluage Ilands." And in *A View* Irenius proposes different ways to tame the savage Irish.

Arguably, the most devastating critique of Elizabeth's recall of Grey and of those opposed to his actions in Ireland is found toward the conclusion of *A View.* There Irenius offers a passionate defense for the right of the Lord Deputy to possess "more ample and absolute" (*View* 168) authority. Set against the historical and political context of Grey's removal from Ireland, Spenser's portrayal of Elizabeth's mercy possesses both positive and negative significations. The exercise of mercy shows the monarch tempering the otherwise cold justice of the law. But it also suggests the queen does not fully appreciate the hard reality of controlling a rebellious and intransigent people like the Irish.

Spenser's portrayal of Elizabeth's mercy is mediated by the presence of a political world in which the queen is not shaping events with sufficient determination and veracity.[6] He suggests that Elizabeth does not understand the difficulty of administrating an Ireland that is culturally backward and vehemently hostile toward the English. And again, in reading Spenser's views on the Irish question, it is important that we not confuse his politics with one that is dominant in the Elizabethan court. Elizabeth did not in fact share Spenser's desire to bring a recalcitrant Ireland to heel through brutal means. She accepted Grey's repeated requests for resignation in 1582 from his duties in Ireland because she did not support his reputedly severe and harsh governance there.

On a larger scale, as already mentioned, there is also the queen's ineffective protection of the Protestant Church's interests abroad.[7] Spenser wanted Elizabeth to consolidate England's role as a principal agent in carrying out the work of Reformation. Immediately following the Mercilla-Duessa episode, he proceeds to allegorize the regaining of Antwerp and the defeat of Catholicism in Arthur's killing of Geryoneo. Geryoneo figures in a transparent allegory aimed to show the stranglehold that Spain is exercising over the European world: he is a monstrous creature who threatens the existence of the recently widowed Belge. Alone and without the possibilities of obtaining any form of succor from without, Belge desperately needs Arthur's assistance in defeating the tyrannical Geryoneo. In the allegorical economy of canto 10, Geryoneo is generally viewed in terms of the tyranny of imperial and Catholic Spain. Thomas P. Roche tells us that, with his triple body, Geryoneo represents the power Philip II exercised over Spain, Portugal, and the Low Countries.[8] The threat posed by Geryoneo over the terrified and defenseless Belge is the danger presented by Catholic Spain to the security of the Low Countries. Belge has seventeen sons, representing the seventeen provinces that make up the Low Countries.

Spain, as Spenser portrays in his allegory, did not force itself upon the Low Countries through violent military aggression. The "bold Tyrant" (5.10.12) took advantage of Belge's "widowhed" (5.10.12) and "her yet fresh woes" (5.10.12) by offering to her "Himselfe and seruice" (5.10.12). Because of the condition of her grief and helplessness, Belge accepts the tyrant's offer of his service. The way in which Belge succumbs to the good things offered by Geryoneo reveals the craftiness and cunning with which Roman Catholicism spreads its destructive hold over a helpless and weakened Protestant Europe. Once inroads have been securely made, this apostate faith is then able to rear its hideous head "To stirre vp strife, and many a Tragicke stowre" (5.10.13); it is also figured as a devouring monster that sets up "an Idole of his owne, / The image of his monstrous parent *Geryone*" (5.10.13). In Spenser's militantly Protestant narrative, the word *Idole* signifies all that is wrong in the Roman Church: its liturgical practices, adorations of the Virgin Mary and the saints, its belief in the doctrine of transubstantiation; it is also possible, Roche tells us, that the "dreadfull Monster" (5.10.13) devouring children allegorizes the Inquisition that Charles V, the last of the Holy Roman emperors, introduced into the Low Countries.[9] Charles's son and successor, Philip II, continued to enforce the tyranny of the heresy-hunting court in his reign. In 1568 this Inquisition condemned to death all the inhabitants except for a few.

Arthur's entrance into the narrative of Belge's apocalyptic plight registers the role played by Protestant England in the defense of the Low Countries. Geryoneo's defeat encodes allegorically the Spenserian desire to find and have the tyranny of Catholic Spain completely destroyed. This vision of the defeat of Catholicism and the tyranny of Philip II does not meld neatly into the historical reality of the inept way with which Queen Elizabeth sent an expeditionary force under Leicester's leadership to the Netherlands to neutralize the Spanish threat in 1584. Leicester's army arrived too late to save the city of Antwerp from being besieged; his efforts to provide assistance really amounted to very little, and the campaign would have been totally forgotten had it not been for the event of Sir Philip Sidney's legendary death in the battlefield of Zutphen. But it must be said that in spite of Antwerp's fall, the joy with which the provinces of the Low Countries greeted Leicester was lavish. They demonstrated their gratitude by offering him a governorship, which he accepted. Elizabeth was infuriated by Leicester's acceptance of the governorship, seeing in it a complete lack of decorum, and recalled him. The implications of England's clumsy defense of the Low Countries were not lost on militant-minded Protestants like Walsingham and Essex. Edmund Spenser saw that Elizabeth I only carried out her duties as professed protector of the Protestant Church in Europe nominally and, at best, ineffectively.

In reality, Elizabeth had never found it easy to commit herself to any action of military intervention on behalf of a group of Protestants who were effectively rebelling against their anointed monarch, even if he was Catholic. Religious ideology was one thing, engaging in action that undermined the authority of sovereignty was another. Elizabeth was placed in a position where she found herself constantly having to negotiate the pressures exerted on her to conduct domestic and foreign policy in particular ways by men drawn to the larger international concerns of the Reformed religion. Respected and influential men of this persuasion included the Earl of Leicester, Sir Francis Walsingham, and Sir Philip Sidney. Leicester, Walsingham, and Sidney were Tudor Protestants identified with the Puritan faction at court. Significantly, this Puritan faction helped to keep at bay potential threats against the body of the queen and security of state: Mary Stuart, Irish recalcitrance, Spanish imperialism and its Catholicism, the Guise faction in France; conversely, they were responsible for pressuring the queen into getting directly involved in the interests of the besieged Netherlands.

That the queen did not give her uncompromising support to combat the threat posed by Catholic Spain and the Hapsburg powers in Europe proved scandalous to England's militant Protestants, one of whom was Sir Philip Sidney. In *A Dedication to Sir Philip Sidney,* published as *The Life of the Honourable Sir Philip Sidney* in 1652, Fulke Greville elaborates on the extent to which Sidney conceived his responsibility as a defender of the Reformed faith.[10] According to Greville, Sidney engaged in contestation with Catholic Spain by recognizing first of all the workings of this evil empire. Spain's "invisible arts and counsels" possess the ability "to undermine the greatness and freedom both of secular and ecclesiastical princes."[11] When contamination of this kind works by stealth instead of by the explicit acts of cruelty exposed in various anti-Spanish tracts and literatures, "a mortal sickness" is inflicted on the political and spiritual bodies of states and nations.[12] Spain is not alone in releasing such destructive effects: it unites with Romish forces in an unholy matrimony, where the military might of the one is wedded to the spiritual tyranny of the other to produce what can best be described as "this brotherhood in evil."[13] Particularly sensitive to the designs and machinations of imperial and Catholic Spain, Sidney—Greville tells us in chapter 8 of his *A Dedication*—undertakes a detailed survey of foreign nations (including such disparate lands and political entities as Poland and the Ottoman Empire) when meditating on the threat it is capable of posing.

Greville's point that Sidney is a courtier especially familiar with the workings of international politics serves to endow him with an authority when proposing ways for England to conduct affairs with Spain: "TO carry war into the bowels of Spain, and, by the assistance of the Netherlands, burn his shipping in all havens as they passed along"; "stirring up spirit in the Portugal against the Castilian's tyranny over them"; and finally and most importantly, forming a united league of nations.[14] The formation of a league, of a united and concerted political body in Europe, to counter and offer an effective challenge to the tyranny of the Spanish empire carries echoes of Luther's appeal to the German nobility to break away from the Roman Church's controlling authority and ground instead the secular government's own legitimate identity. Constituting an important expression of Reformation ideology in *An Appeal to the Ruling Class of German Nationality as to the Amelioration of the State of Christendom,*[15] Luther's endorsement of nonobedience in the face of immoral commands does not figure in Sidney's discourse, but his emphasis on the political imperative to engage in open confrontation with an apostate power certainly does so. In Sidney the will plays a part in making the important decision to build up a concerted and potent force in order to withstand the encroachment of imperial Spain on Europe's freedom. If there is one identity that Greville strives to fashion for Sidney in his idealized portrait in *A Dedication*, it is of this courtier as carrying on the defense of the Reformed faith that began with Luther. For his religious convictions, Sidney was even willing to oppose the proposed marriage match between his queen and the Catholic Duke of Anjou: "in the practice of this [proposed] marriage he foresaw and prophesied that the very first breach of God's ordinance in matching herself with a prince of a diverse faith would infallibly carry with it some piece of the rending destiny that Solomon and those other princes justly felt for having ventured to weigh the immortal wisdom in even scales with mortal conveniency or inconveniency."[16] The analogy of Philip II's marriage to Elizabeth I's sister, Queen Mary, serves to demonstrate that an unequal union of the kind momentarily envisioned by Elizabeth and Anjou can only lead to disaster—it will conclude in the subsumption of England's Protestant polity under the tyranny of the Catholic Church and the power of imperial Spain.[17] What we find in Sidney is the interconnectedness between his Protestantism and the vision of a global imperial politics. In his plans for a concerted and strategic war with Spain, Sidney had settled to extend the confrontation to the shores of the New World. Maureen Quilligan summarizes Sidney's imperial vision and initiative this way: "Sidney's intention was to plant England's empire on the mainland of America, thereby draining England of the excess population that threatened its stability while increasing trade, and hemming in Philip of Spain by cutting off his supply lines from the New World. On Greville's testimony, it would appear that the foundations of the British Empire were laid in Sir Philip Sidney's prophetic imagination."[18]

Like Sidney and his relatives Leicester and Walsingham, Spenser found himself drawn toward defending the interests of the Reformed faith in Europe. And like Essex, he would have liked to see Elizabeth pursue a more interventionist and militant foreign policy. Instead he saw that her defense of the Netherlands was as inconclusive as her subjugation of Ireland. Confronted with these frustrations, Spenser wrote book 5 to communicate his own version of history and propose how things should be. Arthur's defeat of Geryoneo, therefore, can be read as Spenser's recuperation of the narrative of history through an alternative poetic narrative. This allegory in cantos 10 and 11 rewrites the facts of the Netherlands campaign. Spenser portrays Leicester's Calvinist expedition as a triumph of Protestant honor. When he allegorizes

Leicester's acceptance of the governorship offered by the provinces in Arthur's interactions with Belge in canto 11, he highlights the joy with which the Briton Prince was received. Spenser's emphasis amounts to a political statement, for by making Arthur defeat the enemy threatening to undo Belge, he creates the "ideal" allegory of an effective Protestant campaign in the Netherlands. Measured against the historical reality of an unsuccessful campaign, the allegory constitutes an effective critique of Elizabeth Tudor's conduct of foreign policy. The reader is also left to surmise whether the generally positive portrayal of Arthur's encounter with Belge and his acceptance of the gift of her sons actually indicates Spenser's personal feeling that Elizabeth I had been overly harsh in her reaction to Leicester's reception of the gift of the governorship.

Spenser's portrayal of the workings of Catholic Spain as it extends its hegemony through cunning and violence is not restricted to the Belge-Geryoneo episode. Earlier on in book 5, canto 8, he offers another allegorical figure, the Soldan, to represent Philip II and the Pope. As Samient tells Arthur and Artegall, the Soldan "is a mighty man, which wonnes here by / That with most fell despight and deadly hate, / Seekes to subuert [Mercilla's] Crowne and dignity, / And all his powre doth thereunto apply" (5.8.18). King Philip II of Spain is bent on undermining Elizabeth I's sovereignty. Resonating with associations of the Islamic Orient, the name Soldan, when employed to stand for either the Spanish monarch or the papacy, relegates the ruler of Spain and the head of the Catholic Church to the marginalized position of the heathen Other. In *The Life of the Honourable Sir Philip Sidney*, Fulke Greville describes Philip II in a similar manner as "this devouring sultan" and "this Suleiman of Spain".[19] And at the beginning of book 2 of *Paradise Lost*, Milton's portrayal of Satan's throne as the demonic archetype of oriental courts sets the archdeceiver up as an eastern potentate, an epic identity that establishes him as the avowed enemy of truth and that also makes him the symbolic register of all monarchies in general. In Milton also, the monarch and the infidel share a common symbolic identity. In all of these texts the Catholic and the pagan are rendered indistinguishable through naming.

Spenser's portrayal of the Soldan and the chariot that he controls does not point only to his allegorized identity as King Philip II of Spain, but also draws attention to the nature of his defeat. The Soldan's death is more than a generalized fantasy entertained by Spenser to have imperial Spain suffer a complete and effective defeat; it is, significantly, also a direct allusion to the famous and important victory that took place in 1588 with the unexpected defeat of the naval force of the Armada dispatched by Spain. The Soldan's chariot, James Nohrnberg tells us, is Spenser's allegorical representation of this Armada.[20] Especially significant for and relevant to the allegorical meanings encoded in the portrayal of the Soldan's defeat is that he does not die by Arthur's sword. The Soldan is killed by his overturning chariot when the flesh-eating horses drawing it are blinded by Arthur's shield and lose control. Spenser makes an obvious point: the forces of apostasy do not possess the ability to withstand the standard of true faith and are immediately routed. The destruction of the chariot is also Spenser's theological version of Milton's later statement that evil always redounds upon its own rebellious head. A self-reflexive mechanism is built into the very nature of the evil act. The allegorical logic is that Philip II's very plans to confront the standard of the true Reformed faith held by England are doomed to predetermined failure. Justice, Spenser puts it precisely for his reader, "that day of wrong her selfe had wroken" (5.8.44).

Justice is first and foremost a retributive weapon wielded by an omniscient and omnipotent God. And it is also the daughter of Time.[21] The execution of justice on the bodies of the unjust will be taken care of by Time itself, which embeds a principle of inevitability ensuring that God's name will always be vindicated in the self-reflexive destruction of evil. It is significant that in Spenser's allegory, the name of the Soldan's wife, Adicia, stands for "injustice" in Greek. To Spenser, the most grievous injustice perpetrated by the Church of Rome is the Pope's excommunication of Elizabeth I. Injustice (Adicia) is wedded to cruelty (the Soldan) as Spenser's demonic counterpart of the marriage between clemency and true justice in the figure of Mercilla. The ways of injustice arbitrarily and happily practiced by the papacy are joined to the cruelties perpetrated by imperial Spain and its head, King Philip II, in an allegorical marriage; this injustice and cruelty must be combated and destroyed. In book 5, canto 8, the destruction of the Soldan leaves Adicia helpless and insane, raging in "the wyld wood" (5.8.48). Spenser's figure for injustice, the mad Adicia strikes back at the wrong done to her by snatching at everything that crosses her path with "Her burning tongue" (5.8.49). This tongue that "with rage inflamed hath" (5.8.49) resituates the political and ideological warfare waged between Spain and England in the domain of rhetoric and propaganda. Verbal and propagandistic assaults can be just as deadly; only in this particular case, they are delivered by a woman who is identifiably mad. By depicting England's traditional Catholic enemy as being out of control, Spenser attempts to contain through textuality and rhetoric the threat posed by Spain.

In book 5, Spenser is also preoccupied with the subject of justice in its relation to the rule of England's Virgin Queen and the workings of God in contemporary English affairs. Spenser possesses the uneasy feeling that Elizabeth I is not working in complete accord with the divine will that England build up the Reformed Church and set an effective challenge to the Spanish empire. The premise that time always takes care of God's retributive justice may affirm that there is a Christian providence in control of history, but it also suggests the possibility of a distancing between authorial desire for such a providence and the recognition that human agency (Elizabeth I in particular) is not cooperating with this providence. Spenser's unease operates on two fronts: he has a genuine fear of Spain's power and he also possesses the need to articulate a sustained vision of English imperialism. In Spenser's epic romance, theological opposition to Spain's Romish faith cannot be separated from the dreams of empire building. Spenser's concerns are portrayed vividly not only in book 5, but also in the specific episode of Britomart's encounter with Marinell in book 3 of *The Faerie Queene.*

It is important to recognize that the matter of Spain also enters into the epic narrative in Spenser's portrayal of Marinell's defeat by the martial maid Britomart. Through his particular emphasis on this maiden's masculinist attributes and the anxieties experienced by a male-centered society in response to female rule (3.2.2–3), Spenser offers one figuration of Elizabeth I's royal identity. If such associations cannot be easily dismissed in any reading of Britomart's significance in the poem's allegorical economy, then we are asked to read into her overthrow of Marinell certain political motifs. Britomart's Amazonian body links her to the land; Marinell, by contrast, is specifically linked to water. He is the offspring of Cymoent, the daughter of the sea-god Nereus. In stanzas 22 and 23 of book 3, canto 4, Spenser elaborates on the great treasures of the sea bestowed by Nereus on his grandchild Marinell.

The treasures made available to Marinell are the composite wealth of nations swallowed up by the sea. Spenser shows his reader Britomart admiring this booty from the sea and passing on. She does not stop to avail herself of its treasures "for all was in her powre" (3.4.18).

The sea and its treasures constitute an important metaphor in the discourse of colonialism and imperialism in early modern England. The privateers active in Elizabethan England made it a point to raid Spanish galleys in a contest to obtain booty from the sea. And Elizabeth I endorsed and blessed such activities. Very often, Nohrnberg reminds us, the queen greeted the ships of privateers at the dock in her own person in order to exact the Crown's cut of the profits on the spot.[22] Spenser's Britomart differs from Elizabeth I in one significant aspect: she rejects the treasures offered by the sea. Perhaps Spenser wants to impress the point that England's dominion over the sea does not depend on the nefarious methods employed by imperial Spain in its plunder. (This understanding can only be ironic in the light of the activities of the English privateers themselves.) But Britomart's victory may also symbolize the exercise of absolute control over a situation that transcends the contingencies of history embedded in the specifics of the English-Spanish rivalry. If everything now lies in Britomart's power, and Britomart represents one aspect of Elizabeth I's royal identity, then the logic of the analogy serves to propel the queen into that otherworldly and transcendent realm in which her mythological identity is inscribed.

The sea cannot be divorced from the genres of romance and epic in which it plays an especially important function. More than functioning as a medium that transports an epic protagonist to his homeland or toward his manifest destiny, the sea also embodies all the dangers and uncertainties of an unknown that threatens the sojourner with possible destruction. Buffeted on the sea of fortune that is Chaos, Milton's Satan, for example, almost never makes it to Eden when he finds himself suddenly plummeting out of control. If the sea facilitates the fulfillment of personal/ individual as well as national identity, it also functions as a central metaphor for interconnecting activities between nations. When merchandising vessels announce their presence in the ocean, the discourse of international communication comes into its own, notwithstanding the particular social and cultural commentaries made about the status of men who engage in such merchandising activities. By the time Spenser came on the scene, the activities of merchandising vessels no longer existed as markers of class difference, but as the sign of a new mode in the conduct of foreign affairs. The sea may have its romantic charms for Elizabeth's buccaneers, and the naval skirmishes may produce intoxicating thrill for some, but it is also the arena of engagement that must be controlled through acts of metaphorical and literal appropriation.

If the might of imperial Spain is symbolized by the dominion it exercises over the sea, then the English victory over the Armada in 1588 rewrites and reconstitutes the political significations of that symbolism. As a political body, England finds itself compelled to (re)define its identity in relation to a highly suggestive and charged metaphor like the sea, one that many Englishmen recognize should be translated as quickly as possible into the literal activities of commercial undertakings. By having Britomart control everything in her power, Spenser denies Spain symbolic dominion over the sea by asserting, through allegorical extension, Elizabeth's own literal dominion. England's ascendant status is facilitated not only by an event like the Armada, but by the important recognition that the nation must situate and define itself in relation to ever-increasing commercial activities and the interactions of a larger international community.

In his portrayal of the evil represented and perpetrated by the Spanish-Roman union, Spenser consistently points to the role played by England in thwarting the designs of Antichrist. If *The Faerie Queene* is conceived of as a gift that Spenser wishes to offer to Elizabeth I in the hopes of obtaining preferment in the court, then it is also one that expresses the epic writer's desire to enhance England's importance in the arena of contemporary European politics. In this epic poem, encomium cannot be separated from the continuing plea made to England's queen to do much more to propel the nation to the forefront of international politics.

In relation to the discourse of empire building, then, *The Faerie Queene* may describe or represent the destruction of England's enemies in its epic narrative, but it cannot do so by premising that England is operating from an advantaged position as a powerful nation. Underwriting all representations of England's defense of the Reformed faith as protector of the Church is the recognition that Spain continues to remain a daunting oppositional force. That is why when an event like the Armada occurs, the epic poet quickly makes use of the English success to point to God's distinct workings in contemporary historical affairs; this emphasis removes the text from the realm of personal and national dreams and fantasies of success. When there is real success, then the workings of God are given evidential status, and that is why Spenser is able to represent the destruction of the Soldan's chariot as effected simply through an encounter with Arthur's nationalistic body and his symbolic shield of true religion. But if an event like the Armada provides evidence of God's workings in human history, that is not in itself sufficient to ensure continuing and final victory over Catholic Spain. Elizabeth I must also play an active role in ensuring that this victory can finally be made complete. That is why, in *The Faerie Queene*, the destruction of the Soldan and his chariot does not indicate the end of the story. Its significance cannot be extricated from the larger allegorical and political narratives of Elizabeth's weak policies in relating to the threat posed by Spain to the Low Countries, and also to the extratextual proposals advanced by Spenser on how England can enact the complete colonization of Ireland in *A View of the Present State of Ireland*. Reflecting his own Protestantism, Spenser "casts the battle for Ireland as one episode in the continuing war for the soul of Europe."[23]

As a nationalistic epic, Spenser's *The Faerie Queene* propagates the consolidation and crystallization of a distinct English identity by representing imperial Spain as a nation to be prevented from extending its political and religious web of control. Phillip II is the Catholic monarch who must be opposed by the English queen. Patriotism, the theme intrinsic to Spenser's use of Arthurian material, is inseparable from England's identity as a professed Protestant nation. At the core of Spenser's chivalric romance is the desire that his monarch fulfill her role as symbolic repository of a nation's values and the focal point of its national identity. If the creation of a distinct English identity involves demonizing the identity of Catholic Spain, then *The Faerie Queene* must redefine the political meanings of a romance narrative that owes a great deal of its design to its immediate epic antecedent, Ariosto's *Orlando Furioso*. Where *The Faerie Queene* envisions the possibilities of creating a cohesive national identity by relegating Spain to the position of the demonic Other, *Orlando Furioso* celebrates the greatness of Charles V and the Spanish empire. A central desire in the Ariostan text is for the creation of a unified European front that has the power to repel the attacks of the Moslem infidels.

Orlando Furioso is *The Faerie Queene*'s important ideological intertext, and it serves as a useful gloss on Spenser's vision of the Protestant nation expressed in his epic poem. Ariosto's poetic vision of a united European body is vividly portrayed in canto 26 of the *Orlando Furioso*, where Francis I of France, Maximilian of Austria, Charles V of Spain, and Henry VIII of England combined forces to bring about the defeat of the apocalyptic beast that had emerged from the forest and threatened the security of the entire world.[24] It finds its place in a text very much concerned with the story of the defense of Europe by Charlemagne against Islam. In *Orlando Furioso*, Charles V of Spain is portrayed as the historical and spiritual heir of Charlemagne, celebrated as the unifying head of the Christian world. Ariosto responds to Charles V as the last of the Holy Roman emperors to pursue the medieval idea of universal empire. As a backdrop to this celebration of Charles V as the uniter of Christendom lies the memory of defeat in the wars fought against the Islamic forces at Lepanto, Constantinople, in Crimea and Hungary, and at Vienna, all within a hundred-year period from 1450 to 1550.[25] The threat posed by the Islamic infidels is not an imaginary one, and that is why part of the design of the chivalric romance is to represent the clash between the Moslem and Christian forces, and to envision the success of the Christian.

Like *The Faerie Queene* that is its epic successor, Ariosto's *Orlando Furioso* is an imperialist text, but with a distinctly different emphasis. In Spenser, the desire to create a complete and sustained national epic is denied the pleasures of fulfillment. The dreams of national identity and empire are fractured by the performances of a queen inconsonant with Spenser's own perception of what can be done for England. *Orlando Furioso,* by contrast, exhibits greater confidence in its vision of empire. Ariosto's epic poem centers its imperial theme on the greatness of the Spanish empire and its sustained encomium of Charles V. In a vision afforded Astolfo by Andronica in canto 15, Charles the emperor is shown to be the great conqueror of lands in both the East and the West Indies. Ariosto emphasizes the phenomenal outburst of activity happening in navigation and ocean travel by referring to the Spanish galleys as "new Argonauts" (155) venturing forth in search of another golden fleece.[26] Like Camões in *Os Lusíadas,* Charles with his imperialist energies cannot be removed from the place etched out for him in the divine scheme of things. God had specifically concealed the water routes to the East and West Indies from the rest of the world until Charles and the Spaniards came along: "the Supreme Good has awarded [Charles] the crown of the great empire once ruled over by Augustus, Trajan, Marcus Aurelius, and Septimius Severus; not only this, but also that he should rule over every land East and West, however far flung, that sees the sun and the passage of the year."[27] God gives to Spain the mantle of the empire that was Rome because he wants this nation to uphold the faith of the Catholic Church and "the Holy Cross."[28] In Ariosto's treatment of the matter of Spain, Astrœa, the goddess of justice, returns to the earth when Charles is made king. Part of Ariosto's encomiastic treatment of Charles involves making justice, represented by the figure of Astrœa, an intrinsic part of the symbolic economy of "the monarchy of the wisest and most just emperor who ever lived or shall live, after Augustus."[29] By contrast, in book 5 of *The Faerie Queene*, Spenser's Astrœa removes herself from the earth because conditions there have become unfavorable.

Spenser figures himself as a poet fully aware of the cultural potentialities of his historical moment. He finds himself, however, consistently having to deal in his writings with the relationship between potentiality and completion, desire and fulfillment. Completion and fulfillment in *The Faerie Queene* occupy an idyllic space that exists beyond time and history. This is a domain constantly gestured toward but never attained, because the quest of the Elizabethan courtier and his different figurations take place in time and history. In a postlapsarian reality, desire cannot obtain logical fulfillment not only because of the effects of a theological fall, but also because of the particular workings of politics and power. And for Spenser, the most important character at the center of this political universe is Elizabeth I, whose body reifies the monarch's identity as God's anointed in this world as well as the shortcomings of a woman who vacillates dangerously between possibilities in dealing with international relations. In *The Faerie Queene* any celebration of the English Renaissance cannot be removed from the persistent sense that this great cultural moment can be made even more complete, only if the queen does things in certain ways. That she in fact does not is a cause of anxiety for Spenser, one that informs his treatment of the subject of justice in book 5.

JUSTICE AND THE QUESTION OF ROYAL AUTHORITY

The anxieties Spenser experiences as he articulates a very different understanding from the queen about what constitutes a viable foreign policy are also palpable in book 5's representation of the legend of justice. In this legend, Artegall, the image Britomart first encounters in a magic mirror in book 3 and the man she is destined to marry, is represented as having been educated by Astrœa. Artegall will sire the line leading to Elizabeth Tudor. In book 5, Astrœa, the goddess of justice, flees the world's corruption and leaves behind her groom Talus to serve Artegall. With Talus there to serve him, Artegall, like the other knights and "patrons" we have met in *The Faerie Queene* before him, embarks on his adventures and fulfills his symbolic identity in the romance mode that defines him. Astrœa's ascent into another world is an apt figure for the disjunction created by the displacement of Elizabeth's symbolic identity from direct and immediate involvement in a material world where certain demands, like those of justice, must be met. Her ascent, a kind of apotheosis, at the mythological level, gives to Elizabeth Tudor, Astrœa's historical referent, an otherworldly identity and emblematic signification. Because Astrœa is linked to the Golden Age, her disappearance from the earth installs a lack that must be filled by the exercise of justice undertaken by Artegall and the implacable Talus. This lack, concomitant with Astrœa's apotheosis, has the effect of creating nostalgia for an "ideal" order; that nostalgia, affirming Astrœa's symbolic order, dislocates what is from what was, present from past. The associations between Astrœa's and Elizabeth's golden ages are affirmed and celebrated in Spenser's narrative, but Astrœa's removal from the world gives to Elizabeth's symbolic identity a palpable immateriality. Encomium, in other words, is obtained only by relegating Elizabeth to an immaterial space, translating her into an iconic object occupying an imaginary world removed from social and political contingencies. Astrœa's deputation of authority meanwhile displaces the burdens of governance onto Artegall, who produces social order through the violent enforcements of Talus. And of course, through the narrative that projects Astrœa onto a transcendent mythological space, Spenser alludes to Elizabeth's political waffling in exerting her authority over a recalcitrant Ireland and her recall of Lord Grey de Wilton. Book 5's symbolic narrative then gestures in two directions simultaneously: Elizabeth I is celebrated at the emblematic level through association with Astrœa, but the very narrative that facilitates encomium also encodes her "absence" at the material level. The world of time and history in book 5 is, significantly, not the golden age; it is instead the iron one, whose precise embodiment is the mechanical Talus.

Spenser's disappointment with Elizabeth's handling of England's foreign policy then registers itself in an epic text whose ostensible design is to celebrate the Virgin Queen. The different aspects of Elizabeth's glory are figured in such symbolic identities as Una, Belphoebe, Britomart, Mercilla, and Gloriana. But even as Spenser's multiple *mirrours* refer to the positive figurations of the queen's royal identity, they also point to demonic variations of those figurations. Doublings proliferate in Spenser's romance narrative—Lucifera and the Faerie Queene, Malecasta and Britomart, Radigund and Britomart. The presence of these demonic variations means that the queen can never remove from her gaze patterns of what the royal court could degenerate into. If Elizabeth, for example, finds Gloriana set before her as a mirror of majesty, she cannot help but look at the demonic counterpart of that majesty figured in Lucifera. Even though it is a poem of praise to Elizabeth, *The Faerie Queene* extends its educative function as *mirrour* and *ensample* to the queen. (*Ensample* occurs frequently as a word and at different levels in *The Faerie Queene*: the martial prowess of Britomart is described as "th'ensample of that might" (3.4.44) and the destruction of the Soldan and his chariot functions as a cautionary tale: "That all men which that spectacle did see, / By like ensample mote for euer warned bee" [5.8.44].) Encomium is given in a narrative that also relegates blame and delivers warnings. Sometimes the authorial voice even intrudes conspicuously in its critique of the world of the court, a critique that makes its interrogative presence felt within the larger encomiastic framework. In book 6, canto 9, the world of pastoral is invoked and set in opposition to the vanities of life in the court. In stanza 24, Calidore reveals how his idealistic ambition to find a career at the court is shattered by the reality of a glittering world of power in which "vainenesse" is the norm. And in stanza 27, he elaborates on the artifice ("all this worlds gay showes") that is the court's defining characteristic.

The presence of the pastoral idyll in a book that ostensibly announces its purpose to celebrate the virtue of courtesy originating from the queen and returning to her destabilizes the very romance narrative in which different knights journey to find fulfillment and achieve identity in the Faerie Queene, the poem's thematic and ontological center.[30]

The romance narrative by which Spenser's knights are defined and through which they journey in search of the Faerie Queene is shaped by a theological understanding of sojourning in a postlapsarian world and by the figurations of desire. It is desire that drives Spenser's knights, embodiments of the different virtues crystallized in Arthur, to carry on with their journey through trials and hardships. Spenser's romance representation of desire is tied up intrinsically with his personal dreams of obtaining preferment in the court, a dream that can only materialize through Elizabeth's princely condescension. Hoping fervently to obtain his monarch's favor, the poet offers his poetic gift in the form of encomium, where Elizabeth I, figured as Gloriana, is celebrated as an otherworldly and unobtainable "spiritual" genius. The Faerie Queene/Elizabeth I's otherworldliness enhances her mysterious authority and greatness. But again, the same romance narrative that adulates the figure of the queen as transcendent "immaterial" referent toward which all desires gesture, also inscribes the figure of error in its circling and repetitive movements. Suitably, therefore, *The Faerie Queene*'s final resistance to narrative closure places the singular object of the various quests always beyond reach, eternally deferred. Desire is ensconced as the primary controlling figure of the poem, always gestured toward and never attained. The line demarcating encomium from critique becomes a thin and slippery one as we find the first three books of *The Faerie Queene* giving way to the last three books of the second installment. The greater transparency of historical referencing marking the allegories offered in books 4 to 6 entails a shift in political emphasis from the earlier books. The excitement Spenser experiences in writing allegory to celebrate his queen in books 1 to 3 appears to be overshadowed in the second installment of 1596 by a darker and more cynical response to the workings of power. Critics have offered different reasons to explain the cynical registers of the poem's second installment: Spenser's disappointed hopes for procuring personal advancement in the court; his recognition, through the experience of Ralegh's disgrace, of the tremendously slippery world of court favors and political intrigue; his perception that Elizabeth's handling of English foreign policy cancels out by stages her symbolic identity as protector of the Protestant Church in Europe. All have bearing on the matter.

If Sir Walter Ralegh "creates" Virgin-ia for the monarch he loves and offers it to her as a gift, Spenser presents his gift in the form of the chivalric romance. This gift is important because its encomium is delivered with the hopes of influencing the queen into favoring him with preferment in the court. Because there is what we may call a *utilitarian* motive at the center of Spenser's gift, the delivery of encomium becomes a serious matter, not an occasion for trifling. And especially in the first three books of *The Faerie Queene*, Spenser's aim to praise the queen is deeply evident. When finally multiple lawsuits, illness, and extreme disappointment of his hopes for personal advancement contribute to producing books 4 to 6, Spenser's self-interests or their lack of fulfillment do not lead to a deconstruction of his allegiance to an absolutist ideology. The inability of Spenser's efforts to attain closure in his poem reveals both his profound disillusionment in not having things go his way and disappointment with Elizabeth's conduct of English foreign policy, but it does not translate into a critique of the legitimacy of monarchy as a political institution. The shift is a different one. For as I have suggested, if the absence of closure is a mark of Spenserian cynicism, it also signifies the unattainability of Elizabeth I who can only exist as the object of the romance quest but is still desired. Attempting to offer a gift to his queen, Spenser discovers her inscrutability and unattainability. Unlike Ralegh, who has the ability to "play" with the queen because of his privileged position at the center of power, Spenser cannot afford such play or dallying. The *Faerie Queene* exists as a gift offered by a poet who is removed from the world of the court and power, one in which Ralegh, by contrast, moves and has his being. While Ralegh possesses the privilege of venturing forth to colonize lands for his queen, Spenser can only write to plead with Elizabeth I to recognize that territorial acquisition is central to the consolidation of a powerful monarchy.

The trope of making and offering a gift, central to Spenser's purpose in writing *The Faerie Queene,* can therefore be appropriately contextualized with reference to Ralegh's own "creation" of a gift in the form of the American colony of Virginia. Ralegh textualizes Virginia in order to enact the drama of his dalliance with the queen. Virginia signifies as metaphorical Other to the queen as well as her symbolic analogy, so that Ralegh is able to invoke and textualize this colony to create encomium and to impress upon his monarch the extent to which he will indeed proceed to create a colony in her great honor. After losing favor with Elizabeth I, partly because of his marriage to Elizabeth Throckmorton, and desiring to win his way back into the queen's good graces, Ralegh undertakes to appropriate the wealth of Guiana for his monarch. His *Discoverie of Guiana* represents another instance of his attempt to court his monarch, to bring wealth into the coffers of the royal treasury. The difference between the desire to colonize Guiana and Ralegh's literal and symbolic appropriation of Virginia for his queen is that the Guiana project is conceptualized in relentlessly literal terms—the actual effort generated to find and procure gold—while the Virginian project has all the trappings of a literary romancing. Faced with loss of princely favor, Ralegh replaces symbolic wealth—the gesture of going out to win colonies for his queen—with literal wealth, the tangible commodity that he hopes can move his estranged monarch toward conciliation. Ralegh's symbolic appropriation of Virginia and the literary dallying encoded in the Virginian project register, therefore, an important preliminary moment in the history of English colonial ambitions. Here a courtier is able to play up the activity of colonial expansion to define his "love relationship" with his beloved monarch.

The colonial motif of Ralegh's *Discoverie* cannot be extricated from his desire to translate the text into encomium. Ralegh expands for the Arromaian king's benefit Elizabeth's "greatness," "justice," and "charity," the very same attributes and virtues Edmund Spenser deals with in book 5 of *The Faerie Queene*. Spenser identifies the queen's justice as the necessary basis for and originating center of social order as well as requisite for the expansion of empire. In *A View* he advocates the importance of extending those effects of the queen's justice to Ireland to bring about order and control. In his *Discoverie*, Ralegh focuses on that aspect of the queen's justice that is linked to the protection of rights and liberation from Spanish oppression. Yet it must again be emphasized that while the *Discoverie*, and *The Faerie Queene* are gifts "created" for Elizabeth I, they come from givers who are situated in very different social positions. Ralegh wants to impress upon Queen Elizabeth that he is still her subject and servant, that he is seeking out gold and wealth in order to dedicate these to her honor, while Spenser tries textually to persuade Elizabeth to expand her royal identity beyond the geographical confines of England.

In the event, however, both positions were dashed. Queen Elizabeth did not support Ralegh's desire to obtain her blessing for the colonization of Guiana, just as she could not accede to Spenser's programmatic proposal for the subjugation of Ireland. Ralegh had to live with the fact that he could no longer enjoy the queen's favor as he once did, and Spenser had to retain his disturbing sense that the queen was ineffective in running foreign affairs. And again, we must stress that the fact that Elizabeth refused to support Ralegh and Spenser in their pleas for endorsement did not translate at any moment into either the courtier's or poet's interrogation of monarchical authority. After he lost princely favor, Ralegh's writings began to focus on the themes of lost love and the arbitrary inclinations of the monarch. Spenser's writings would also represent the dark workings of court politics.

What we find Ralegh and Spenser doing in their writings—*The Discoverie of Guiana* and *The Faerie Queene*—is coming to terms with the compelling power of the royal charisma, one from which they cannot be extricated in spite of their monarch's arbitrary impulses and incomprehensible ways. But even Elizabeth's royal charisma, central to the crystallization of her authority and power, must give way shortly after, in 1603, to a different mythologizing of royal identity. The lavish display, pageantry, and symbolism intrinsic to the creation of Elizabethan charisma will, with James I's accession, become part of England's nostalgic past. In spite of its energy and vitality, Elizabethan charisma—associated interestingly by Shakespeare with the mythically-charged world of Cleopatra and Egypt—is replaced by the pragmatics of James's Roman present in 1603, the originating moment of Stuart rule. Now irony begins to proliferate. An ardent supporter of royalist ideology, Spenser inadvertently introduces into his criticism of the queen's foreign policy the subject of efficacious and inefficacious action. Without knowing it Spenser, in criticizing Elizabeth's effectiveness, contributes toward defining an emerging anti-royalist discourse. In the anti-episcopal tracts of the early 1640s, before he forged his ideas on regicide, Milton was, for example, preoccupied with the effectiveness or ineffectiveness of the monarch in bringing about a change in church government.

Slightly over half a century after the publication of both parts of the *Faerie Queene*, the symbolics and iconology of the royal identity were fractured beyond recuperation with the execution of Charles I. After the Interregnum of Cromwell's Protectorate, the charisma of monarchy never regained the symbolic power it possessed before 1649. The breaking of sociological taboos with Charles's regicide led to the creation of a social plasticity that enabled the industrious in England to rise high on the social ladder, a rise that consolidated the primacy of financial institutions such as banks, stock exchanges, and insurance companies.[31] Social coherence now hinged on economics and mercantilism: post-Restoration England witnessed the beginnings and establishment of "technique"—Jacques Ellul's term to describe "the prime instrument of performance"[32] that imposes centralism upon the economy—and the rise of a commercialized society predicated on impersonality. "Technique" is a symbolically laden term denoting an ideology distinctly separate from the authority-wielding power and influence of the royal charisma. Even though Edmund Spenser reacted to Elizabeth's inefficacy in defending Protestant interests abroad, he was unable to propose a "technique" to rectify the situation because he wrote within a social and cultural milieu and moment when the needed structures for generating this "technique" were unavailable. Elizabeth Tudor still wielded authority very much on the basis of the royal charisma and not on any strength extended by a viable mercantilism. When Spenser, therefore, created his own version of "technique," it could only assume the symbolic form of Talus, Elizabethan England's relentless iron man whose function was to enforce and validate this charisma. The passage of authority from charisma to capital was negotiated by John Milton who reduced the monarch to a tragic actor forced to leave the stage of life because of his tyranny. Unlike Milton, Spenser produced his romance epic within the boundaries and strictures afforded by the royalist ideology that formed him as subject.

Nevertheless, it is important for us to recognize, when considering *The Faerie Queene*'s encomiastic treatment and critique of Elizabeth, that the poet's views on empire building fail to coincide with his monarch's at different points. There was in reality no unified Elizabethan world picture defining England's internationalist ambitions in the latter half of the sixteenth century. (Indeed, it is highly probable that the conflicts existing between Spenser's and the court's views on English colonial practices in Ireland brought about a censorship that led to the printing of *A View* only in 1633, well over three decades after its most likely date of composition in 1596.)[33] Figuring himself as the English Virgil writing in praise of the Elizabethan Golden Age, Spenser finds he cannot simply celebrate the idea of national greatness, if a central requisite in consolidating that greatness—the expansion of an overseas empire—is lacking in some way. Any Virgilian poet can only find himself at a loss if his "emperor" or "monarch," the subject of encomium, is not in complete sympathy with the project of building a powerful *imperium*. Destabilized in the conception of himself as Virgilian poet, Spenser attempts to accommodate his anxieties by consistently linking imperial authority and English greatness to the expansion of empire. The metonymic relationship Spenser sets up between Elizabeth's power and the expansion of the English *imperium* generates encomium in a narrative that also identifies the threats posed to the consolidation of that *imperium*.

A question that interpolates itself at this juncture in my discussion of Edmund Spenser's envisioning of the English *imperium* is the extent to which considerations of gender politics are brought into play in the poem. This query is partially addressed by Louis Adrian Montrose in an essay, "The Elizabethan Subject and the Spenserian Text," in which it is argued that Spenser's encomiastic treatment of Elizabeth I cannot extricate itself from the poet's inscription in a culture for which gender hierarchy exists as the natural order of things.[34] Montrose proposes that part of *The Faerie Queene*'s contestatory and subversive discourse can be located in the poet's particular use of genre and myth, leading to the creation of a poetics in which the male gaze scrutinizes as well as constructs female subjectivity. In the example of the blazon of Belphoebe in book 2, Spenser's combination of the figures of the engulfing Amazon and nurturing Virgin produces an ambivalent celebration of female power when it reaffirms masculine capacity to exert mastery over that power. The very fact that the literal, symbolic, and female body of the queen is necessarily made subject to the male gaze in order to enable poetic and narrative representation(s) places the monarch in her rightful situation in a male-centered cultural schema. Montrose's reading of Edmund Spenser as Elizabethan subject and the monarch as poetic subject accords tremendous power to a text that possesses the ability to scrutinize, interrogate, and subvert. It is recognized that this power resides fundamentally in the text's linguistic structure, a point I agree with, but do not see as adequately explaining the complex interactions functioning between this text and the political conditions enabling its production. I propose that a fuller picture can be obtained, for example, if we consider how the queen might have received the "gift" of The Faerie Queene offered by Spenser in her praise, which opens up, of course, the whole dimension of how textual meanings are tied up with the awareness that anything a poet says may very well incur the monarch's disapproval. And that is the last thing you want if you do not wish to experience the terrible pain that various instruments of torture can inflict. Later on in this chapter, I will elaborate on how The Faerie Queene was produced within the context of the realities of censorship and the intricate negotiations worked out between poet and the royal gaze in the offering of the poem as "gift."

If part of The Faerie Queene's subversive energies is enabled by Spenser's masculinist understanding of gender politics, that does not mean that the position of the Other in the poem's narrative economy is filled completely by the symbolic maternal body toward which the male is necessarily antagonistic. The Other is identified in this poem as that uncharted space beyond England's geographical and political confines that the queen should occupy through an extension of her literal and symbolic body. Anxieties about gender get dimmer whenever the epic impetus is charged by the poet's desire to have his queen venture forth and appropriate lands in the New World. The poetic imagination is itself identified as a prescient faculty foretelling and enabling the expansion of empire. Spenser's desire for English expansionism has the interesting effect of heightening the queen's mystical status and her absolutist identity. Constituted by culture and its innate prejudices, Spenser may express male anxieties relating to female rule. Ideologically, however, he believes inherently in the divine right of Elizabeth Tudor to reign. This belief is embedded in an epic narrative whose basic impulse is to expand the English queen's political body instead of diminishing it. And Spenser's dream of territorial expansion is expressed in a narrative that conflates the queen's body with England's political one into the unitary metaphor of a devouring machine. Elizabeth I, *The Faerie Queene* proposes, can only succeed as a monarch if she is, like the faculty of the poetic imagination, prescient enough to literalize the metaphor of devoration as political action.

In choosing the specific mode of the Arthurian romance, Spenser initially affirms England's greatness by conflating its contemporary "sundry place" (2.Proem.4) with its "famous antique history" (2.Proem.1). Despite his recognition that the creation of this poem may be viewed by readers as "th'aboundance of an idle braine" (2.Proem.1) and "painted forgery" (2.Proem.1), Spenser defends his creative efforts by pointing out that the imagination can exert a powerful influence over material reality. England, Spenser's argument implies, can be "that happy land of Faery" (2.Proem.1) even though, of course, no one has yet seen it. But not to have seen something does not negate its existence. Central to the experiences of early European imperialism is, after all, the verification of rumors, and the actual voyaging from one's home base to authenticate what has only existed in the popular cultural imagination. Christopher Columbus, prototype of the European voyager and discoverer, set off in search of the New World not only with a version of paradise etched in his imagination, but also with maps to translate his fantasized landscape into material reality. The imagination is central to originating any dream of possession. It projects individual as well as cultural fantasies onto conceptual space and works to materialize that space through the physical act of colonial appropriation. Spenser recognizes that not to have seen fairyland does not mean England is not the great realm of legend and history, just as not to have heard of Peru, the Amazon, and Virginia does not mean these places do not exist. For it was as late as 1540 that the Amazon was first sailed by Europeans, and not before 1584 did Sir Walter Ralegh, Spenser's intimate friend, present to Elizabeth those lands he had discovered in North America. The proem to Spenser's Legend of Temperance is a defence of the imagination's ability to translate fictions into reality, tied to the specific exhortation for England to recognize there is an empire out in the larger world waiting to be carved. The imagination, in other words, as Spenser sees it, serves a utilitarian function. "Faeryland," as Maureen Quilligan puts it, "is located in the place of the questing human imagination, a peculiar Renaissance creature that does not, Spenser reminds us . . . , confine its quests to mental realms alone but sallies out to seek new continents."[35] Spenser locates England's colonial interests at the point in which the world of the imagination intersects with reality. In the twenty-second stanza of book 4, canto 11, he exhorts the British to follow Ralegh's urgings to colonize in South America:

> Ioy on those warlike women, which so long
> Can from all men so rich a kingdome hold;
> And shame on you, ô men, which boast your strong
> And valiant hearts, in thoughts lesse hard and bold,
> Yet quaile in conquest of that land of gold.
> But this to you, ô Britons, most pertaines,
> To whom the right hereof it selfe hath sold;
> The which for sparing litle cost or paines,
> Loose so immortall glory, and so endlesse gaines.

Ralegh's *The Discoverie of Guiana* asserts that wealth can be obtained in the Americas, if only England recognizes the urgent need to enter into and compete for land in which the Spaniards and the French have already made incursions.

In spite of the anxieties Spenser betrays in responding to Elizabeth's foreign policy and the ways in which she conducts affairs at court, Spenser cannot free himself from the imperial ideology to which he subscribes and in which he is inscribed. His criticisms of the queen are not designed to destabilize the monarch's authority, but made to serve the interests of advancing the Protestant cause and increasing England's territorial boundaries. The justice that Spenser celebrates when it works to protect the security of the state and to crush crime and rebellion legitimizes and consolidates the monarch's authority. We realize that Spenser believes that the prince cannot be touched by the law because he or she is God's anointed in the civil realm and has the responsibility of administering God's law on earth. Francis Bacon shares Spenser's understanding of monarchical authority when he writes: "Let judges also remember that Solomon's throne was supported by lions on both sides: let them be lions, but yet lions under the throne, being circumspect that they do not check or oppose any points of sovereignty."[36] Accepting implicitly the royalist premise that the monarch is God's anointed on earth and the custodian of justice in time, Spenser subscribes wholly to the Homily, *Concerning good Order, and obedience to Rulers and Magistrates* (1547), which identifies rulers and magistrates as the guardians of civil order:

> Take away Kings, Princes, Rulers, Magistrates, Judges, and such estates of GODS order, no man shall ride or goe by the high way unrobbed, no man shall sleepe in his owne house or bedde unkilled, no man shall keepe his wife, children, and possession in quietnesse, all things shall bee common, and there must needes follow all mischiefe, and utter destruction both of soules, bodies, goodes, and common wealthes.[37]

This homily endorses a hierarchical view of human society with its macrocosmic correspondence in the universe, telling the common people that supporting the authority of their ruler protects them from crimes committed against their bodies, properties, and souls. In this hierarchical society, the subject always remains the possession of the monarch.

It is clear to Spenser, witnessing Robert Devereux's political career in the court, that Queen Elizabeth will not allow herself to be threatened or "unseated" by the tremendous rise in popularity of any of her courtiers, even if this happens to be her favorite second Earl of Essex. When Francis Bacon writes in October 1596 that Essex is a "man of nature not to be ruled; of an estate not grounded to his greatness; of a popular reputation; of a military dependence," he captures those characteristics Elizabeth I can only be wary about. In an assessment that reveals something about the ambivalence of a male-centered court culture to the fact of a reigning female monarch, Bacon continues: "I demand whether there can be a more dangerous image than this represented to any monarch living, much more to a lady, and of her Majesty's apprehensions."[38] If like Bacon, Spenser is aware of Elizabeth's displeasure with Essex's liberal conferral of knighthoods on the Cadiz expedition, his praise of Essex as "a noble Peer, / Great *Englands* glory and the Worlds wide wonder, / Whose dreadfull name, late through all *Spaine* did thunder"[39] in "Prothalamion" (published in the fall of 1596, in the wake of Cadiz) indicates his support for spreading God's Reformation on the international stage at the same time that he risks antagonizing the queen. The admiration expressed for Essex in "Prothalamion" reveals a pattern of political engagement characteristically Spenserian. "Prosopopoeia: or Mother Hubberds Tale" and "Colin Clouts Come Home Againe" reveal Spenser's disapproval of affairs transpiring at the court—the queen's flirtations with her courtiers, rise of serious factionalisms, increasing love for ostentatiousness, intensi-

fied financial manipulations; "The Shepheardes Calender" celebrates the queen even as it critiques the effects of her
government.[40] As a poet who recognizes that any hope of preferment in the court depends fully on the whims of the monarch's
favor, Spenser knows that the production of any literary text must
take into serious consideration its reception by the world of the
court. If it so pleases her, the queen can react to a text critical of
her by ordering the bodily mutilation of its author.

That Spenser makes explicit his recognition that the poet operating in society can never be freed from his subject position enforces the status of his epic poem as a gift made by a loyal servant
to his queen even as it destabilizes the monarch-subject relationship. For any suggestion that textual production is enabled by
pressures exerted from without has the effect of compromising
the constructions of poetic praise. One obvious reminder of the
poet's relationship to the world of court politics is given in
Spenser's allegorical representation of the nailing of the poet
Bonfont's tongue to a post in Mercilla's court. This painful example jostles the otherwise cohesive allegorical framework of Mercilla's grand court and her just reign. If acknowledging the poet's
subject position ratifies the hierarchical conception of society, it
also disrupts encomium by suggesting that poetic praise is given
under the conditions of censorship, surveillance, and control.

In an instance of deep historical irony, Spenser's depiction of
the royal monopoly of the authorial voice materializes in James
VI's demand that he be punished for allegorizing Mary Queen
of Scots as Duessa in the Mercilla/Duessa episode. This demand
can be read as James's attempt to rewrite the narrative of history
by making Elizabeth disavow symbolically her support for and
approval of Queen Mary's execution. If the queen should punish
Spenser as he demanded, James would obtain the symbolic affirmation that he enjoyed the privileges of sovereignty; he could
then extrapolate from this concession the fact that Elizabeth supported him as her successor to the English throne.[41] James's response to Spenser's allegory clearly shows that ownership of the
poetic text does not belong solely to its author; the text can serve
as a pawn in the contest of power between monarchs. Like all
other subjects in society, the poet is conceptualized here as possession, one that compromises encomium and identifies the social
conditions and political pressures that enable and shape textual
productions.

Spenser's preoccupation with power and its social articulations
is expressed even further in the episodes of Artegall's encounter

with Pollente and Talus's with Munera. Here royal possession assumes the form of a physical sign imprinted on the body of the
subject. In book 5, canto 2, Spenser significantly describes Artegall as the knight "Who now to perils great for iustice sake pro-
ceedes" (5.2.1). Following his encounter with Sanglier, Artegall
meets Pollente at the start of this canto. Alluding to monopoly
patents granted to corporations, Pollente, whose name means
"powerful" in Italian and puns on the word "poll" (tax), is
Spenser's allegorical sign for the abuse of political power. Pollente
extorts from both rich and poor travellers who wish to cross over
his bridge. Artegall's encounter with Pollente ends in the latter's
decapitation, described by Spenser in vivid and graphic detail
(5.2.18–19).

Of particular interest in Spenser's description of Pollente's execution is the example Artegall makes of Pollente. Artegall fixes
Pollente's head on a pole for all to see. There this head, Spenser
tells us, remained for many years to serve as "a mirrour to all
mighty men" (5.2.19). The *mirrour* which reflects the true state of
nature is also Spenser's synonym for *example*. Defending Lord
Grey's regime in *A View of the Present State of Ireland*, Spenser's
Irenius explains the importance of setting up *examples* to instill
fear into those inclined to become rebels. Lord Grey "spared not
the heads and principals of any mischievous practice or rebellion,
but showed sharp judgement on them, chiefly, *for ensample sake,*
that all the meaner sort, which also were then generally infected
with that evil might by terror thereof be reclaimed and saved, if
it were possible" (*View* 107; italics mine). Sir Humphrey Gilbert,
Ralegh's stepbrother and a soldier who served as captain in Ireland under Sir Henry Sidney, understood instinctively the colonial
terrorism advocated by Irenius when he slaughtered Irish non-
combatants in order to reduce popular support for rebellion. Familiar with the ritual spectacles of dismembered bodies often ex-
hibited publicly in his contemporary England to strike terror into
those with rebellious thoughts, he would cut off the heads of Irish
soldiers taken in battle and have these laid alongside the laneway
leading to his tent. Gilbert recognized clearly that the production
of terror led to the making of short wars. A pamphleteer, Thomas
Churchyard, who accompanied Gilbert to Munster, provides a
graphic description of Gilbert's use of the spectacle of dismemberment to exercise social control:

> that the heddes of all those (of what sort soever thei were) which were
> killed in the daie, should be cutte of from their bodies and brought

to the place where he incamped at night, and should there bee laied
on the ground by eche side of the waie ledyng into his owne tente so
that none could come into his tente for any cause but commonly he
muste passe through a lane of heddes which he used *ad terrorem,* the
dedde feelying nothyng the more paines thereby: and yet did it bring
greate terrour to the people when thei sawe the heddes of their dedde
fathers, brothers, children, kinsfolke and freinds, lye on the grounde
before their faces, as thei came to speake with the said collonel.[42]

In book 5 of *The Faerie Queene,* Artegall exhibits the ghastly spectacle of Pollente's head as *mirrour* and *ensample.* His act finds its
political and social analogy in the power the prince exercises over
the body of the subject.

Spenser's depiction of Pollente's punishment points to a discursive field in which the manufacturing of body parts is loaded with
heavy symbolisms. Directly linked to the capital crime of treason,
spectacles of dismemberment were designed to remind the citi-
zenry of their subject position in the body politic and to serve as
grisly warnings. Thomas Wyatt's plans to overthrow the government of Catholic Queen Mary, for example, resulted in his imprisonment, torture, beheading, disembowelment, and quartering;
the different parts of Wyatt's quartered body were displayed on
gibbets in various parts of London. In the reign of Elizabeth I,
the pamphleteer John Stubbs and his printer Page were ordered
by the queen to have their right hands cut off for writing and
publishing a pamphlet against the proposed Anjou match. In the
Stuart period, an indirect attack on the Caroline court and its
theatricals lost William Prynne both his ears.[43] Curt Breight summarizes the pervasiveness of mutilation as punishment and symbolism in Renaissance England: "Although there were more
executions for treason in the 1530s than in the whole of Elizabeth's reign, discursive productions of treason—arrests, trials,
executions, displays, pamphlets, sermons—pervaded the socio-
political environment of the entire second half of Elizabeth's reign
and the first few years of James's government. In this sense the
overall numbers are less important than the regularity of and
the attendant discourse about treason cases after 1580—i.e., the
almost annual parade of demonized conspirators to the scaffold,
frequently preceded and/or followed by ideological disputes between the regime's apologists and its opponents."[44] London
Bridge frequently displayed body parts, exhibits promoted by the
royal court to create paranoia and undermine dissent. It was always useful to produce traitors for almost yearly execution: this

ritual helped to strengthen the prince's literal and symbolic authority.

Consistent with what we have already seen, the terror wielded by the monarch to crush dissent and procure compliance is a principle understood by Spenser as central to the creation and consolidation of social order. His Irenius likewise advocates terror as a means of procuring discipline. In envisaging an Ireland with no expressive form of idleness, Irenius, for example, wants all stragglers who roam aimlessly to be picked up by the sheriff. He wants them to be punished with stocks for a first offence and with whipping for a second. Should a straggler be apprehended a third time, he is given "the bitterness of the martial law" (*View* 160). Meted out by the marshall, this martial law, which can involve the death penalty, will inflict terror on the loafers that mere whipping fails to accomplish. The terror of death serves as an effective deterrent; but capital punishment fulfills the more practical and utilitarian purpose of ensuring that the jails are not packed to overflowing.

That justice makes spectacles and examples of the bodies of the condemned is not confined to the Pollente episode. Munera, Pollente's daughter, is also subjected to the same fate. When Talus starts battering down the gate of Munera's castle, she attempts to appease him by bribing him with bags of gold. Talus cannot be bought with riches and, representing a justice that penetrates all the secret places (5.2.25), he discovers Munera hiding "Vnder an heape of gold" (5.2.25). Once again Spenser describes graphically Talus's violent treatment of Munera. In the account given in stanza 26 of book 5, canto 2, Talus, who represents inexorable justice, is unable to stay the course of Munera's execution because he is totally incapable of feeling pity. Despite Munera's supplication by kneeling at his feet, this executive agent of justice ends up chopping off her limbs and nailing them in a position so "that all might them behold" (5.2.26).

Recalling for the reader Artegall's action, Talus's treatment of Munera symbolizes an important aspect of the prince's demonstration, wielding, and exercise of power. Spenser conceptualizes justice as imperial virtue, grounding its significance in the governance of the body politic. In canto 4, for example, Talus, "that great yron groome," is described as Artegall's (or justice's) "gard and gouernment" (5.4.3). Spenser's use of the word *gouernment* to describe Talus links the executive force of justice to rulership. Significantly, he refers to "the right hand of Iustice" (5.4.1) as "powre" (5.4.1). Justice must "be perform'd with dreadlesse might" (5.4.1).[45]

Because the monarch is the originary source of justice in civil society, "it is a capital crime to devise or purpose the death of the king" (*View* 21). The indisputable head of the body politic, the monarch is not subject to laws. In *A View*, Spenser's Irenius says significantly that it is "in the power of the prince, to change all the laws and make new" (*View* 141). We encounter a radically different tenor in Milton's figurations of justice. For the republican and antiroyalist Milton, an inverse relationship governs monarch and subject. The king holds his position in society only so long as he fulfills his God-given function and ensures the subject's welfare. Subject to law, the monarch who betrays the people who delegated power to him to protect "the Common good of . . . all"[46] must be brought to justice. *The Tenure of Kings and Magistrates* equates justice with "the Sword of God" (*Yale* 3.193); Milton writes: "be he King, or Tyrant, or Emperour, the Sword of Justice is above him; in whose hand soever is found sufficient power to avenge the effusion, and so great a deluge of innocent blood. For if all human power to execute, not accidentally but intendedly, the wrath of God upon evil doers without exception, be of God; then that power, whether ordinary, or if that faile, extraordinary so executing that intent of God, is lawfull, and not to be resisted" (*Yale* 3.197–98). Unlike Milton who, in equating justice with the sword of God, argues for the subject's right and obligation to dethrone the prince who is a tyrant, Spenser puts the sword of justice in the monarch's hand. In *A View*, he specifically identifies as treason any act that involves consorting with the monarch's enemies to the detriment of his royal dignity and danger to the crown. Spenser's politics cannot accommodate Milton's contractual model of kingship.

UNSTABLE STRATEGIES/STRATEGIC INSTABILITIES

In interpreting the expressions of Spenser's colonial views in his writings, we often find ourselves aligning with one of two critical positions: Spenser is the preeminent English poet of empire,[47] or he is responding realistically to the threat posed by Irish rebelliousness and intransigence, a position that reads his endorsement of the brutal suppression of the Irish as a matter of expediency and necessity. I want to respond to the colonial theme in Spenser by relating it to the contradictions encountered in his definition of the colonialist project and also to views held on the subjection of Ireland supported by the Elizabethan court. For arguably, a major force disrupting Spenser's attempt to produce a powerfully coherent blueprint for the colonization of Ireland is the absence of a sustained and consensual court ideology concerning the Irish question.

Spenser's *View* begins by providing an exposé of the degenerate state of Ireland and a critique of Elizabeth's "soft" attitude toward its control and subjection. Spenser argues that because the state of Ireland is beyond any hope of recovery, it must be salvaged through the logical project of colonization. Irenius begins his dialogue with Eudoxius by asserting that the Irish do not understand the basic nature and function of laws, and have never learnt obedience to them. If laws serve to restore and secure order in society, a people without laws have no access to the benefits provided by a legal institution. Even the task of imposing good and sound laws in Ireland is doomed to failure in a society that cannot understand their significance. Once Irenius has established that laws are central to any civilized society and culture, Ireland, with its absence of a coherent legal system, is immediately categorized as uncivilized.

Spenser's Irish are not only barbaric and uncivilized, they do not possess an identifiable ethnic or national identity. The origins of the people who have come to be known as the Irish are lost as a result of different ethnic interactions, a point to which I have already drawn attention in my discussion of the racist discourse of *Othello* in chapter 3. Spenser's Irish are defined then by their nature. Culture is powerless to effect any change for good in this intransigent and unmalleable nature. The relationship between nature and culture, a commonplace topos in English Renaissance literature, is meditated upon and represented not only in the *View,* but also in *The Faerie Queene,* its powerful political and ideological intertext. In book 6, Spenser offers us the figure of the savage man, one who has ties with Shakespeare's Caliban. Like Caliban, who first shows Prospero how to survive on the island to which he is exiled, Spenser's savage man seeks "all the woods both farre and nye / For herbes to dresse [Calepine's and Serena's] wounds" (6.4.16). In *The Tempest,* Prospero makes Caliban his slave once he learns how to survive on the island and after discovering that Caliban cannot assimilate the benefits of culture and civilization taught by language. In *The Faerie Queene,* the savage man innately recognizes innocence, and so he comes "creeping like a fawning hound" (6.4.11) to Serena, a kind of allegorical analogue to the lion (representing amoral nature) who recognizes that Una is

Truth and protects her in the Legend of Holiness. In the allegorical economy of Spenser's Legend of Courtesy, the savage man can be read as "nature" harnessed to advance the interests of "culture" and "civilization," associated with the world of the court and the genre of the chivalric romance. The savage man is first set up to provide a contrast to a villain like Turpine, whose unreasonable cruelty symbolizes absence of courtesy or *gentilesse;* he also exists for Spenser not only to dramatize the violent deaths visited on the bodies of villains who violate the virtue of courtesy, but also to show how even "nature" obeys unquestioningly the authority of the courtly ethos, as represented in the figure of Arthur.

Spenser finds himself compelled to explain to his reader how "this wyld man, being vndisciplynd," is able to "shew some sparkes of gentle mynd" (6.5.1). The savage man "was borne of noble blood" (6.5.2); like Pastorella, whose true parentage explains her inherent nobility, his capacity for "gentle vsage" (6.5.2) can only be explained through his parentage, which the text does not proceed to elaborate upon. Spenser finds he has no need to offer an explanation because the savage's significance lies in his ability to respond to the heroic attributes and virtues possessed by the courtier, all of which are linked to the authority of Gloriana. Unlike the savage man who, interestingly, possesses a capacity for gentleness, Spenser's Irish occupies a primitive and uncivilized world described in book 6 as the "saluage nation" (6.8.35). The denizens of this "saluage nation" are unable to respond to beauty; seeing the naked Serena only whets their cannibalistic appetite. Significantly, in *A View of the Present State of Ireland,* Eudoxius's very first utterance refers to Ireland as "that savage nation" (*View* 1), drawing self-conscious attention to Spenser's Ariostan episode of Serena's handling by the savages in book 6, canto 8. Certain thematic constants readily connect the *View* to the episode of the "saluage nation": the practice of superstitious rites and ceremonies (*View* 7–8), the love of reveling in licentious barbarism (*View* 11), the delight in making terrible noises (*View* 54). Calepine's entry into the narrative of Serena's plight leads to the destruction of the savages, an allegorical representation of the uncontestable power that knighthood and the charisma of civilization enjoy over savagery and inchoate nature.

Ireland's uncivilized, anarchic, and nationally indistinct state is further alluded to in the "Mutabilitie Cantos," where the ambition of the titaness Mutability to control the gods in addition to her dominion over the world leads to a gathering of the gods in council. In this gathering, Nature is invited to hear and adjudicate

Mutability's plea on Arlo Hill, a setting which refers to Galtymore, the highest peak in the mountain range near Spenser's home Kilcolman in County Cork.[48] The reference to Ireland in Colin Clout's digressive tale about Arlo is significant because it enacts the myth of lost glory and degeneration. Ireland is a society caught irreversibly in a state of chronic regression. Canto 6, stanza 38 accepts that "IRELAND florished in fame" for her learning throughout Northern Europe from the sixth to the ninth century; that was when Cynthia/Diana, the virgin goddess of the hunt, frolicked and played unhampered on the grounds of Arlo. When the voyeuristic Faunus views Diana naked at her bath with the help of Molanna, he is punished. But even worse than the retribution visited on Faunus is Diana's decision to abandon her old haunt, a departure that brings "an heauy haplesse curse" (Mutabilitie.6.55) upon the place. Because of this curse, Ireland is filled with wolves and thieves up to this day. Combining the Ovidian stories of Actaeon and Diana, Calisto's punishment, and Alpheus's love for Arethusa, Spenser's mythologizing of Diana's departure from Arlo reduces Ireland to a cultural wasteland. Spenser does the reverse of what an extoller of British greatness like Alexander Pope will do years later when, in celebrating the Peace of Utrecht, he portrays Windsor Forest as the hunting ground of monarchs as well as haven of the Muses. The presence of the Muses establishes not only the forest's timelessness, but its possession of a cultural heritage as great as that of classical Greece and Rome. In his "Mutabilitie Cantos," Spenser tells us that Ireland lost that heritage a long time ago.

The corollary follows: If Ireland cannot be recuperated in any way, then it might be well for a civilizing power to consider the possibility of recreating the entire realm of Ireland anew. There is much discussion of this recreation in A View, one that can be described as the Machiavellian fantasy of founding a new society ex nihilo. Of Moses, Cyrus, Romulus, and Theseus, Machiavelli writes in The Prince: "And examining their deeds and their lives, one can see that they received nothing from fortune except the opportunity, which gave them the material they could mould into whatever form they desired."[49] In the last chapter, he stresses: "no other thing brings a new man on the rise such honour as the new laws and the new institutions discovered by him."[50] In The Discourses, Machiavelli writes that anyone who proposes to set up "una potesta assoluta" (a despotism) must renovate everything; men who steer a middle course face the grave danger of losing their authority.[51] Articulating an anti-Machiavellian perspective,

Spenser's Eudoxius finds all forms of radical innovation perilous (*View* 94). In contrast, Irenius advocates the complete overhauling of Irish society because it is an impossible task to prescribe laws for a people who have no respect whatsoever for a viable legal institution; the Irish violate and do not keep the laws. That is why Irenius calls for a reformation of the entire realm of Ireland before the institutionalization of laws. Once the reformation of Ireland has taken place—and reformation is employed here by Irenius to mean a transformation of human nature (Irish barbarism and intransigence in particular)—there will be no problem with the imposition of laws because the subjugated Irish are in no position to resist.

While Eudoxius and Irenius have, then, spoken at length on the importance of laws to civilized society, their responses to how and when these laws are to be introduced differ. Eudoxius cannot conceive of the beginnings of a new society apart from erecting laws and ordinances. Irenius advocates first using the sword to eradicate those evils that make the erection of good laws and ordinances impossible to start with. He defends the use of the sword: "for all those evils must first be cut away with a strong hand before any good can be planted, like as the corrupt branches and the unwholesome boughs are first to be pruned, and the foul moss cleansed or scraped away, before the tree can bring forth any good fruit" (*View* 95). Later on in the text, the proposal to clean up the filth in Ireland is replaced by the staggering statement: "For the English, having been trained up always in the English government, will hardly be enured unto any other, and the Irish will better be drawn to the English than the English to the Irish government. Therefore, since we cannot now apply laws fit to the people, as in the first institution of commonwealths it ought to be, we will apply the people and fit them to the laws, as it most conveniently may be" (*View* 141–42). Because the Irish are completely intransigent, no effort should be wasted on civilizing them. Put simply, England should use whatever means it has at its disposal to force the Irish to conform to its laws and accept whatever plans it has for that society. Moreover, Spenser's view of the intransigent Irish is a commonplace cultural perception in English society. In his fragment, "A Discourse on Irish Affairs," Sir Philip Sidney prioritizes the use of "severe meanes" over "lenity" because the Irish are obstinate and no other passion can prevail but fear:

> Truly the generall nature of all contreys not fully conquered is plainly against it. For untill by tyme they fynde the sweetnes of dew subjection,

it is impossible that any gentle meanes shoolde putt owt the freshe remembrance of their loste lyberty. And that the Irishe man is that way as obstinate as any nation, withe whome no other passion can prevaile but feare besydes their storye whiche plainly painte it owt, their manner of lyfe wherein they choose rather all filthiness then any law, and their owne consciences who beste know their owne natures, give sufficient proofe of.

The Irish cannot be moved or affected by "any gratefull love."[52]

The exercise of violence as an intrinsic aspect of colonial policy is advocated in *A View* even though a dialogue is formally set up to discuss its viability and morality. The dialogue set up between Irenius and Eudoxius creates the effect of a fruitful discussion taking place, even though the reader is fully aware that Irenius's voice is Spenser's.[53] So predictably, Spenser makes Eudoxius question Irenius's assertion that use of the sword is necessary to England's colonization of Ireland: "Is not the sword the most violent redress that may be used for any evil?" (*View* 95). Articulating the Spenserian perspective, Irenius argues that the use of military might is imperative when no other remedy is available for reforming the evils of Ireland. Force and violence occupy an important place in Irenius's schemes for the subjugation of Ireland. Irenius, for example, imposes a twenty day limit for the Irish rebels to surrender themselves, a period of grace not extended to the rebel leaders. He wants to kill the ringleaders and their followers who do not capitulate at the right moment.

Spenser's emphasis on the use of force and violence to bring about the suppression of the rebellious Irish translates into an interesting redefinition of the word "reformation" in the *View*. His contemporary reader would immediately respond to the theological significations of this term, but the *View* deliberately subverts its conventional meanings. The Protestant stance assumed by Spenser when he attacked the idolatrous practices of Catholicism in *The Faerie Queene* is downplayed in *A View*, where Irenius specifically says he is no authority concerning matters of faith: "Little have I to say of religion, both because the parts thereof be not many, itself being but one, and myself have not been much conversant in that calling, but as lightly passing by I have seen or heard" (*View* 84). Toward the end of *A View*, he repeats that he has little to offer on the subject of religion. What he needs to communicate, however, is that the dissemination, what Spenser calls "planting" (*View* 161), of faith should not be undertaken with "terror and sharp penalties" (*View* 161), but rather with "mildness and gentleness" (*View* 161). This would ensure that the people to be brought to the true faith are first made to understand the new religion. It is never a good strategic move to get a people to respond with hate to a faith you wish to propagate.

Even though Irenius and Eudoxius do discuss briefly the apostasy of Irish Catholicism, they show no interest in amplifying England's symbolic role as defender of the Protestant faith in order to justify the proposed prosecution of any brutal Irish campaign.[54] A large part of this reapportioning of emphasis, the text's redefinition of the word "reformation" in glaringly secularized terms, is shaped by Spenser's very own deep fantasies concerning the complete restructuring of Irish society and its institutions. Irenius envisages overhauling the entire fabric of Irish society in terms of salvaging the diseased body, which must, he stresses, precede saving the diseased soul: England is figured as the physician who holds the mandate to excise Ireland's original body. "Reformation," for Spenser, involves nothing less than recreating Ireland *ex nihilo*.

Throughout most of the *View*, Irenius presents the picture of a rebellious and intransigent Irish to persuade the English that it is necessary to bring them under tight control. Such control can take a variety of forms, ranging from forcing the Irish against their choice to subscribe to English laws and governance, to prosecuting military action or even full-scale massacres. Interestingly, however, this theme cannot sustain itself without interruption. Toward the end of *A View*, for example, the portrait of the intransigent Irish who must be forced to accept an English system of laws is softened. The rude Irish can, in fact, be made to become more civil (*View* 151). The focus of criticism now falls on the English-Irish, that detested product of intermingling. Spenser's view, as we have seen, that this particular group is degenerate because of its tendency to get assimilated into the indigenous Gaelic population, was a prevailing one. When Spenser produced *A View*, Palesmen had begun to turn away from the English culture to which they had clung tenaciously, albeit at the same time, they continued to see the need to eliminate the Gaelic traits in their midst. Nevertheless, from the 1570s onward, the English-Irish began to move slowly but surely toward Counter-Reformation Catholicism.[55] Spenser's representation therefore reinforces his general construction of the Gaelic Irish as irretrievably mixed. The anxieties Spenser expresses concerning the status and position of the English-Irish do not represent a response to a social elite in Ireland beginning to lose power because it is displaced by the injection into Irish society of the New English. His distrust of intermingling can be traced to the more general and real problem of the defections of Englishmen and their assimilation into the indigenous Gaelic Irish culture. This problem of defection and assimilation was as real in Ireland as it was in the New World, where many disenchanted colonists joined and made new lives for themselves among the American Indians. Many of the Englishmen who were sent to take care of Ireland were unemployed or underemployed; others were discharged soldiers who frequently sold their weapons to the enemy. When news, for example, of Tyrone's rebellion arrived at London in the fall of 1598, replete with accounts of Irish brutality committed upon the English settlements, an order went out for a levy of soldiers to be taken and sent to Ireland. The exercise carried on into 1594. The queen's recruitment of soldiers revealed one important fact: in general, the common soldier, forced to perform military duty in foreign territory marked out for colonization, did not always fall in love with his job. As Joel B. Altman points out in his discussion of *Henry V*, a war play performed at the time of the Irish war, many of the soldiers Elizabeth I sent into Ireland to contain the rebel elements there were unwilling participants in the national effort.[56] Dreams of effecting the subjugation of Ireland were not shared by all alike. If the queen had problems with Spenser's brutal blueprint for the colonization of Ireland, the common soldier had problems with being sent to fight the rebels there. According to one historian, the Irish war "was the most hated war of their era: England's Vietnam. The country, the elements, the general populace and adversaries skilled in the arts of guerrilla warfare were all pitted against them."[57]

And yet in spite of the fact that Irenius has spoken so much about the potential and actual evils of intermingling, the interactions of the Irish and the English appear to be an option Spenser, in the voice of Irenius, must entertain. At one especially interesting moment in *A View*, Irenius states that since the indigenous Irish are never going to be rooted out of their "own nation" (*View* 153), and because Ireland is a place in which a sizeable number of English also live, it may not be a bad idea to make the two groups of people "one" (*View* 153) by "an union of manners and conformity of minds" (*View* 153). This model of intermingling imagined by Irenius will have the beneficial effect of creating amity between the Irish and the English in Ireland. The project of intermingling, which also involves scattering the Irish in small numbers among the English, can also serve to neutralize threats posed by the hostile Irish.

Eudoxius's response to Irenius's new vision of intermingling repeats what the latter has been saying throughout much of the dialogue up to this point: that the Irish and the English can never merge without producing disastrous results. His reiteration of Irenius's political position is especially ironic as Spenser's spokesman for Irish colonization has now produced a counter-narrative that undermines the thrust of his own general discourse. The shift in Irenius's position provides an instance of how the desire to create a new society ex nihilo, following the lines of Machiavelli's deep fantasies, runs aground when confronted with the economic reality of obtaining support for and actualizing the colonial enterprise. Spenser is forced to recognize that it is difficult to sustain the view that Irish nature is completely impervious to acculturation, just as it is impossible to realize the fantasy of re-creating a new Ireland out of nothing.

Spenser also runs into problems trying to argue out a colonial policy that makes use of force and violence in Ireland. In writing about expanding the scope of the queen's exercise of justice as an inherent royal prerogative, Spenser had represented that justice in terms of suppressing the Irish. At this moment in the text, however, Spenser's representation runs into trouble as his narrative finds itself unable to bring literal and symbolic meanings into viable conjunction. We see this cogently expressed in the rewriting of the literal meaning of force: "for by the sword which I named I do not mean the cutting off of all that nation with the sword" (*View* 95). Irenius assumes a defensive stance when he asserts that he had never found occasion to advocate the use of the literal sword in the conquest of Ireland. He explains that when he talks about "cutting off . . . all that nation with the sword," he is employing figurative language, referring specifically to "the royal power of the prince" (*View* 95). The extension of this power is necessary for remedying and excising the evils inherent in Ireland. To sustain the logic of his figurative language, Irenius makes a distinction between evil as a theological principle and a people who are evil. Whereas an evil people like the Irish may be transformed for the better by "good ordinance and government" (*View* 95), evil, as a principle, can never become good.

Here, literal signification is forced into a metaphorical framework, a backpedaling that suggests Spenser had a sudden need to deal with the ethics of his proposition or accommodate a court audience that might be averse to such violent schemes.[58] Spenser also finds he is not always able to sustain the premise that the Irish are completely impervious to the effects of acculturation and civilization.

One of the most vocal expressions of Spenser's forced recognition that any colonial project must work with existing structures already in place in England is found toward the conclusion of *A View*, where the use of military force to compel submission is replaced by a program of ordering the work patterns of the Irish and improving the shambled layout of the land. The earlier emphasis on violence is mitigated as the text now focuses on domestic life and geographical planning. At this point, the reader is forced to interpret the nature of the shift in perspective: Has Spenser discovered he is unable to push his program of military action in Ireland to its logical conclusion? Or does this shift represent yet another strategy in the overall thrust of the narrative toward procuring absolute control over Ireland? The answer is found in a conjunction of these two possibilities, for Spenser's inability to sustain his program of militaristic intervention means he has to produce an alternative program, one which in this case does not erase the English ability to exercise surveillance and control. Irenius advocates promoting the practice of husbandry because he believes this would help to civilize the Irish; he also speaks as a humanist when advancing the importance of education. According to Irenius, it would be ideal for an able schoolmaster to be kept in "every country or baronry" (*View* 158) in order to provide instruction in grammar and the sciences. These adults who have been instructed should be compelled to send their young to be educated in a similar way, for education offers a sure means of enabling discipline. Through education and discipline, children will quickly learn to recognize and detest the conditions of their barbaric upbringing; they will be instrumental, then, in helping bring about the requisite change to their native society. Transformed children also function as powerful examples to their parents, who are now forced to recognize "the foulness of their own brutish behaviour" (*View* 159). What education finally succeeds in accomplishing is create a society that legislates itself by slowly erasing the deadly hold of a barbaric nature; when this happens, the Irish love of *liberty*, translated by Irenius as *licentiousness* (*View* 152), will be broken. Learning, as the humanist Irenius celebrates with unrestrained exuberance, "hath that wonderful power of itself that it can soften and temper the most stern and savage nature"(*View* 159).

Crucially, the project of civilizing a savage people through education cannot be separated from Spenser's preoccupation with the need to install a network of surveillance and control in Ireland. Once garrisons are put in place, securing the presence of a military machine to fall back on in times of rebellion and violent unrest, then discipline can be exercised by redefining the geography and infrastructure of the land. Irenius proposes clearing pathways through woods, building market towns by the highways, repairing ruined churches, and erecting schoolhouses. Clearing pathways in the woods controls the activities of robbers; setting up watch stations along the straits obstructs rebel movements; erecting market towns promotes greater civility. The difference between having the presence of a military machine and procuring control of the infrastructure of a land is the difference between the open expression and concealed exercise of power.[59] Spenser knows that power is exercised most effectively when the body of the individual is controlled by documentation and made subject to analysis. We have seen how, in Spenser's England, this power is expressed symbolically in the spectacular rituals of torture and execution.

As a blueprint for the colonization of Ireland, *A View* performs the rhetorical function of arguing for an imperialistic English foreign policy, but it does so by criticizing openly as well as indirectly opposition encountered in the court. It supports the actions and practices of Lord Grey, and concludes its polemic by calling for greater autonomy for the Lord Deputy to carry out his duties in Ireland. Exclusive right should be given to the Lord Deputy to exercise power when "present occasions" (*View* 168) demand and necessitate it. Without giving him "more ample and absolute" (*View* 168) power, Ireland's reformation cannot be carried through to its conclusion. Irenius argues that time is an important factor that must be contended with in governing and administrating a hostile land. It is not always possible for the council in England to direct the actions of a governor who is stationed in Ireland. The problem of distance is a serious one, and the governor sometimes finds himself compelled to act in certain ways in response to social and political contingencies. He may not enjoy the privilege of time, of waiting for endorsement of his actions from England. Invoking Machiavelli's animadversions on Livy in *The Discourses*,[60] Spenser outlines the repercussions of interfering with the Lord Deputy's duties—possible defeat for the colonial administration. Significantly, the Machiavellian context Spenser invokes is the context of war. Livy had written that apart from the power to initiate fresh wars and confirm peace treaties, the Roman Sen-

ate gives to its consuls, dictators, and army commanders full discretionary powers. Wars are won or lost depending on the degree
of discretionary powers enjoyed by the commanders. The force
of the analogy is communicated with clarity. Grey's need to control
the anarchy in Ireland is no different from operating under conditions of war. The court may have men who possess considerable
experience in matters of governance and war, but they do not
operate directly in the field of action. To be in this field is to be
placed in the position of having to make snap judgments in response to circumstantial exigencies. The luxury of waiting for
orders to filter down from above after lengthy deliberations does
not exist.

In book 5 and *A View*, Spenser's conception of justice is tied up
immediately with the establishment of civil order and the expansion of empire. Spenser, then, also anticipates Clausewitz's key
insight: that politics is war continued by other means. When he
associates Elizabeth's mercy with an antique past, or when he con-
trasts it with the ideality of an interventionist foreign policy,
Spenser wants the queen to recognize that England's expansionist
ambitions are essential for creating a powerful monarchy.[61] That
is why the exercise of martial force is central to Spenser's figurations of justice: only force can quell rebellion and enforce obedience. Yet in the event, it is not enough. For Spenser, justice is also
exercised by putting in place a well-defined system of surveillance
and control. Book 5 and *A View* reveal how strategies of surveillance and control are already well understood by the monarch
who instills fear, undermines dissent, and procures consent.
These strategies operate in England, and they are also proposed
by Spenser for enabling English colonial rule in Ireland. When
Spenser addresses the subject of civil order and social stability in
The Faerie Queene, he never separates their enforcement from a
consideration of the consolidation of the English *imperium*. When
he writes about enacting the demands of justice to secure this
order and stability, he wants to extend that justice to control an
intransigent Ireland. In Spenser's writings and political thought,
justice functions as a synonym and metonymy for *power* in both its
raw and highly polished forms.

Spenserian Influences

The colonial energies of Spenser's text cannot be questioned,
but too often these energies are read and interpreted as a reflec-

tion of policies endorsed by the court. Elizabeth's court is divided in its responses to the colonization of Ireland. The tensions one finds in Spenser's *View* can be attributed to pressures exerted on the production of the text by opposing views found in the court. Ludovick Bryskett, we said, had identified Lord Grey as the embodiment of a justice required to salvage a lawless Ireland. Then we have Sir Walter Ralegh who, in conjunction with Lord Burghley, drew up a plan to confiscate four thousand acres of Munster and distribute this land to English tenants; this plan was based on Ralegh's proposals for settlement in the New World.[62] The colonial ambitions shared by Burghley, Ralegh, Bryskett, and Spenser were not accepted by everyone. We remember that Spenser's *View* was written in response to Queen Elizabeth's vacillating and placatory policies in dealing with the Irish question.

In general, Elizabeth's attitude toward Ireland was more defensive than aggressive. She simply wanted to ensure that Ireland would not become a jumping-off point for her enemies.[63] Renwick comments on the permanent strategic problem posed by Ireland: "England was at war with Spain, and the flanks of England rest beyond the narrow seas, in the Low Countries and in Ireland. Nobody has ever wanted Ireland very badly, but no English government could feel secure while the long western seaboard was open to invasion from across St. George's Channel; and every foreign enemy—Scots, Spanish, French, German—has attempted to open that flank."[64] Not liking wars, Elizabeth was also never keen on spending vast sums of money. It is especially significant, for example, that England never occupied any territory claimed by Spain after the defeat of the Spanish Armada in 1588. England had the resources to win victories, but Elizabeth recognized that she did not possess the financial means required to retain any conquest. The Spanish and Portuguese possessions still remained intact when James I made peace with Spain in 1604. The reluctance to ransack her coffers for money to be spent on wars duly influenced Elizabeth's attitude toward Ireland. The revolt that smouldered for several years in Munster with James Fitzmaurice Fitzgerald's rebellion was made possible because Elizabeth could not afford a major expedition. Only after Ireland threatened to become independent with assistance from King Philip of Spain, who sent money and even another armada (which never reached Ireland because of storms) to support the cause of Hugh O'Neill, Earl of Tyrone, did Elizabeth dispatch the Earl of Essex to Ireland with about twenty thousand men. Before this, she had already spent one million pounds on Ireland.[65] And Essex, to her tremendous anger, lost nearly three hundred thousand pounds in his march about Ireland to subdue Tyrone.[66] That the expenses of the Irish war proved to be a great embarrassment for Elizabeth is evidenced by the letter she wrote to Henry IV, the French monarch, in December 1600 pressing him to pay back the money she had lent him for his wars. Shortly after, in January 1601, she sent him another letter once again pressing for repayment of the French debt.[67]

While the colonization of Ireland constituted the primary expansionist project of Elizabethan England, there was really no distinct nor coherent policy concerning the method and the scope of conquest. I have argued in this chapter that even though Spenser's views on the subjugation of Ireland found support among different members of the court, the queen herself remained opposed to his schemes. The absence of a consensual position on the Irish question did not relegate Spenser's *View* to oblivion. About half a decade after Spenser's composition of the *View*, the quarrel over Ireland reasserted itself in similar terms, but in a new and different political context. Radical groups like the Levellers now made it a point to oppose the plan of any military body to prosecute the violent suppression of the Irish. This led to inevitable conflict between army commanders like Cromwell and Fairfax, and radical agitators among the rank and file. In the instance of this specific conflict, Cromwell and Fairfax responded swiftly and decisively by suppressing the mutineers and their radical leaders. At this point, an analogy immediately suggests itself between the commanders' brutal reaction and Spenser's textual representation of Artegall's encounter with the egalitarian giant in book 5 of *The Faerie Queene*. Spenser's giant is hurled down a cliff by Talus because he speaks in the language of egalitarianism. According to the allegorical meanings of Spenser's text, the giant must be destroyed if an inherent hierarchical system is to remain inviolate. Both Spenser's giant and the Leveller leaders are ruthlessly suppressed to prevent any subversive idea about equality from taking root.

The Levellers identify England's ambition to extend their political reach as the manifestation of outright tyranny. William Walwyn, one of the Leveller leaders, was alleged to have said "[t]hat the sending over Forces to Ireland is for nothing else but to make way by the blood of the Army to enlarge their territories of power and Tyranny, That it is an unlawful War, a cruel and bloody work to go to destroy the Irish Natives for their Consciences, (though they have kill'd many thousand Protestants for their Consciences,)

and to drive them from their proper natural and native Rights."[68]
And it was also reported of Walwyn:

> that is his constant endeavour to hinder the relief of Ireland, by exhib-
> iting arguments and reasons in justification of that bloody rebellion,
> and in puzzling the judgements and Consciences of those that oth-
> erways would promote that happy work, arguing that the cause of the
> Irish Natives in seeking their just freedoms, immunities, and liberties,
> was the very same with our cause here, in indeavouring our own res-
> cue and freedom from the power of oppressors.[69]

Walwyn's opposition to any projected Irish campaign cannot be
separated from his belief that "a quiet and cheerful conscience,
. . . is above all honor and riches."[70] Because living in a fallen
world inevitably involves possessing only uncertain knowledge,
rendering any belief in the existence of "an unerring spirit" pre-
sumptuous, liberty of conscience must be allowed to every person.[71] Walwyn responded to the passing of the 14 August 1644
ordinance reestablishing licensing of the press by writing *The
Compassionate Samaritan* (1644), decrying the tyranny not only of
censorship but also of oppression of the conscience. The body of
left-wing Protestants or sectarians—Anabaptistical, Brownistical,
or Independent, as Walwyn itemizes them—must be allowed to
enjoy a free conscience. This common freedom and Christian
liberty to be experienced by every man must not be restricted to
any self-serving interest. Walwyn writes: "Methinks every man is
bound in conscience to speak and do what he can in the behalf
of such a harmless people as these [referring to left-wing separat-
ists and sectarians]."[72]

Walwyn produced *The Compassionate Samaritan* in the same year
that Milton published *Areopagitica*. While both texts constitute a
reaction to the Parliamentarian legislation of censorship, their
emphases are distinctly different. Walwyn's *Compassionate Samaritan* articulates a vision of Christian liberty and freedom of the
conscience Milton will only crystallize much later on in his polemical career. Even though Milton's figuration of Truth as the dismembered Osiris reveals a revision of his earlier understanding
that Scripture is God's revealed Word that communicates its
meanings unambiguously, he ultimately centers his polemic on
the optimism that God's Englishmen still function as a composite
body in the defense of Truth: England is a mighty nation of
prophets. Milton also reacts to Parliament's retrogressive legislation by arguing for the importance of obtaining a knowledge of
evil and of undergoing purification by trial. Virtue, like the Lady

in *Comus,* must not be "fugitive and cloister'd" (*Yale* 2.515), but exercised and tested. Only by being exposed to evil can men and women exercise their prerogative of choosing, and choice in Milton is always synonymous with reason. Unlike Milton's critique of the tyranny of censorship, Walwyn's particular attack is predicated on the right of the sectarians to adhere to their understanding of Truth. For Walwyn, this right, linked to the freedom of the conscience and reason, is set in opposition to all forms of tyranny, whether papist, prelatical, regal, even Parliamentarian or Presbyterial; it is significantly extended also to the beleaguered Irish. The same rhetoric of contestation applies to opposing Cromwell's design in Ireland. Both sectarians and Irish must not be deprived of their freedom of conscience or their "proper natural and native Rights."

Fairfax and Cromwell's annihilation of the radical opposition within the army earned them honorary degrees and a banquet from Oxford. Cromwell's efficient conduct of military affairs also made him the subject of Andrew Marvell's politically indeterminate "An Horatian Ode Upon Cromwell's Return from Ireland." The "Horatian Ode" was apparently written in the early summer of 1650, after Cromwell's Irish campaign (executed between August 1649 and May 1650) and before the decisive invasion of Scotland on 22 July 1650.

In his Ode, Marvell describes the Protector as "restless *Cromwel*" (line 9) who "could not cease / In the inglorious Arts of Peace" (lines 9–10). Through "adventrous War" (line 11), Cromwell burns through the air "like the three-fork'd Lightning" (line 13), renting palaces and temples, and most importantly, blasting the laurels on Caesar's (Charles I's) head. The Protector's warlike energies cannot be resisted; he is specifically associated with "angry Heaven's flame" (line 26), a reference that associates Cromwell with the forces of nature and implies the divinely sanctioned nature of his enterprise. If "restless *Cromwel*" breaks in upon the English political scene like lightning, he also falls upon the Irish with the same kind of intensity and destructive fervor. In one year, Ireland found itself completely tamed.

Based on the images and metaphors Marvell uses to portray Cromwell in this poem, Michael Wilding argues for a consistent poet who is unambiguously supportive of the Protector and anti-Royalist in his politics. Marvell is certainly not, Wilding goes on to elaborate, the New Critic's poet of ambiguity like the one posited by Cleanth Brooks; he celebrates the "Sword erect" (line 116) with which Cromwell prosecutes not only his Irish campaign, but also his suppression of the radical opposition within the army and the mutinies incited by the Levellers.[73] Wilding's construction of an unambiguous Marvell who is filled with praise for Cromwell does not, however, begin the important critical task of addressing the poem's numerous unstable and indeterminate moments: the association of Charles I's cause with a "Justice" (line 37) that cannot overturn the dictates of "Fate" (line 37); the double-edged significations of Cromwell's "wiser art" (line 48) as both positive design and artificial scheming; the sympathetic treatment given to Charles's execution. Even Marvell's poetic treatment of the Irish campaign is not without ambiguity. We read, for example, the highly ironic lines:

> And now the *Irish* are asham'd
> To see themselves in one Year tam'd:
> So much one Man can do,
> That does both act and know.
> They can affirm his Praises best,
> And have, though overcome, confest
> How good he is, how just,
> And fit for highest Trust.
>
> (lines 73–80)

Marvell appears to be saying that the Irish now have no choice but to accept unconditionally England's colonial jurisdiction and control over them; their praise for Cromwell, after the fact of the brutal Irish campaign, also creates, however, the ironic effect of interrogating the very ruthlessness of the enterprise. Cromwell's unappeasable warlike energies are positive, but they can also be disturbing. The Irish have had first-hand experience of those disturbing energies in their disastrous defeat. And the Scots can find no place to hide from Cromwell's fiery passage: "The *Pict* no shelter now shall find / Within his party-colour'd Mind; / But from this Valour sad / Shrink underneath the Plad" (lines 105–08).

Cromwell's militarism is cause for celebration, especially as it enabled the overthrow of monarchical tyranny, but it is also terribly disturbing because of its absence of remorse. Ironically, Marvell's inability to celebrate Cromwell without intimating his uneasiness concerning the Protector's uncontainable energies points to a facet of English colonial policy missing in Elizabethan England, and that is the distinct willingness to endorse direct military intervention to effect the subjection of another people or culture. Cromwell learnt from Spenser the best way to proceed in order to subjugate a rebellious Ireland, and he gave symbolic recognition to that tutelage by restoring some lands to Spenser's grandson. In bringing about the complete subjection of Ireland, Cromwell effected in a remarkably short time what Tudor England only succeeded in discussing, debating, and caviling over. But it was in Elizabeth's reign that one of the most sustained and programmatic blueprints for the colonization of Ireland, Spenser's own *View,* was produced. And what Cromwell did a few decades later was to reread the Spenserian text and translate into action its invaluable lessons.[74] Cromwell, Spenser's ideal reader, materialized what Spenser could only dream about. He enabled the creation of the Act of Settlement of Ireland, which confiscated the estate of every Irish landowner, both Protestant and Catholic, unless it could be proven that this landowner had been supportive of England's political interests. Cromwell's reconquest of Ireland also restructured the system of plantation. With the majority of Catholic landowners expelled from their property, English soldiers now became landowners by accepting land in compensation for arrears of pay. Catholic Ireland became a country dominated by Protestant landlords.[75]

5

"Space May Produce New Worlds": Theological Imperialism and the Poetics of Colonialism in *Paradise Lost, Paradise Regained,* and *Samson Agonistes*

IN A RECENT STUDY ENTITLED *MILTON'S IMPERIAL EPIC*, MARTIN EVans argues that Milton is fully aware of England's expansionist and colonial designs in the New World, and that his knowledge of these makes its presence felt in *Paradise Lost* through direct references and allusions.[1] If Milton, for example, portrays Satan as the archetype of the evil colonist and imperialist, he also depicts his God as the ultimately benevolent and "sovran Planter" (*PL* 4.691).[2] And if he makes Adam and Eve the victims of a destructive colonist and slave-owner, he also portrays them as colonists in turn, enjoying dominion over the earth. *"Paradise Lost,"* Evans then concludes, "contains, in short, almost every conceivable permutation of the colonial experience available in the seventeenth century."[3] For Milton ultimately, Evans continues, "In and of itself, colonialism was neither good nor bad. Everything depended on the identity of the colonizer, the nature of the colonized, and the purpose of the colony. And so it is in *Paradise Lost*. Imperial expansion, the poem implies, is morally neutral. When it is practiced by the virtuous, it is entirely admirable. When it is practiced by the wicked, it is one of the greatest evils that the human race can endure."[4] The idea that there is such a thing as good colonialism and virtuous imperialism needs further commentary and elaboration. This is because any rationalization of the rightness of one's duty or mandate to colonize another people necessarily involves responses and reactions from those marked out for subjection. The treatment of colonialism and imperialism in Milton's writings does not allude and refer only to activities in the New World. Milton also takes a special interest in neighboring Ireland.

The New World is, for him, not only the site toward which much of England's colonial energies are channeled, but also the New England that Puritans, fleeing the apostasy of the Old England, sail to in search of refuge. The significance of the New World is not limited, then, to its ability to generate commercial profits; it also obtains much of its meanings from a theological framework and an apprehension of history mediated through a typological perspective. Ireland's significance is, by contrast, different: Milton views Ireland as a subject state and an established colony of England.

In this chapter, I propose to comment on the distinctive features of Milton's colonial temperament and on his debt to a theological tradition favorable to the dreams of expansionism. Intrinsic to Milton's political and religious thought is the ethic of what can be called Christian imperialism, predicated on the exclusivist doctrine of the one true God and salvation obtained only through the one true Christ. In his polemical writings, Milton's political antagonists are figured in terms of the Satanic as well as apostate men and women of the Old Testament, and where the earthly and cosmic contestation between good and evil will inevitably conclude in the victory of God's prophets. When events in history are interpreted with reference to "us" against "them"— with "us," of course, enjoying God's divine sanction—then a categorical space, associated with hell, is created for conveniently dumping the enemies of Truth. The moral and ethical judgments imposed by Milton on different people who occupy the stage of biblical and contemporary history are made on the basis of a dichotomized view of the world. Apostates who belong to the other side of the moral and ontological divide must be fought against and vanquished. The theological rhetoric that Milton employs to mark, marginalize, and demonize difference also belongs to a colonialist discourse that involves more than simply converting unbelievers to Truth through the power of the Word; it is directly linked to the interests of consolidating a viable Commonwealth, and also of pushing for a sustained project to effect, for example, the subjugation of Ireland. Milton's prose writings reveal to the reader not only his early dreams of spreading Reformation from England to Europe and the world, but also his colonial view of Ireland. Any commentary on the relationship of Milton's thought to the discourse of colonialism and imperialism must take into account his treatment of the subject of Ireland.

The exclusivist rhetoric of the Judeo-Christian tradition also shapes the narratives of Milton's major poems—*Paradise Lost,*

Paradise Regained, and *Samson Agonistes*—except that now, it is the possession of God's lonely prophet: Milton, standing like Abdiel, solitary in the midst of an apostate society. But this emphasis on the isolation of God's faithful prophet also produces narratives that appear to be unsympathetic toward any sustained vision of expansionism and colonialism. Where Martin Evans concludes that *Paradise Lost* inscribes the multivalent strains of colonialist discourse, I wish to emphasize that the text strongly encodes the energies of an antiimperialist one. It is possible to link the antiimperialist narratives identifiable in *Paradise Lost* and *Paradise Regained* to Milton's sense, accentuated especially after the failure of the Puritan experiment, that England has lost its cultural mandate to stand as a beacon of God's Reformation. In such a condition, its immediate task should be to try and get its own house in order instead of attempting to engage itself with the projects of overseas expansionism.

THE COMMONWEALTH, SPAIN, AND IRELAND

When James VI of Scotland became King James I in 1603, he immediately sought to establish friendly relations between England and Spain. The bitter English-Spanish rivalry that had marked its presence deeply in the literature of Elizabethan England did not, however, disappear completely. Conflict with Spain continued into the Interregnum, this time precipitated by Oliver Cromwell's Western Design. Martin Evans reminds us, however, that by the time Cromwell daringly challenged the supremacy of Spain in the New World, England was no longer attempting to make its political presence felt, as in the days of Elizabeth I: "the conflict with Spain . . . served as a vivid reminder that England, too, was a major colonial power."[5] Anti-Spanish sentiment was rekindled in a big way in the period of the Commonwealth.[6] In 1655, for example, a document was produced—titled *A Declaration of His Highness, by the Advice of His Council; Setting Forth, on the Behalf of This Commonwealth, the Justice of Their Cause Against Spain*—employing the contestational language found in writings that aimed to represent the treachery and apostasy of imperial Spain. This document proclaims Spanish colonialism and imperialism invalid and defends England's rightful settling of colonies in America.[7]

Milton's relation to Cromwell's *Declaration* is unclear. The Columbia editors of *The Works of John Milton* actually accept him as the author of the text, but the Yale editors of the *Complete Prose Works of John Milton* do not. According to the Yale editors, "The authorship of both the Latin and the English versions of Cromwell's declaration against the Spaniards is unknown"; the reader can never be completely certain about Milton's connection with the authorship of either or both of them (*Yale* 5:2.711–12). But Martin Evans makes the point that "As Secretary for Foreign Tongues [Milton] had almost certainly heard Cromwell rehearsing the arguments for his disastrous attempt to drive the Spanish out of Hispaniola in 1654, and he may even have had a hand in translating the Lord Protector's rationale for his Western Design in the following year."[8] Whatever the precise nature of Milton's involvement in the production of the text may have been, *A Declaration* remains an important cultural document because it reveals something about the Lord Protector's expansionist ambitions. Milton would certainly be familiar with these. The immediate occasion for the production of *A Declaration* is Cromwell's haranguing of Parliament for support in his ill-fated attempt to conquer the West Indies. The text registers the continuing tensions existing between England and Spain in the politics of empire building, and serves well as a context for and preamble to my discussion in this chapter of Milton's treatment of Ireland and of his attitudes toward the colonial themes in *Paradise Lost* and *Paradise Regained.*

Cromwell's *Declaration* criticizes Spain for its refusal to respect peace and to observe the commercial arrangements expressed in a Treaty that took place between Henry VIII and Charles V in 1542. Arguing that Spain's imposition of an embargo requires England to go to war, the document provides an account of major differences between the designs of Spanish and English imperialism. Certain themes recur. Borrowing from the legend of Spanish imperial cruelty given great impetus by Bartolomé de Las Casas in his *Brevísima relación de la destrucción de las Indias* (1551), the *Declaration* focuses on the cruelty and unworthiness of Spanish dealings with the English in the West Indies, and their barbaric treatment of the American Indians: "And certainly, at one time or another, by some hand or other, God will have an accompt of the Innocent Blood of so many Millions of Indians, so barbarously Butchered by the Spaniards, and of the Wrong and Injustice that hath been done unto them."[9] We see Hakluyt similarly portraying the Indians as meek and gentle when he foregrounds Spanish atrocities by reproducing accounts provided by Las Casas.[10] Las Casas had preached that the Spaniards who held Indians in encomiendas could not obtain salvation. He himself decided to emancipate his slaves in 1514 in the name of Christianity. The question of "title," characteristic of the articulations of colonialist discourse, is given prominence in both the *Declaration* and Hakluyt's *Discourse of Western Planting*. In his *Western Planting*, Hakluyt asserts that Pope Alexander VI had no authority to give to the rulers of Spain all the islands and lands of the West Indies. He employs the theological argument to buttress this assertion: only God distributes kingdoms and empires. God laughs to scorn and reduces to dust Charles V's pride in desiring to be "the universall and onely monarch of the world."[11]

Employing an understanding similar to the one expressed in Hakluyt's *Western Planting,* the *Declaration* rejects papal authority and the Pope's Donation giving Spain right of dominion over the Indians. It recognizes no such right and argues that the Indians have had their liberty taken away from them. Where Spain has deprived the Indians of their liberty, it has taken away from England "the Right which We have by the Law of Nature, and of Nations, of Converse and Commerce with them."[12] The *Declaration* continues:

> But as to the state of Our Quarrel in the West-Indies; Whereas We have Collonies in America, as well in Islands as upon the Continent, upon as good and a better Title then the Spaniards have any, and have as good a right to Sail in those Seas as themselves; yet without any just Cause or Provocation (and where the Question of Commerce was not at all in the Case) they have notwithstanding, continually invaded, in an Hostile maner, Our Collonies, slain Our Countreymen, taken Our Ships and Goods, destroyed Our Plantations, made Our People Prisoners and Slaves, and have continued so doing from time to time, till the very time that We undertook the late Expedition against them.[13]

England, not Spain, possesses the inherent right to be in America. This is because the Spanish claim their legitimacy to the land through coercion and bloodshed. Spain's power is built "out of the bowels of the first Inhabitants, in whose bloud they have founded their Empire."[14] Unlike the Spanish who have been extremely cruel, the English settle plantations in lands that are unpeopled and unoccupied. For this reason, England possesses "a very clear Title to their Plantations, especially to divers Islands, which the Spaniards have assaulted, and slain their Colonies in, which either never had any Inhabitants, or if destroyed by the Spaniards, were also deserted by them, and left unpeopled; so that by the Law of Nature and of Nations, they rightfully accrew to the Occupiers, and possessors thereof."[15]

The discourse of the *Declaration* validates the program of English colonizing ventures and ambitions in the New World by invoking the medieval concept of natural law, supporting the logic that uninhabited territories become the possession of the first nation to discover them. Columbus subscribes to this medieval idea of natural law by discursively constructing a *terrae nullius* in those lands inhabited by the natives. Not possessing the language and linguistic framework of the European, the American native Columbus encountered was unable to contradict the proclamation of possession he made through ceremony and ritual, a proclamation resting on the fact that no native in the New World contradicted him at that central moment of originary symbolic and literal appropriation of the Americas. The natives were unable to challenge Columbus because they were excluded from the linguistic universe and specific set of legal concepts of the European.

The context of the *Declaration* differs from Columbus's prototypical colonial appropriation because, in the case of the English-Spanish contestations for empire, interventions have already been made in new lands through the colonizing activities of the Spanish. In terms of historical chronology and the scope of empire building, the Spanish, of course, were established imperialists long before the English. When England decided to contest Spain for the possession and expansion of empire, it had to challenge the hegemony of the Spanish *imperium* either through literal confrontations on the seas and on land, or through the subversive modes of discursive representation. A large part of the rhetorical strategy employed in the *Declaration* relies upon demonizing the Spanish imperialists. Spanish cruelty has led to the reduction of a once-inhabited land into *terrae nullius,* a blank slate that must be inscribed with the benefits of English culture and civilization. A theological argument is advanced to support the reverse transformation of *terrae nullius* into a full text inscribing specific cultural identity, in this case English. Because God made the world for man's use and ordained him to replenish the same, arable land left untenanted should rightfully be appropriated for cultivation. The *Declaration*'s affirmation of its right to appropriate lands left empty as the result of a brutal Spanish imperial politics iterates a similar colonial program, but situates it in the context of an absolutist theology. In other words, the validity of the colonial enterprise for Cromwell comes from God's own divine legitimation. God puts his stamp of approval on an English cultural and political project that he withholds from the Spanish, who are authenticated by the demonic Church of Rome and the papal Antichrist.

A Declaration obtains its significance in relation to Cromwell's colonial designs that include the prosecution of the infamous Irish campaign between August 1649 and May 1650. If Milton's position as Secretary for Foreign Tongues in Cromwell's government makes him unavoidably aware of England's place in the world of seventeenth-century geopolitics, it also involves him in articulating and supporting the Lord Protector's colonial policies. At the same meeting in which Cromwell was named "the commander-in-chief of the troops for Ireland," the Council of State appointed Milton "foreign secretary." A fortnight after this event, Parliament authorized Milton to write the *Observations Upon the Articles of Peace* as a pamphlet.[16] The colonial conception of *Observations* could very well have come from an opportunistic author working with gusto to fulfill the demands of his office. But the specificity of this particular experience does not negate the larger reality of Milton's general perceptions on the subject of the Irish question. Associated in his mind with Romish practices and destructive rebels, Ireland deserves its place as a subject colony. This means that any program proposed to suppress the inhabitants effectively obtains his complete support. Despite its brevity when compared to *A View of the Present State of Ireland,* Spenser's very important colonial intertext, and in spite of the absence of a coherent and detailed program of strategic interventions, Milton's *Observations* feeds directly into Cromwell's brutal Irish campaign by being situated at a particular historical circumstance. The *Observations,* Thomas Corns tells us, "works as a preemptive justification for that Cromwellian ruthlessness manifest in the storming of Drogheda, where the garrison of 2,600 were given no quarter, and of Wexford, where, in almost indiscriminate slaughter, about 2,000 people were killed by the victors. By 1653, the last resistance had been overwhelmed and the conditions prepared for the wholesale confiscation of the property of Irish landowners and its transfer to London financiers and parliament's supporters in arms."[17] All that Cromwell needed was a statement, which Milton's pamphlet conveniently provided, on the state of Ireland that necessitated military intervention; incidentally, when Cromwell appealed to the *Observations* as a symbolic (pre)text for ratifying his plans for the brutal suppression of the Irish, he also made the appreciative gesture of restoring some lands in Ireland to Spenser's grandson. The symbolization of gratitude played out in this act of restoration not only shows Cromwell giving due recognition, which Elizabeth I did not, to Spenser as the great apologist for empire, it also reveals the complicity of poets and literary artifacts in ratifying the politics of colonialism.

Milton's *Observations* elaborates at length on the threat posed by Irish Catholicism and its perversion of true Christianity to the security and freedom of Protestant England. If we compare Milton's *Observations* with Spenser's *View*, we find that although both poets share a common colonialist view on the subject of Ireland, their emphases on the problems with the Irish differ subtly. Spenser is very much concerned with the absence of any coherent social structure in Ireland, a state of affairs that demands English colonial intervention. Such intervention is necessary to contain the rebellious energies of the barbaric Irish and prevent these from getting out of control. For him, the effective subjugation of the rebellious Irish is requisite to the consolidation of monarchical authority. Spenser also significantly downplays the theological motifs in *A View*, a point I have discussed in chapter 4 of this book. Milton, by contrast, is strident in his attacks on the Romish faith in his treatment of Ireland. He is able to describe a "blasphemous . . . Popery, plung'd into Idolatrous and Ceremoniall Superstition, the very death of all true Religion; figur'd to us by the Scripture it selfe in the shape of that Beast, *full of the names of Blasphemy*" (*Yale* 3.316). Elsewhere in *Observations,* Milton writes: "All men who are true Protestants, . . . know not a more immediate and killing Subverter of all true Religion then Antichrist, whom they generally believe to be the Pope and Church of *Rome,* he therefore who makes peace with this grand Enemy and persecutor of the true Church, he who joynes with him, strengthens him, gives him root to grow up and spread his poyson, removing all opposition against him" (*Yale* 3.309). The narratives that Milton creates of Ireland in the prose works are consistently shaped by his emphasis on the anti-Christian papal practices rife in the land.

For Milton, an unambiguous display of the dire threat posed by Irish Catholicism is the brutal massacre of Protestant English and Scots at the outbreak of the infamous Irish rebellion on 23 October 1641 in Ulster. In the early *Reason of Church Government,* for example, Milton sets up an analogy between the harm wrought by this massacre on the physical bodies of the English and the carelessness with which the prelates of the church look after the souls of believers. What is transparent in the physical assaults made on the English and Scots is the dark condition of Romish forces working to overwhelm and destroy the English church. Because Ireland is the home and haven of these dark spiritual forces, it must be contained and reduced to a state of complete subjection to the English. Furthermore, Charles I himself, Milton elaborates, had seriously threatened the security of Protestant England by entering into political negotiations with the Irish. In chapter 12 of *Eikonoklastes*, Milton specifically accuses the Stuart monarch of encouraging the continuing Irish rebellion against England that had begun with the massacre of 1641. In *Observations*, Milton writes that "no true borne *English-man*" (*Yale* 3.301) can read the Articles of Peace "without indignation and disdaine" (*Yale* 3.301) because they were "made with those inhumane Rebels and Papists of *Ireland* by the late King, as one of his last Masterpieces" (*Yale* 3.301). Milton reminds his reader that these same rebels and papists were responsible for "the mercilesse and barbarous Massacre of so many thousand *English*" (*Yale* 3.301). This historical example of the brutality that the Catholic Irish are capable of perpetrating, not to mention their involvement in the politics of Charles's tyrannical and treacherous reign, deprives Ireland of ever hoping to gain "full liberty" (*Yale* 3.301) for itself.

Milton's *Observations* constitutes a response to the Earl of Ormond's *Articles of Peace,* produced thirteen days before Charles I's execution, negotiating for greater freedom for Ireland from English control. For Milton, Ormond's proclamation of peace involves nothing less than seeking virtual independence for the Irish: an impossible situation. Ormond had sought such rights as allowing the Irish to sit and vote in Parliament (Item 5), allowing them to take and receive degrees (Item 8), and giving Catholics access to ministerial offices (Item 9). Milton's response to Ormond indicates there is no space for dialogue between the colonial master and a conquered people, which is the relationship he perceives to exist between England and Ireland. He refers to Ireland in this text as England's "Feudary Kingdome" (*Yale* 3.307); the Irish are a conquered people, and can, therefore, never presume to ask for those liberties that belong by inherent right to their conquerors. The Irish, Milton elaborates, were first transformed into vassals because of their own shortcomings and propensity for treachery and disruption of social order: Irish practice of piracy and raids on coastal Britain had early on necessitated their suppression. Milton remembers distinctly the consequent severe restrictions imposed on Ireland by Sir Edward Poynings, the deputy sent by King Henry VIII to govern his unstable fiefdom directly. In the Parliament summoned at Kildare on 1 December 1494, Poynings passed a number of remarkably harsh laws: chief Irish castles were put into English hands; the Irish were forbidden to carry arms and to wage private wars; they were also forbidden from marrying English colonists. Poynings also enacted a law that completely reduced the power of the Irish Parliament: in the future, it could not pass any law without the express permission of the king of England and validation of the Privy Council.[18]

In order to emphasize the intrinsic difference between the conqueror and a conquered people, Milton even appropriates the motif of racial superiority to describe England's relations with Ireland. He figures the Irish as surging with all the destructive energies of barbarism, treachery, and hostility. The Irish demonstrate

> a disposition not onely sottish but indocible and averse from all Civility and amendment, and what hopes they give for the future, who rejecting the ingenuity of all other Nations to improve and waxe more civill by a civilizing Conquest, though all these many yeares better shown and taught, preferre their own absurd and savage Customes before the most convincing evidence of reason and demonstration: a testimony of their true Barbarisme and obdurate wilfulnesse to be expected no lesse in other matters of greatest moment. (*Yale* 3.304)

Ireland's identity as the uncivilized and apostate Other gives to Milton a convenient metaphor that can be used to undermine rhetorically the positions of adversaries like the Earl of Ormond and the Presbytery at Belfast. Suspicions and fears of Roman Catholicism and of Irish hatred of the English generate powerful emotions that can always be harnessed to compromise and subvert oppositional politics. That is why even though Ormond and the Ulster Presbyterians have their own political interests and programs, they are identified in Milton's polemic as papal sympathizers. Indeed, throughout the *Observations*, Milton reiterates the point that both Ormond and the Ulster Presbyterians belong to the Romish party. By linking the Ulster Presbyterians to "the Pontificall See of *Belfast*" (*Yale* 3.333), Milton seeks to annihilate the specificity of the Presbyterian political agenda, one not in accord with his own politics and ideology. The Presbyterians, for example, criticize the proliferation of sects fracturing the English religious establishment as well as the execution of Charles I. In *Observations*, Milton evokes the specter of a larger and darker conspiratorial agenda threatening England's social stability and its national interests.

Familiar with Cromwell's West Indian campaign and his Irish policy, Milton is an apologist for the Commonwealth and also an unabashed advocate of English colonialism. He makes it very clear in *Observations* that Ireland is a "Feudary Kingdome" that must never be given any degree of political freedom, and that rightly instead should be made completely subject to English jurisdiction and colonial control. All the arguments and reasons—theological, social, and political—are mustered to support Milton's conviction that Ireland should be locked into a state of perpetual subjection.

When Milton gives his endorsement to Cromwell's ambition to effect the decisive conquest of Ireland, he implicitly and explicitly affirms his faith in the mandate possessed by the Commonwealth to extend England's cultural and political boundaries. The right to colonize cannot be separated from a nation's and people's possession of a viable culture and political system. To the republican Milton, the Commonwealth is such a system, sanctioned by God himself. And this God who had reduced England's monarchy to the dust is also the same deity who commands the demolition of idols and destruction of the enemies of Truth. As Milton makes abundantly clear in *Observations,* Ireland's adherence to the Romish faith is one important reason why it should be colonized. But where Milton registers clearly what Willy Maley refers to as his "colonial disposition" in the production of a text like *Observations,* he no longer does the same in the major poems like *Paradise Lost* and *Paradise Regained,* texts forced to come to terms with the bitter experience of political defeat.[19]

Ocean Travel and the Deconstruction of an Epic Motif

Very early on in book 1 of *Paradise Lost,* Milton's Satan introduces the subject of a newly created world that he has heard about:

> Space may produce new Worlds; whereof so rife
> There went a fame in Heav'n that he ere long
> Intended to create, and therein plant
> A generation, whom his choice regard
> Should favor equal to the Sons of Heaven:
> Thither, if but to pry, shall be perhaps
> Our first eruption, thither or elsewhere:
> For this Infernal Pit shall never hold
> Celestial Spirits in Bondage, nor th' Abyss
> Long under darkness cover.

> (*PL* 1.650–59)

This topic will be resurrected by Beelzebub in book 2 within the context of a demonic council convened for the primary purpose of getting back at God for his arbitrariness and tyranny, and for driving them into hell. Interestingly and significantly, the "ancient and prophetic fame" (*PL* 2.346) concerning this other world refers to rumors circulating about the existence of new lands. Such rumors form an intrinsic feature of colonialist discourse. Many colonial ventures were undertaken to ratify the validity of rumors circulating about land and treasures. Accounts of the boundless wealth of the Americas that fired Renaissance England's imagination and fueled her colonial appetite can be traced back to Columbus's day, when stories about the new world were told long before its existence could be confirmed. The reader is then introduced to the discourse of colonialism from the very start of the epic because Satan wants to avenge the wrong done to him by God by undertaking a project of colonization: bringing the new world under the dominion of hell and enlarging hell's boundaries to assimilate its bounties. Characteristically also, colonial ventures were involved in fighting rival powers for control and possession of territory. In the council in hell, Moloch is the demon who speaks about the need to wage "open war" (*PL* 2.51) against God, also described elsewhere in the epic as "the sovran Planter." If the demons agree to endorse Moloch's argument, they will effectively go to war against a plantation owner and master colonist. And when Mammon talks about tapping the resources of hell, an allusion is made to those explorers who expected to find readily available treasures when they arrived at the legendary Indian cities they had heard so much about.

The colonial themes inscribed in Milton's portrayal of Satan's plans to destroy the garden of Eden are not limited to the debates of the demonic council. Milton reinforces them throughout *Paradise Lost*. In book 3, for example, he portrays Satan as embarking on an arduous reconnaissance mission, succeeding finally in obtaining a good view of the land that is the end of his quest:

> *Satan* from hence now on the lower stair
> That scal'd by steps of Gold to Heaven Gate
> Looks down with wonder at the sudden view
> Of all this World at once. As when a Scout
> Through dark and desert ways with peril gone
> All night; at last by break of cheerful dawn
> Obtains the brow of some high-climbing Hill,
> Which to his eye discovers unaware

> The goodly prospect of some foreign land
> First seen, or some renown'd Metropolis
> With glistering Spires and Pinnacles adorn'd,
> Which now the Rising Sun gilds with his beams.
>
> (*PL* 3.540–51)

A passage like this evokes the experience of wonder described in different literatures of travel. Wonder, the experience of witnessing new, exotic, fascinating, and marvelous things and spectacles can be a spontaneous and sincere response, just as it can also function as a strategic reaction, carefully fashioned to legitimate and enact the politics of empire. Aware of the discourse of travel, Milton alludes to the literatures of discovery in his portrayal of the wonder with which Satan responds to the view of Paradise.

This passage also echoes the biblical account of Israel's survey of the promised land it was preparing to take over. We remember that chapter 13 of the book of Numbers in the Old Testament begins with God commanding Moses to send men to search the land of Canaan, which he had promised to Israel. The mission of the spies is to evaluate the strength of the people who inhabit the land. Where Numbers 13 concludes with Israel rejecting the opportunity to enjoy the bounty of the land of promise—the large cluster of grapes from Eshcol signifying the terrible might of the inhabitants rather than the joy of plenitude—Milton's Satan immediately recognizes the riches to be offered by the new land he stumbles upon. The discourse of spying is central to the Old Testament accounts of the preparations made for the conquest of the promised land. At the beginning of the book of Joshua, for example, one of the first acts performed by Moses' successor even as he prepares to assault the promised land is to send two men to spy on the land. In Numbers and Joshua, reconnaissance is a necessary prelude to the conquest of a foreign land. We have said that in *Paradise Lost*, Satan engages in a reconnaissance activity inseparably intertwined with the voyeuristic motif. Where the early books of the Old Testament present the conquest of Canaan as Israel's birthright, *Paradise Lost* depicts Satan's conquest of Eden as an act of unlawful usurpation. If Milton portrays Satan as a demonic parody of Moses promising to lead the children of Israel into the promised land, he also depicts Satan's covert activities in Eden by alluding to the activities of Israel under Joshua's leadership, surveying the land it is in the process of conquering. In relation to his identity as a spy specifically scripted for him by Milton, Satan's act of intruding into Eden then expresses itself in parodic terms; in a parody of Joshua, Satan sets the ground for the eventual taking over of the land he promised his followers.

In *Paradise Lost,* Satan, the archetypal evil colonist and antagonist against the authority of heaven, embarks on an epic journey. He makes his way across Chaos to destroy God's newly created Eden in a narrative that recalls the journeyings of such celebrated characters as Odysseus, Aeneas, Jason, and Da Gama. His journey is also linked specifically to the designs and practices of European colonialism and imperialism.

Writing within a tradition in which the epic poet asserts that his poetic endeavor addresses a subject far greater than any antecedent epic, Milton implicitly makes Satan occupy a theological narrative infinitely greater in scope than the narratives of the *Odyssey, Aeneid, Argonautica,* and *Os Lusíadas.* But Satan's epic journey across Chaos must situate itself in relation to contestational notions of epic heroism. In so doing, his flight to Eden becomes the demonic parody of the narratives of Odysseus's successful homecoming to Ithaca and Aeneas's laying the foundation for building the New Troy. Odysseus's and Aeneas's heroic accomplishments are greater than the sum of Satan's deconstructive and nihilistic energies precisely because the archetypal antagonist of all good obtains his identity only in the narrative domain of parody. Instead of reestablishing social order with a homecoming like Odysseus, Satan returns to hell to be greeted by the hisses of his followers metamorphosed into snakes; and instead of founding an empire like Aeneas, he destroys the garden of Eden. The author of Eden's destruction is, as Maureen Quilligan qualifies, not only a colonist but also a slave master: Satan wants to own not only Adam and Eve, but the population that will derive from them as well.[20] Situated also in a narrative that is a parody of the epic exodus of Israel, Satan is figured as a demonic Moses who fails to lead his followers into the promised land.

When the heroic narratives of the antecedent epics of the classical tradition are evoked, however, to contextualize Satan's own epic undertaking, they become themselves contaminated by association with the demonic: in other words, the traditional epic metaphor of the journey across water is no longer unambiguously heroic. By making Satan go on a journey across Chaos, Milton recasts the voyagings of discovery in a demonic light, interrogating familiar epic structures that celebrate the foundation of empire and definition of individual and social identity. Using the central epic metaphor of the journey to compromise and destabilize its own literary and symbolic meanings, Milton calls into question the colonial ambitions of an England that does not have the ability to shape its own destiny. The significance of Milton's demonization of colonialism in *Paradise Lost* is linked to his general critique of England's colonial ambitions after the failure of the Puritan experiment and the collapse of the Commonwealth. A nation that has lost its cultural mandate should not presume to extend its political influence to other peoples and other lands. Milton's epic poem then renders its critique in a text that still grounds its prophetic vision in the structures of a theological imperialism. But while the rhetoric of "us" against "them," central to the discourse of theological imperialism, continues to be forcefully expressed in *Paradise Lost*, it is now registered with an emphasis different from the rhetoric of Milton's earlier anti-episcopal tracts and regicide pamphlets. This rhetoric now belongs to the remnant prophet, whose views are no longer shared by the rest of society.

To elaborate on the relationship between the existence of an anticolonial narrative and the discourse of theological imperialism in *Paradise Lost*, I wish at this point to consider in some detail Milton's particular representation of Satan's flight out of hell and its symbolic relation to the central metaphor of the epic journey in general. The journeyings of Odysseus and Aeneas are significant to this representation, but so is Da Gama's voyage to India celebrated by Camões in his *Os Lusíadas*. *Paradise Lost* specifically describes Satan's flight to the gates of hell by evoking Da Gama's voyage depicted in the *Lusíadas*:

> Meanwhile the Adversary of God and Man,
> *Satan* with thoughts inflam'd of highest design,
> Puts on swift wings, and towards the Gates of Hell
> Explores his solitary flight; sometimes
> He scours the right hand coast, sometimes the left,
> Now shaves with level wing the Deep, then soars
> Up to the fiery concave tow'ring high.
> As when far off at Sea a Fleet descri'd
> Hangs in the Clouds, by *Equinoctial* Winds
> Close sailing from *Bengala*, or the Isles
> Of *Ternate* and *Tidore*, whence Merchants bring
> Thir spicy Drugs: they on the Trading Flood
> Through the wide *Ethiopian* to the Cape
> Ply stemming nightly toward the Pole.
>
> (*PL* 2.629–42)

In book 4, lines 159–65, Satan, skirting the garden of Eden, is described once again with reference to a simile that points to the Indian Ocean world that constitutes the locus of Camões's epic poem:

> As when to them who sail
> Beyond the *Cape of Hope,* and now are past
> *Mozambic,* off at Sea North-East winds blow
> *Sabean* Odors from the spicy shore
> Of *Araby* the blest, with such delay
> Well pleas'd they slack thir course, and many a League
> Cheer'd with the grateful smell old Ocean smiles.

In the *Lusíadas,* Da Gama stops at the court of the king of Malindi asking for directions to India; in *Paradise Lost,* Satan, in a gesture that recalls not only Da Gama's search but also Herod's desire to know where to find the newborn king of the Jews, asks Uriel the way to God's newly created world. The reference Milton makes to the Cape of Good Hope in book 2, line 641, also points to the account given by Camões of the terrible dangers promised by Adamastor to the Portuguese sailors who must travel round the Cape. Personifying the Cape of Storms in the metamorphosed figure of Adamastor, Camões emphasizes the great difficulties encountered by the Portuguese in undertaking their voyages of discovery. Only by experiencing dire hazards and excruciating toils can a hardy people who love fame achieve immortal honor and esteem. The quest for fame central to the imperial conception of the *Lusíadas* also forms part of the overreaching ambition of Milton's Satan.[21] In the case of the Satan of *Paradise Lost,* the approval of one's followers is much sought after. Like Da Gama, Beelzebub speaks about the tremendous difficulties involved in negotiating the treacherous tumult of Chaos to arrive at the garden of Paradise. Milton's invocation of the Camões subtext reinforces the difficulties Satan encounters crossing the murky realm of Chaos.

Milton's allusion to the *Lusíadas* also invokes the world of mercantile commerce inseparable from the vision of Portuguese imperialism celebrated by Camões.[22] Cantos 7 and 8 of the *Lusíadas* provide a useful context for reading Milton's representation of Satan as a merchant adventurer. These two cantos give an interesting expression of the imperial vision of the *Lusíadas.* Da Gama arrives in India, described specifically as the land of wealth. Indian wealth is measured not only in terms of its possession of spices, but also by the ostentatious display of gold and precious stones in the courts. Calicut, the last city Da Gama visits in India, is famous and wealthy because of its trade. Camões is obviously fascinated by the wealth of India that comes from its trade: "As for the country, it is bursting with merchandise of every kind, thanks to its maritime traffic with other lands from China to the Nile."[23] His Da Gama is especially interested in negotiating trade between Portugal and India—that is the thematic focus of Da Gama's relationship with the Samorin of Calicut. In fact, the mercantile motif is reinforced by the Samorin's thoughts of the gain that can be obtained by concluding an alliance with the Portuguese; the treacherous Catual sets Da Gama free after the merchandise brought by the Portuguese has been bartered and sold.

Even though the *Lusíadas* recognizes the importance of trading ventures and merchandising activities in the expansion and consolidation of empire, it nonetheless registers anxieties about fitting the celebration of wealth through trade into the religious matrix of the poem. Throughout Camões's epic poem, the greatness of the Portuguese empire is linked to a Catholic vision of God's providential control and blessing. The Portuguese are renowned for holding the fort of true religion against the pagans and infidels. God is always there to protect Da Gama from the schemes and practices of treacherous Moslems, whether at Mozambique or in Calicut. The fame of the Portuguese comes from their determination "not to be beaten by the toils and perils that attend great enterprises," such as launching "voyages of discovery across the restless ocean in the resolve to ascertain its farthest boundaries and the whereabouts of the most distant shores it lapped."[24] Their martial prowess and valor in war are linked to their defense of the Catholic faith. Canto 7 begins with an indictment of Germany, England, France, and Italy for fracturing the solidarity and coherence of Christendom. Yet the voyages of discovery undertaken by the Portuguese to open up new channels of trade to India and the East also assume an ambiguous status for Camões, whose understanding of faith brings him to question the motive forces energizing the quest for wealth. That is why at the end of canto 8 of the *Lusíadas*, the Catual, associated with Moslem treachery, gets transfixed as an allegorical figure representing depraved self-interest linked to the fatal appetite for gold. Even the celebration of fame that marks the particular epic identity of the *Lusíadas* evokes anxieties in Camões. Just as Da Gama's crew is about to leave the harbor of Lisbon and embark on its voyage of discovery, a venerable old man speaks out passionately against the acquisition of fame and glory, linking it to overreaching ambition, Satan's primal sin.

It is possible to read in Milton's allusion to Da Gama's journey when describing Satan's flight a critique of the motifs celebrated in the *Lusíadas*—fame, ambition, and military might. (Jesus significantly rejects all of these in *Paradise Regained*.) More to the point, however, Milton's portrayal of Satan's journey out of hell with reference to the experience of Da Gama's voyaging celebrated by Camões casts the Portuguese voyage of discovery in a demonic light in order to interrogate the Catholicism that shapes and informs Camões's epic vision. In the *Lusíadas*, religion is central to the expansion of empire because the latter is linked to the workings of divine providence. Here Camões's epic is closely related to Tasso's *Gerusalemme liberata,* a work that celebrates the Renaissance Age of Discovery. Like Tasso's *Liberata,* which places Columbus's discovery of the New World within the context of God's grand providential design, the *Lusíadas* relates the prophecy concerning the grand expanse of the Portuguese empire to the sanction and workings of a similar design. Milton's antagonism toward Roman Catholicism means he would have immediate difficulties relating to the structures of authority celebrated in the *Lusíadas*.

On the symbolic level, Milton's use of sailing imagery, with its allusions to such texts as the *Odyssey,* the *Aeneid,* and the *Argonautica,* depicts Satan as the demonic epic archetype, but it also signals the end of the Golden Age of Eden. In classical mythology, the loss of the golden age necessitates the building of the first boat, Jason's Argo, launched in search of the golden fleece. Satan's voyage across the ocean of Chaos then registers his ontological status as a fallen being. According to David Quint, this status is registered in Satan's figuration as a ship sailing through the seas of Fortune; Satan is depicted as a boat of romance in *Paradise Lost.* The voyages of discovery to which Satan's figuration as a ship alludes accomplish only temporal needs and ends, and as such are locked into the circles and errancies of the romance narrative.[25]

When Milton makes an associative link between Satan's voyaging and Da Gama's ocean travel, he shows himself still accepting the norms of a literary tradition that ties epic grandeur and heroism to the exploits of an aristocratic class. In epics that celebrate the glories of this class, the merchant is marginalized, defined by his trade, which does not enjoy a positive reputation in society. Even though *Paradise Lost* is not an epic of the aristocratic or ruling class, its treatment of the merchant reveals a perception not very different from one usually found in such an epic. The point is worth further elaboration because this particular representation of Milton's response situates itself against the important practice of merchandising activities in the economic life of England in the seventeenth century. Among the different contemporary social currents and practices that exert their pressures on the creation of the epic poem, one that I wish to highlight for the purposes of this discussion is the location of epic heroism in the domestic economy exemplified in the family life set up by Adam and Eve. As husband and wife, Adam and Eve entertain guests like Raphael, and share a deep concern for the welfare of their children yet to be born. Milton's portrayal of Adam and Eve, one that can be usefully read in relation to the social phenomenon of the emerging nuclear family in Renaissance England, focuses on the domestic space of the family. The spiritual dimensions of the text—centered on the cosmic conflict between the forces of good and evil—are depicted in relation to the ramifications of temptation and disobedience experienced by the first family. My point is that *Paradise Lost*'s location of the heroic in family and domestic life—a feature that shows the text's embeddedness in a specific cultural moment—curiously fails to assimilate the new "heroism" of the merchandising class to its epic vision. This is striking because of the contribution made by the trading activities of Stuart England and the Interregnum toward forging England's identity as an emerging viable political entity.

When Milton began writing *Paradise Lost* in earnest and intensity sometime in 1658, the situation of English merchandising activities was markedly different from that under James and Charles Stuart. Under the Stuarts, England was just beginning to enter into trade in the oceans with some degree of enthusiasm. Christopher Hill tells us that in the 1640s, much effort was generated to transform London into an entrepôt for the re-export of colonial produce; the passing of the Navigation Acts of 1650 and 1651 showed an England challenging the Dutch in fighting for the world's trade. Over two hundred ships added to the British navy between 1651 and 1660 built a substantial fleet employed deliberately to obtain commercial advantages.[26] The national importance of commerce was recognized when the navy began to provide regular convoys, from 1649. Milton's association of merchandising activities with the Satanic flight refers to a world very different from the one responded to by earlier dramatists of the period. With many of these earlier writers, the ambivalence marking their response to overseas mercantile activities comes from having to react to new ways of doing things and to entry into a larger world existing beyond the boundaries of England. Milton's immediate referential frame is different. The advantages of a robust overseas trading activity are obvious. If Milton's particular representation of Satan's journeying to Paradise as a merchandising activity provides a commentary on England's trading ventures, it is not one shaped nor influenced by any misgiving about the positive gains to be obtained by such ventures. Rather this negative rendering of merchandising activities is linked to Milton's disillusionment with the Protectorate and the later experience of defeat that will color his representation of any event or narrative tied to the expansion of empire. The demonization of colonialism is, I want to suggest, a direct expression of Milton's disillusionment with England's inability to remain in the freedom bestowed by a republic. What Satan does in journeying across Chaos derives its political meanings from the historical situation to which Milton is reacting.

Of immediate relevance is the portrayal of Satan that draws self-conscious attention to Charles Stuart, the contemporary antitype of Pharaoh and numerous other Old Testament types of the evil king. But Satan does not only exist in a republican narrative, designed to undermine the central figure of charisma in royalist ideology. Even as the figuration of Milton's Satan points to the kingship of Charles I in its allusions and symbolisms, it also touches the politics and social practices of those republican heroes who created the English Commonwealth, but who also contributed to its demise. As the prototype of all demagogues, Satan also bears a resemblance to Cromwell, his fellow radical and revolutionary parliamentary dictator. Christopher Hill reminds us that Satan is not a flat allegorical character that can be equated systematically with Royalists or Ranters or major-generals; Milton saw the Satanic in all three, and we must respond to the portrayal of Satan by recognizing the ambiguity intrinsic to its wide range of allusions.[27] In Milton's figuration of Satan, then, representation, the narrativizing of ideologies and political stances subjected to scrutiny and critique, is made radically complex by the range of allusive possibilities constituting the referential field. If Satan's portrayal draws attention to the evils and shortcomings of both royalist and republican ideologies, it encodes the devastating trauma sustained by Milton, who found himself compelled to justify God's ways to humankind in the face of an unfolding history that makes little or no sense.[28]

Milton's sense that England had lost its cultural mandate when it decided to embrace the return of the monarchy in 1660 can be seen in his changing understanding of England as a nation over the years. In the early 1640s, the years of the antiprelatical tracts, Milton saw himself as one prophet in a nation of prophets. This nation of prophets would bring about the consummation of Reformation in England, and then proselytize Europe and the rest of the world.[29] His prose works, like *Of Reformation* and *The Reason of Church Government*, reveal the young and eager polemicist's confidence that as a people who shared one understanding of God's ordained system of church government, all Englishmen would act in concert to remove prelates from the church. This confidence was predicated on the understanding that God's Word communicated itself to all true believers plainly and unerringly.[30] Milton's early confidence was, however, shaken when his painful experience of an incompatible marriage led to the writing of the divorce tracts, a writing that compelled a strained recontextualizing of Christ's injunction against divorce by appealing to the spirit rather than the express letter of the scriptural text. The uneasy realization that the Word might not be the repository of the plain Truth, that Scripture needs hermeneutical mediation and by implication individual interpretation, now made itself felt in the *Areopagitica*, where Truth loses the immediacy of presence to the unfolding of process. Only at Christ's Second Coming can dismembered Truth be viewed and experienced in its totality. But despite the emerging recognition in *Areopagitica* that Truth is not always readily available to the believer, Milton nevertheless still conceived of England as a nation that possessed the ability to exercise a concerted will to advance the cause of Truth—the figure of England as Samson awakening after sleep and reviving in power attests to this hope and optimism. Samson, the figure of the fallen judge whom Milton evoked in *The Reason of Church Government* to allegorize King Charles's danger of being shorn of his royal authority by the prelates, is in *Areopagitica* transformed into an allegory of the might of England as a nation.

About one and a half decades will intervene between the publication of *Areopagitica* (1644) and the stridently desperate *Readie and Easie Way* of 1660. By the time *The Readie and Easie Way* was published, Milton could only see himself as belonging to a prophetic remnant. *Paradise Lost* resonates with the loneliness of the prophet crying out in the wilderness that is contemporary English society. The poet-prophet in this epic aligns himself with the faithful remnant of the Old Testament; in *Paradise Regained*, divorce from political activism is rationalized with reference to the vision of obtaining a future spiritual kingdom; and in *Samson Agonistes*, Israel is accused of not fully comprehending the divinely ordained role of the judge whom God had chosen to be his oppressed people's deliverer.

Despite the presence of a distinct quietist undercurrent in both *Paradise Lost* and *Paradise Regained,* readers of these two texts recognize in general that Milton was still very much propagating political activism even in those painful moments of defeat; the iconoclastic temper of *Samson Agonistes* is often evoked to substantiate this point. One feature that has not been elaborated upon is how, in Milton's poems, there appears to be a distance separating the construction of prophetic subjectivity from its logical mooring in a nationalist identity. Because contemporary society has moved in a direction away from the right path propagated by the prophet who is society's rightful spokesman, the gap between prophet and society appears wider than ever. The prophet in possession (or thinking he is in possession) of God's Truth defends it by embracing a powerful sense of alienation. It is true that an interesting rhetorical feature occurs in *Paradise Regained* and *Samson Agonistes.* In these companion poems, the enemy is identified as the colonizing or pagan Other: the Romans in *Paradise Regained* and the Philistines in *Samson Agonistes.* Whenever a poetic or dramatic text defines the enemy in terms of a tribe or people who threaten the security of one's countrymen or homeland, it deals with the fundamental impulse to stand up as a nation in order to overthrow and rout the intruder.

What we recognize almost immediately in Milton's major poems, however, is that when a distinction is made between Israel and its enemies, any suggestion that nationalistic sentiments are somehow expressed is destabilized and complicated. For Milton can no longer hold on to any sustained understanding of an England that exists as a unified and cohesive national body. That, of course, is not true of his early writings. Lawrence Lipking rightly observes that the young Milton who wrote *Lycidas* worked with strong nationalistic sentiments: Lycidas is the genius of the shore whose one function is to stand guard over Ireland; the late Edward King functions in the elegy as a guardian spirit in a cartographic discourse in which the positioning of names on a map "kindles thoughts of ownership, of empire, of routes of trade and invasion."[31] Also found in other early writings like the antiprelatical tracts is the rhetorical maneuver of identifying the prelates as the enemies of a nationalistic England; the argument against prelacy is specifically built on an appeal to a people's consensual identification of an external threat to the well-being of the nation. Milton's use of the Samson-Dalila analogy as cautionary tale for the threat presented by the prelates in *The Reason of Church Government* obtains, for example, much of its rhetorical power from the hermeneutical response to Dalila as an interloper from a foreign tribe. In *Samson Agonistes* Milton plays up the motif of Samson's betrayal of his own people when he succumbs to his libido by yearning after the women of foreign tribes. It is clear that in the parabolic significations of *Samson Agonistes,* a great divorce must be enacted between God's heroic champion and the enemies of Truth. Likewise, the Roman conquerors in *Paradise Regained* do not function so much as an allegory of enemies existing outside of the geographical and political entity of England as they stand for the forces arrayed against Truth operating within England itself: archbishop Laud's "idolatrous" practices and the apostasy of the Anglican establishment, Charles I and the monarchy, anything offensive to and opposed by God.

Milton's criticism of the failure of the Puritan experiment was not levelled primarily against the common and ignorant masses who led England back to the tyranny of Egyptian bondage by restoring the monarchy; it was aimed also at the Parliamentarians and military leaders who made the demolition of the institution of monarchy possible in the first place. It had become obvious to Milton, long before 1660, that God's kingdom would not be established in England so quickly. Christopher Hill tells us that Milton's hopes of preserving the English Commonwealth were offset by such factors as the disunity of the radicals, the ambitions of the generals, the "self-interested a-politicism" of most middleclass Englishmen, the failure of revolutionaries to allow for the resilience and adaptability of the English gentry, and the error of depending too much on the leadership of individuals who turned out to be avaricious, ambitious, or hypocrites. Ultimately, then, the political failure that led to the Restoration was viewed by Milton as a moral failure, hence the trenchant critique of ambition, passion, appetite, self-serving interests, hypocrisy, and willful blindness in *Paradise Lost.*[32]

Linking political failure to moral failure, *Paradise Lost* traces the collapse of the Commonwealth to the English people themselves: their degenerate condition and sinful state. If the blame for failure lies with the English people, then it is necessary to identify sin and participate in the discipline that can bring about regeneration. God will teach a regenerate people how to resolve political problems. These themes are expressed in an epic narrative also embedded with anxieties. For Michael's internal Paradise, removed from the external world of politics and historical contingency, is also a defensive space set up to offset the encroachments of incomprehensible earthly events. At the same time that *Paradise*

Lost and *Paradise Regained* advocate the importance of cultivating and nourishing the internal Paradise and inner man to obtain needed regeneration for the individual, they also express the belief that God's kingdom is not going to be inaugurated in England any time soon. Millenarianism has been replaced by a futuristic vision of history, a motif cogently expressed in Jesus' assertion that his spiritual kingdom is not of this world and will not be established in time.[33] The emphasis on the establishment of an otherworldly kingdom also appears to shape Milton's association of the colonial enterprise with the demonic. If colonialism and imperialism are expressions of national ambition, and if all human political aspirations are doomed to failure, then there is really no place for any venture that glorifies individual achievement and national pride.

It would be useful at this point to invoke the distinctions David Quint makes between two forms of epic—the epic of the victors and the epic of the defeated—to elaborate on our discussion of Milton's reactions to the experience of defeat. According to Quint, the example par excellence of the classical epic of the imperial victors is Virgil's *Aeneid,* and the text exemplifying the epic of the defeated is Lucan's *Pharsalia.* The relationship between these agonistic traditions is a complex one. For even as Lucan writes the *Pharsalia* to attack both the ideology of the one-man rule of the emperor and of Virgil's *Aeneid,* he can do so only on Virgil's terms: no degree of parody can break the epic continuity running through Virgil's and Lucan's texts. But while Lucan seems able to conduct his agon only within the strictures defined by the powerful Virgilian text, the very generation of opposition to Virgil's encomiastic celebration of imperial ideology produces and consolidates an alternative republican or antimonarchical discourse.[34] How does *Paradise Lost* fit into Quint's useful definitions when the Miltonic epic encodes the frustrations of a defeated republican in a generic form associated with victors and the glories of empire? I will respond to this question by first identifying *Paradise Lost* as a poem of defeat that struggles to be made right through the reshaping and compensatory gestures of establishing a teleological narrative that strives after closure and meaning. Yet when we look carefully at how *Paradise Lost* ends, we find that any closure that the narrative attempts to achieve is problematized by the expulsion of Adam and Eve into the postlapsarian world, which is also the condition of exile. It is the immediacy of this fallen world that presses itself most urgently upon our attention; the Apocalypse, anticipated by the preexistent Son in book 3,

continues to remain in the narrative domain of prolepsis even
after book 12 has been reached. The world of the fall, human
choice in conducting affairs both individual and social, the consequences of actions that violate divine injunctions—all these are
tied to Milton's anxious efforts to come to terms with and apprehend God's mysterious ways in ordering the affairs of history.
Milton finally decides it is not God who is responsible for the
collapse of the English Commonwealth, but men and women
themselves who, because trapped in the fallen world of sin, have
exercised a perverse choice in subjecting themselves to the tyranny of monarchical authority. As Milton sees it, human agency,
governed by a perverted will and fallen reason, is also responsible
for bringing about the lapse of the Commonwealth itself from
parliament to dictatorship. The devils in the demonic council are,
significantly, not the victims of a Restoration, but of a usurpation
by their own Lord Protector.

By generalizing colonial undertakings as negative and demonic,
Milton not only identifies greed, ambition, and pride as aspects
of human sinfulness contributing to the collapse of the English
Commonwealth, he also critiques an entire nation's loss of cultural
identity. The expansion of empire can come about only when a
nation possesses cultural vibrancy, something Spenser recognizes
when linking absolutist ideology to the colonizing mandate. When
Milton argued in favor of regicide, he did so by figuring himself
as an authoritative prophetic voice for all of Europe. He delighted,
for example, in challenging Europe's spokesmen for monarchy,
like Salmasius. England will set a political model for Europe to
emulate in deposing and executing a king who is a tyrant. After
the restoration of the monarch, however, England can no longer
claim for itself the privileged position of enlightening the rest of
the European world. The failure of the Puritan revolution also
involves the loss of a nation's cultural and moral mandate. England is now confronted with the severe problem of keeping its
own house in order before it can even presume to consider acting
as a light to the outside world. Associating the colonialist enterprise with the Satanic comes, then, from despair and confusion
as Milton finds himself forced to make sense of God's inexplicable
workings on the stage of history. The early epic plans for an
Arthuriad glorifying the English people are replaced in *Paradise
Lost* by a poem that recognizes no newly united nation is about to
succeed and replace the much-detested monarchy. Affirming the
faithfulness of the prophetic remnant and solitary servant of God
comes hand in hand with condemning a nation for succumbing

to anti-Christian apostasy. Milton's traumatic response to the failure of the Puritan experiment and his loss of faith in England as a nation obedient to God's will account for his intriguing demonization of colonialism in the epic.

The colonization of Eden is the cowardly act Satan must undertake and fulfill to be avenged of his defeat by the warrior Son. Interestingly, that venture is identified as an activity not different from the diversionary engagements of the demons after the conclusion of their council. As Satan proceeds to expand the dominion of hell, the fallen angels spend their time playing games, singing songs about their own heroic deeds, or discoursing on matters of high theology and philosophy. Ultimately, all these activities will lead nowhere, for hell and its condition are defined in terms of "wand'ring mazes lost" (*PL* 2.561). Evil always redounds upon its own rebellious head, and Milton's hell is significantly figured through the conspicuous metaphors of self-consumption: Satan impregnating Sin, his daughter and express image; Death feeding on the entrails of its mother; the devils chewing "bitter Ashes" (*PL* 10.566), the fruits of Satan's labor. The activities of the devils in hell resemble engagements in the human world, and the analogy Milton sets up between the demonic and terrestrial domains enables him to critique a social order lost in the intricacies of intellectual discussions and confusion of self-serving interests. The point Milton makes is that the colonizing and imperial impulse forms an intrinsic part of a cultural ethos that lacks the cohesiveness needed for building up a viable society. The "Song" of the demons, interjects the epic narrator, "was partial" (*PL* 2.552).

The anticolonial and antiimperial narratives present in *Paradise Lost* can be read not only in relation to Milton's experience of defeat and his general pessimism about recuperating a vibrant national culture, but also as a critique of royalist ideology in particular. When Milton portrays Satan's journey across Chaos by invoking the metaphors and images of ocean travel, he alludes to Aeneas's passage across water to set the foundation for the building of the new Troy. Barbara Kiefer Lewalski emphasizes that Satan is the epic antagonist who falls far short of the heroism exemplified by Aeneas who sets up a beachhead in Italy, enabling the creation of empire.[35] I wish to adjust Lewalski's reading by proposing that we can read Satan's subversive venture as a metaphor that compromises the meaning and symbolic significance of the journey motif in the *Aeneid*. By appropriating the metaphor of ocean travel in the *Aeneid* and rewriting it in terms of the Satanic

undertaking, Milton contaminates the significance of that metaphor in the Virgilian intertext, a significance linked to the ultimate founding of Rome.[36] The relevant context here is that the
Aeneid functions as the paradigmatic text of empire for readers
of the English Renaissance. It is the central text in a typological
discourse that constructs England as the contemporary and second Rome, an envisioning that celebrates the rise of an *imperium*
that will become a great world power. Renaissance England
worked out in elaborate and self-conscious detail the conception
of England as the New Troy, already obvious in English medieval
literature. If the effect of demonizing ocean travel in book 2 of
Paradise Lost is to bring into question the *raison* for the elaborate
use of that metaphor in the *Aeneid,* one linked to the founding of
empire, it does so as part of a political rhetoric interrogating any
celebration of *imperium.* The glories of Rome, which Virgil's *Aeneid*
was written to celebrate, are significantly cast in a generally negative light in Milton's writings.

THE POETICS AND POLITICS OF IMPERIAL ROME

To understand more fully the deep level of political engagement generated by Milton's appropriation of Roman imperial
structures to represent Satan and his rule, it is important to contextualize the symbolics of power employed for the legitimation
of monarchical authority in Stuart England. The Stuart monarch
James I made self-conscious use of the symbolics of imperial
Rome to fashion the specific political identity of his reign, setting
it in contradistinction to Elizabeth Tudor's previous rule. The
depth and extent of the monarch's appropriation of this symbolics
is considered in detail by Jonathan Goldberg in *James I and the
Politics of Literature.* Significantly, James I even represented his
royal identity as Caesar Augustus. On his coronation medal was
inscribed the following: "IAC : I : BRIT : CAE : AVG : HAE
CAESARUM CAE. D. D." ("James I, Caesar Augustus of Britain,
Caesar the heir of the Caesars"). Paul Yachnin elaborates on
James's use of Augustan image-making to identify his reign as
one committed to peace-making and to uniting the realms of England and Scotland:

> Panegyric poems on the occasions of James's accession to the English
> throne introduced an imperial motif: and royal encomium became
> explicitly Augustan when Jonson undertook to lionize the King in the

1604 royal entry. Here, in the streets of London on March 15, 1604, and in the most elaborate and costly procession of the age, Jonson's Temple Bar Arch (the last of seven) and his panegyric of welcome in The Strand heralded the King as the new Augustus. A fourfaced head of Janus crowned the Arch; at James's approach, the gates closed on Janus, signifying the peculiarly Augustan peace-making attendant upon the onset of James's reign. On the gates was written: "IMP. IACOBVS MAX. CAESAR AVG. P. P." ("Emperor James the Great, Caesar Augustus, Father of the Country").[37]

The use of Roman motifs was not restricted to Jacobean image and myth-making. The revival of triumphal architecture and lavish pageantry in the English Renaissance, begun in self-conscious earnest in Elizabeth's reign, provided a legacy that was also appropriated by the Caroline Court. Charles I was presented with a number of extravagant masques, all performed to glorify the monarch and the aristocracy by linking them to heavenly counterparts. The Caroline Court also emphasized the authenticity of the triumph within the original Roman tradition, an emphasis that served to represent the Stuart monarch as a modern Caesar.[38] If indeed the Roman motif is deeply embedded in the construction of royal identity in the Stuart court, any negative rendition of it can be interpreted as a critique of sorts. Finally, the Roman imperial motif figures in complex ways in Renaissance England's political and cultural life, appropriated for fashioning political identity in the Jacobean and Caroline courts, and also for enabling the larger conception of England as the new and contemporary Rome.

When he was seventeen years old, Milton himself had written "In Quintum Novembris" to commemorate the failure of Guy Fawkes's attempt to blow up a session of Parliament; in this poem, James I is portrayed as a monarch who had come from the remote north and assumed lordship of the Troy-born race, which is the English nation.

And in *The History of Britain,* probably written in 1647–48 but revised for the press in 1670, Milton included a verse celebration of England as the Second Rome. Expressing a deep interest in the origins, history, and destiny of his native country, an obviously optimistic Milton also recognized the English nation's potential as an imperial power, like the first Rome, which is its type. Other poems like "Mansus" and the "Epitaphium Damonis" also register feelings that reveal patriotic pride and that communicate confidence in England's cultural viability. When Milton refers to the English as descendants of the Trojans, and to England as another

Troy, he gives implicit recognition to the centrality of Virgil's *Aeneid* in the construction of the patriotic theme. Virgil's celebration of the founding of the new Troy exists as the typical epic text enabling England's envisioning of itself as an *imperium*.

In his *Aeneid*, Virgil celebrates the Roman empire by making the exploits of his hero far greater than the capacities of man in the human world. Much of the amplification of the heroism in the epic depends on his consistent use of the rhetorical trope of hyperbole. Hyperbole, Philip Hardie writes in his excellent study of Virgil's expression and celebration of Roman power, signals the sheer impetus of the growth of Rome not only from its insignificant and humble beginnings to become the city ruling the entire civilized world, but also from an identification of the Roman *imperium* with the natural world and realm of the gods.[39] The *Aeneid*'s encomiastic framework is enforced by a narrative preoccupied with dimensions and size. Virgil presents Aeneas's realization of his role as the leader responsible for creating the new Troy and champion of cosmic order by politicizing and moralizing physical space. The dimensions of physical space, then, defined by the coordinates of the horizontal and vertical axes, enable Virgil to create an epic narrative that both celebrates the sheer geographical magnitude constituting the Roman empire and identifies *cosmos* with *imperium*. By creating identity between the Roman *imperium* and *cosmos*, Virgil implicitly celebrates the capacity of the Roman empire to last forever.

Milton also moralizes physical space in *Paradise Lost*. But the conception of space in *Paradise Lost* does not support a vision of world empire like the one given in the Virgilian epic. Where Virgil's depiction of Rome's control of the totality of all four divisions—heaven, earth, sea, and hell—represents his identification of world empire with the order of the cosmos, a representation central to the construction of his epic encomium,[40] Milton's portrayal of Satan's fall into hell is figured as a descent into incarceration within a "horizontal" existential condition. That condition is figured in the flat surface of burning hell upon which the apostate angels find themselves sprawled in disarray. There is no escape for Milton's Satan from this condition. In desiring to climb up the existential chain of being by aspiring to godhead, Satan finds himself reduced instead to a dragon-like figure, stretched out in hell. Milton's theology cannot accommodate the Virgilian identification of *cosmos* and *imperium*.

If in order to represent the glory that is Rome, Virgil's narrative strategy involves imbuing the affairs and actions of his epic char-

acters with a significance that assimilates to them cosmic resonances, Milton's use of the trope of hyperbole has the dual effect
of bestowing on his poetic endeavor grand epic stature and down-
playing it at the same time as being associated with the demonic.
Specifically, in portraying the war in heaven, Milton draws self-
reflexive attention to the epic trope of hyperbole as part of the
Satanic discourse. The point is that so long as the good angels
insist on fighting their battles with recourse to this trope, the
eternal contestation between truth and falsehood, good and evil,
can never be resolved. Breaking the stalemate is the devastating
entrance of the Son riding the Father's chariot. Milton's epic narrative finds its significance only in relation to the transcendent
Father and Son just as his historical narrative finds its meaning
only with reference to the Christian God. This Christian God that
is *Paradise Lost*'s transcendental signified is the sole controlling
authority of history.

In Milton's epic, the most succinct expression of ascent up the
vertical axis is given in the preexistent Son's prophetic and apocalyptic anticipation that his *kenosis* will redeem nature and a fallen
human race:

> I through the ample Air in Triumph high
> Shall lead Hell Captive maugre Hell, and show
> The powers of darkness bound. Thou at the sight
> Pleas'd, out of Heaven shalt look down and smile,
> While by thee rais'd I ruin all my Foes,
> Death last, and with his Carcass glut the Grave:
> Then with the multitude of my redeem'd
> Shall enter Heav'n long absent, and return,
> Father, to see thy face, wherein no cloud
> Of anger shall remain, but peace assur'd,
> And reconcilement; wrath shall be no more
> Thenceforth, but in thy presence Joy entire.
>
> (*PL* 3.254–65)

This vision of the redemption of the saints will, however, be fulfilled only at the end of time and history. When Michael reveals
to Adam the world's future history, the Apocalypse the Son introduces in book 3 is a long way off. In fact, as book 11 gives way to
book 12, the reader experiences a sense of receding immediacy
as Adam's ocular apprehension of history is replaced by the auditory. In book 11, Adam is allowed to watch human history unfolding up to the end of the flood; in book 12, Michael continues
revealing the history of the world through narration. Where Vir-

gil's Aeneas sets up a beachhead in Italy at the end of his journeying, Adam and Eve begin their lives in exile at the close of
Milton's epic. The lessons Michael imparts in book 12 are designed to lead toward forging a theology of Christian stoicism that
can provide strength in a postlapsarian existence. This stoicism—
described in the proem to book 9 as "the better fortitude / Of
Patience and Heroic Martyrdom" (*PL* 9.31–32) and the "paradise
within . . . , happier far" (*PL* 12.587)—introduces a conception
of space very different from Virgil's. Milton's "paradise within"
privileges a moral space removed from the externalized spaces of
history and temporal contingencies, the very spaces that, for Virgil, are imperative for the consolidation of Rome as a great imperial power. The themes of enlargement and expansion we find in
Virgil, figured through a national hero's and city's occupation of
physical/geographical as well as cosmic space, are linked to the
Satanic aspiration in Milton's epic.

When discussing cultural conceptions of England as the New
Rome, it is important to locate their basis in a typological view of
history. In this view England, interpreted as antitype, fulfills and
makes complete an earlier version or type in historical time. "Typology," Northrop Frye summarizes in his exacting formulation
in *The Great Code*,

> is a figure of speech that moves in time: the type exists in the past
> and the antitype in the present, or the type exists in the present and
> the antitype in the future. What typology really is as a mode of
> thought, what it both assumes and leads to, is a theory of history, or
> more accurately of historical process: an assumption that there is
> some meaning and point to history, and that sooner or later some
> event or events will occur which will indicate what that meaning or
> point is, and so become an antitype of what has happened previously.[41]

Typology is a mode of thought as well as a way of responding to
history by a nation like Old Testament Israel, never very good at
the game of empire. The idea that one day in the future will bring
consummation to and bestow meaning on history enables such a
disadvantaged nation to accommodate suffering in its cultural
experience. But the same typological vision of history can, of
course, also be easily appropriated to validate a nation's imperialist
dreams and ambitions. When the English Renaissance looks back
to the Roman empire as a type of its own contemporary cultural
and political experience, it borrows the necessary narrative and
symbolic structures used to celebrate the great world empire that
was Rome. This is why Virgil is such an important poet for the

literary imagination of the English Renaissance, and especially for those poets who possess a passionate nationalistic bent. It is true that we find in our consideration of Milton that types are, for him, found much less in the mythology of imperial Rome than they are in the Old Testament. The indispensable model for this trans-position, or superimposition, is Augustine's *City of God*, in which Christian typological history is written over Roman.

In both Milton's polemical prose and major poems, Old Testa-ment characters and their narrative situations are evoked to serve as mirrors through which contemporary seventeenth-century En-gland can obtain lessons on how to live and observe God's work-ings with his people in history. Toward the close of *Paradise Lost* the archangel Michael reveals to Adam a group of faithful men who stand up in defence of Truth in the midst of an apostate world: Enoch, Abraham, and Noah. These Old Testament figures instruct Milton on how to stand firm as a member of the faithful remnant in a world that has forsaken God's will. It appears that Milton's need to emphasize the important role still played by the prophet who stands alone, like Abdiel, in the face of insurmount-able odds, goes hand in hand with a rhetorical negation of the imperialist energies normally associated with a distinctively vi-brant culture. When Milton figures Charles I's tyrannical rule with reference to the wicked Roman emperors, he interrogates implicitly the raison d'être of the *Aeneid* because the celebration of the emperor/monarch lies at the heart of the Virgilian text. The struggle Milton must undergo to come to grips with an En-glish nation that has willfully embraced the Egyptian slavery from which it has just recently been liberated translates in *Paradise Lost* into a destabilization of the centrality of Virgil's *Aeneid* to which, as epic writer, Milton is indebted through the literary tradition. That destabilization in turn encodes a critique of the colonialist and imperialist enterprise.

When Milton links Charles I to the evil Caesars in his regicide *apologia* and portrays Satan as demonic archetype of the emperors in *Paradise Lost*, he casts a dark shadow over the entire celebration of monarchy and empire represented by the Roman order. Not coincidentally, the Roman theme is once again invoked and inter-rogated in *Paradise Regained* when the Incarnate Son repudiates Satan's offer of the kingdom of Rome. In this poem, Milton treats the Roman theme in a fascinating way. First, Rome is presented by Satan as the great imperial power that Jesus as a Jew and colonized Other must defeat in order to bring Israel liberation. In Augustinian theology, Israel is a type of the Church as alien sojourner in the city of this world, raped by imperial Rome. If Israel displaced Rome, it would become Rome, as for Milton the Catholic Church had done. Shaping Milton's portrayal of Satan's temptation of Rome is Augustine's understanding in *The City of God* that generic social and political order is defined by the struggle for power; Roman history, as surveyed in *The City of God*, never achieved anything other than playing out this endless struggle. Milton's Satan wants Jesus to be locked irretrievably in this struggle as he proposes different ways by which the Incarnate deity can become king. If Rome in *Paradise Regained* represents the culmination of Satan's temptation of the kingdoms of the world, it does so not only because it is the sole imperial power dominating the world at that time, but also because it represents in full the politics of power ravaging every human society in the postlapsarian world.

Significantly, Jesus' rejection of the temptation of Rome must also be read in terms of Milton's critique and interrogation of royalist ideology and of the monarchy that is its material manifestation. Theology cannot be separated from politics in Milton's major poems. The example of *Paradise Regained* reveals how theological structures facilitate and enable political engagement with the restored monarchy. One can expand on the politics encoded in Milton's interrogation of the Roman motif by contextualizing it in relation to Spenser's own use of that motif in *The Faerie Queene*. We remember that when Spenser wrote in praise of the monarchy in his romance epic, he specifically envisaged himself as contemporary Virgil celebrating the English *imperium*. Unlike that of *The Faerie Queene*, *Paradise Lost's* relationship with the *Aeneid*, its great epic antecedent, is much more subversive. For any critique of empire unavoidably undermines the paradigmatic imperial structures constituting Virgil's epic text.

ABSOLUTIST AND REPUBLICAN POETICS AND POLITICS

Rome occupies an important place in the imagination of the English Renaissance because it can be evoked to bolster or legitimize different political and ideological positions. First and foremost, Rome serves as a kind of cultural mirror held up to sixteenth and seventeenth-century England to appreciate the magnitude of its own glory and splendor. In holding this classical mirror up to the nature of contemporary society, Renaissance England also discovers its identity as a nascent colonial and potential imperial power. In the same way that the old Romans had once civilized the ancient Britons, the English, now the new Romans, possess the mandate to civilize the barbaric Other, one of whom is the Irish. The typological relationship existing between the first and second Romes is a rhetorical construct especially conducive to ratifying England's conception of its imperialist potential. When the Roman empire appears in the literature and polemical tracts of the English Civil Wars, however, its significance becomes much more ambiguous. The Rome that is the classical example par excellence of *imperium* will signify in the narrative of a republican text in an uneasy way because any celebration of the Roman empire endorses the rule of the emperor that constitutes the originating and primary source of its greatness.

Paradise Regained's epic narrative embeds Milton's republican ideology in its attack on an imperialism inextricable from monarchical authority. This narrative engages in conflict with an absolutist narrative like the one formulated by Francis Bacon in his *Advancement of Learning*. Reading *Paradise Regained* next to the *Advancement*, we find a succinct abbreviation of the political and theological conflicts involved. Published in 1605, Bacon's *Advancement* specifically celebrates James I's identity as a great humanist prince; he suggests that only a prince with such learning has the capacity to rule England. Bacon's panegyric does not end there: much of the text is given to providing a definition of power. Specifically, Bacon finds that learning and discipline form an essential part of the military project, a view that translates itself into an equation between knowledge and power. Where a republican writer like Milton evokes the Roman empire to critique the monarchy, a royalist author like Bacon conjures it up to celebrate the greatness of monarchical authority and empire. We find that two historical figures Bacon consistently invokes side by side in his *Advancement* are Alexander the Great and Julius Caesar. His unqualified admiration for these characters stems from the recognition that their power derives from the very close and intrinsic relationship established between learning and martial prowess:

> experience doth warrant, that both in persons and in times, there hath been a meeting and concurrence in Learning and Arms, flourishing and excelling in the same men and the same ages. For, as for men, there cannot be a better nor the like instance, as of that pair, Alexander the Great and Julius Cæsar the Dictator; whereof the one was Aristotle's scholar in philosophy, and the other was Cicero's rival in eloquence.[42]

Equating "learning" metonymically with "utility," Bacon advocates that the learning that can bring order, peace, and freedom should also adapt itself to life and practicality; and an important aspect of social life is linked to the conception of greatness and power:

> Neither hath learning an influence and operation only upon civil merit and moral virtue, and the arts or temperature of peace and peaceable government; but likewise it hath no less power and efficacy in enablement towards martial and military virtue and prowess; as may be notably represented in the examples of Alexander the Great, and Cæsar the dictator.[43]

Bacon's writings invite comparison with Milton's because they ratify a royalist and absolutist ideology by appealing to the greatness of empire. We remember that in *The Faerie Queene*, Spenser tries to convince Queen Elizabeth that the greatness of the monarch cannot be separated from the ambition and project of empire building. Francis Bacon elaborates on the importance of building an empire in his essay, "Of the True Greatness of Kingdoms and Estates," where the advice is given:

> Therefore let any prince or state think soberly of his forces, except his militia of natives be of good and valiant soldiers. And let princes, on the other side, that have subjects of martial disposition, know their own strength, unless they be otherwise wanting unto themselves.[44]

The means of attaining ability in arms is to be distinguished from the need to "intend" or pay constant attention to arms; for this is necessary to transform a nation into the greatest empire of the world. For Bacon, "no estate [can] expect to be great that is not awake upon any just occasion of arming."[45]

Bacon goes so far as to say that the health of the body politic can only be maintained through conducting a foreign war; "slothful peace," he insists, only effeminizes courage and corrupts manners.[46] Aggression is built into Bacon's conception of national greatness. For Bacon, the Roman empire affords an ideal model of this greatness. Reasons are provided for Rome's ability to secure, consolidate, and maintain its imperial might. Rome not only moves "into the soil of other nations" by planting colonies, it enables the larger world to "spread upon the Romans" themselves by granting naturalization or the *jus civitatis*.[47] Spain's strength as an imperial power approximates the Roman practice of assimilating other nations into itself; in the example of Spain, all nations are employed in its militia of ordinary soldiers.[48] Bacon recognizes that the building of empire cannot be an independent and self-sufficient project. And it certainly cannot be removed from the necessity of social and national interactions. Bacon's writings show that he has no difficulty advocating the conquest of foreign territory as a means of enlarging England's national boundaries. He sees such conquests as central to the consolidation of monarchical authority. In *Oracles of Empire,* David Shields tells us that Bacon propagates English domination of commerce as a means to securing national prosperity. The emphasis on commerce, however, offers only one angle on the discourse of colonization in his writings. There is always a place for military action in Bacon's conception of the expansion of empire.[49] Indeed, Bacon possesses a strikingly imperial conception of greatness.

The *Advancement of Learning* and *Paradise Regained* employ similar metaphors and rhetorical structures to communicate antithetical and opposing ideological convictions. The Roman theme enables Bacon to articulate his endorsement of royalist ideology and conception of empire, while it encodes Milton's critique of the monarchy and fallen human aspirations. In *Paradise Regained,* a vision of Christ's universal and timeless kingdom is given with reference to two metaphors found in the Old Testament book of Daniel. Christ describes his kingdom this way:

> Know therefore when my season comes to sit
> On *David's* Throne, it shall be like a tree
> Spreading and overshadowing all the Earth,
> Or as a stone that shall to pieces dash
> All Monarchies besides throughout the world,
> And of my Kingdom there shall be no end.
>
> (PR 4.146–51)

This description borrows from Daniel's vision of the tree "in the midst of the earth, and the height thereof was great" (Dan. 4:10). "The tree grew," the vision continues, "and was strong, and the height thereof reached unto heaven, and the sight thereof to the end of all the earth" (Dan. 4:11). At the same time, it alludes to Nebuchadnezzar's vision of the stone that fell upon and crushed the great image of worldly power representing the four empires of the world:

> Thou sawest till that a stone was cut out without hands, which smote the image upon his feet that were of iron and clay, and brake them to pieces.
> Then was the iron, the clay, the brass, the silver, and the gold, bro-

ken to pieces together, and became like the chaff of the summer threshingfloors; and the wind carried them away, that no place was found for them: and the stone that smote the image became a great mountain, and filled the whole earth. . . .

And in the days of these kings shall the God of heaven set up a kingdom, which shall never be destroyed: and the kingdom shall not be left to other people, but it shall break in pieces and consume all these kingdoms, and it shall stand for ever.

(Dan. 2:34–35, 44)

Milton's Christ evokes Daniel's image and metaphor of worldly power to remind Satan that his kingdom of nations, conquerors, and arms is transitory when set against the kingdom of the Church. His repudiation of the world's kingdoms also reinforces Milton's rejection of heroic arms in *Paradise Lost*[50] and the attack on the monarchy in his regicide pamphlets. We remember that in *Eikonoklastes*, Milton had referred to the people of England as those true Christians who "are the Children of that Kingdom, which, as ancient Prophesies have foretold, shall in the end break to peeces and dissolve all thir great power and Dominion" (*Yale* 3.509).

Where a republican text like *Paradise Regained* evokes Nebuchadnezzar's tree to represent the fragility of the world's empires, an absolutist text like Bacon's essay, "Of the True Greatness of Kingdoms and Estate," will allude to it as an example of the consolidation of empire:

By all means it is to be procured that the trunk of Nebuchadnezzar's tree of monarchy be great enough to bear the branches and the boughs; that is, that the natural subjects of the crown or state bear a sufficient proportion to the stranger subjects that they govern. Therefore all states that are liberal of naturalization towards strangers are fit for empire.[51]

Daniel's metaphor instructs on the process by which a nation can interact with the larger outside world to build up and strengthen its *imperium*. Bacon borrows from Machiavelli's *Discourses* when he writes about the importance of enlarging the population of a nation by grafting foreigners onto its civil society. Machiavelli had promulgated the expansion of one's population by incorporating foreigners through friendliness or force; it is important that the numbers of a nation's population are always kept large because that is indispensable to maintaining the strength of a society's military force. The Machiavellian counsel advances three methods for expanding empire: forming a league consisting of several republics in which no one enjoys preference, authority, or rank above the others; forming alliances in which one reserves headship, prerogative, and right of initiative; and making other states subjects instead of allies. For the last method to be successful, the imperially ambitious state needs to ensure that it possesses the strength of a powerful army to compel obedience if needed.[52] Bacon borrows his conception of the need to ensure that the imperialist state possesses the ability to absorb the foreigner into its society from Machiavelli. For Machiavelli, forming alliances can make possible the disempowerment of one's allies by the covert development of a political strength built on military might. When that strength makes itself visible, the states now reduced to subjection are powerless to offer resistance.

In *Paradise Regained,* Satan offers Christ the Machiavellian counsel of entering into league as a stratagem, for example, to gain control of Parthia, a move that can then be utilized to defeat Rome (*PR* 3.359–80). Control of Parthia would provide the Incarnate Son with the military might needed to overthrow Rome; it would also enable him to realize the patriotic dream of reuniting the ten tribes of Israel with the Jewish remnant, for Parthia controls the territory in which now dwell the ten lost tribes of Israel. Satan also calls upon Christ to use his "Regal Virtues" (*PR* 4.98) in order to overthrow the power of the childless, "Old, and lascivious" (*PR* 4.91) Emperor Tiberius. His promulgation of the breaking of trust and the importance of dissimulation in the game of politics is a position espoused by Machiavelli, one that even Bacon has difficulties accepting in his *Advancement,* a text that provides one of the most sustained praises of the Machiavelli of the *Prince* in the early 1600s. Bacon allows for dissimulation in politics, but this dissimulation must not be a sustained one.[53] Milton's Satan is portrayed then as the archetypal father of Machiavellian politics, as he has been in books 1 and 2 of *Paradise Lost.* Significantly, Satan speaks as the great and experienced opportunist in his lecture on fame and glory (*PR* 3.31–42) and on the exercise of zeal and duty (*PR* 3.171–80). Satan is not only the Roman historian and political theorist who emphasizes the predominance of *fortuna* in dictating the processes of history, he is also the Machiavellian counselor who argues that any prince who is in absolute control of fortune can never lose his power. In Machiavelli's political philosophy, the prince who wishes to entrench himself immovably in power cannot possess a stable and grounded character or identity.

If the use of the Roman imperial motif in *Paradise Lost* affords

Milton the generic structures for building his epic poem, it also enables him to critique the tyranny of monarchy by demonizing the splendour of the *imperium*. Similarly, *Paradise Regained* depicts the world of time and history with reference to Roman imperial terms, once again inscribing a rhetorical attack on royalist ideology and Roman Catholicism, the apostate faith to which that political ideology is literally and figuratively intertwined. Milton does not rest comfortably in the quietist position, the most logical space in which a beleaguered republican can hope to obtain refuge. In *Paradise Lost* and *Paradise Regained*, a rhetoric of political engagement and confrontation occupies singular space with another narrative linked to quietism and patience. The redaction of the Roman imperial motif provides a narrative that encodes Milton's critique of kingship and the political structures monarchy represents. This sheds light on the central significance of *Samson Agonistes* (published simultaneously with *Paradise Regained* in 1671), a tragedy that represents God's agonist and heroic champion rising up after self-inflicted defeat to destroy the enemies of Truth.

Sexual/Textual Politics in *Samson Agonistes*

In *Samson Agonistes*, the experience of moving toward a reaffirmation of self-identity is enabled by the tragic protagonist's confrontation with and exorcism of the ghosts of his past. The entrance of Dalila and her pleas for him to accept the care she is willing to provide as penitential gesture must be repudiated by Samson even as he matures in the understanding of his role as Israel's deliverer. Interestingly, the development of Samson's redefinition of subjectivity depends on the rejection of the female body rhetorically demonized as quintessential whore. Dalila stands for the fallen woman who entices and destroys men as well as for the foreign tribes God always warns Israel against commingling with. Samson's marriage to Dalila exists as a powerful symbol of the stains of a contaminated match, what the New Testament refers to as an unequal yoking. *Samson Agonistes* is a tragedy that makes much of the sense of Israel's exclusivism as God's chosen people. Samson, the judge responsible for protecting this exclusivist national identity, unfortunately possesses a liberal view of intermarriage. But more than that: if Israel is privileged as God's elect nation in *Samson Agonistes*, and Samson is chosen to be its liberator, then one would expect the tragedy to furnish an uncompromised affirmation of Israel's national identity in which the individual and the state exist as a singular and concerted body. But *Samson Agonistes* refuses to offer such an affirmation, for the uneasy sense continues to exist that the individual apprehension of subjectivity does not coincide and cohere with the tribe's. No character, for example, has access to the state of Samson's relationship with his God at the end, an opacity that suggests that all reactions to historical and social events are interpretative and subjective. Dalila recognizes the subjectivity and relativity of historical readings when she says that she will be celebrated as a timeless heroine among her own people. If Samson is a character Milton associates with his own personal and historical experiences, the inability of this judge to obtain cohesiveness of identity in relation to his tribe betrays the fracture Milton must experience between his conception of self-identity and the discordant social energies of the English people.

It has been said that, in *Samson Agonistes*, Milton textualizes his fantasies of revolutionary terrorism, vicariously destroying Jehovah's enemies through cathartic narrative. His tragedy also sets up a private space between the agonist and his God, transforming the experience of defeat into victory by participating in theatrical display before the judging and approving eye of deity.[54] The relevant context to situate Milton's representation of Samson's iconoclasm would be the experience of the regicides in the face of trial and imminent death in post-Restoration England. For like Samson and the other characters in Milton's tragedy, radical clergy, intellectuals, and writers struggled to make sense of their defeat in relation to their original interpretation of the divine will for history. The regicides who had to face the fact of their executions expressed strong millenarian convictions. These convictions had in fact been necessary for them to commit such an unprecedented act as the killing of a king.[55] If millenarian belief provided the strength needed for regicide, it also gave the necessary spiritual support in the face of trial. Regicides like John Carew, Thomas Harrison, John Jones, and John Cook were, therefore, able to believe that their deaths would persuade the English nation about the truth and invincibility of their cause. The present trial would not last long, for Christ would return quickly and reverse the roles of judge and persecuted in history. The divine tribunal at the Apocalypse would ensure the triumph of righteousness. With Christ's return, the regicides who had been condemned would judge their judges.[56]

Because of their millenarian convictions, the regicides can face the agony of their trials and the prospect of their executions with heroism, courage, and strength. Christopher Hill describes their demeanor as "an art of dying," an art carefully studied in the seventeenth century, when death could be a far more public affair than it is today.[57] The concept of dying as an art transforms death into a kind of theater, practiced as a legitimate expression of martyrdom in the sixteenth and seventeenth centuries. Samson's death takes place in the "spacious Theater" (*SA* 1605) of Dagon's temple, in which he had been forced by his captives to provide displays of his tremendous strength. The messenger refers to Samson's display of his strength as a "spectacle" (*SA* 1604). The theatricalization of his strength forced upon him by his captors turns into a theatricalization of iconoclasm when Samson finally declares:

> Hitherto, Lords, what your commands impos'd
> I have perform'd, as reason was, obeying,
> Not without wonder or delight beheld.
> Now of my own accord such other trial
> I mean to show you of my strength, yet greater;
> As with amaze shall strike all who behold.
>
> (*SA* 1640–45)

Making use of a convention in Greek tragedy, Samson's theatrical iconoclasm, only reported to the reader through the mediating account of the messenger, translates into a private performance dedicated to his God. A divinely sanctioned theatricalism is distinguished from the love for outward appearances, finery, and "disguise" that the regicides and Milton found in popery and the practices of the Roman Catholic Church. "To court martyrdom," Jonas Barish writes in *The Antitheatrical Prejudice,* "was to claim a starring part on the stage of history, to become a 'visible saint,' theatricalizing one's sanctity by revealing it triumphantly before the Supreme Gaze."[58]

Reading *Samson Agonistes* as a text that embeds Milton's deep fantasies concerning the destruction of apostasy and victory of the righteous champion of Truth, we also find the tragedy inscribing the marginalization of the demonic Other central to the rhetorical structurings of the controversialist pamphlets. From the time he began writing the antiprelatical tracts in the early 1640s, Milton had evoked evil types of the Old Testament to delineate contemporary figures in his own day. In the regicide tracts, Charles Stuart shares with Saul, Rehoboam, Ahaziah, and Amaziah the common experience of losing God's favor; the gradual erosion of the king's authority by the encroaching power of the prelates is figured in terms of the shearing of Samson's locks by the treacherous Dalila. (Adam's loss of spiritual strength and native righteousness after the fall is also portrayed through the analogy of Samson's deprivation of physical strength.) Biblical analogues shape Milton's narrative representations of evil. They introduce dramatic and theological contexts within which Milton is able to redact the stories of apostasy in contemporary English society. Because Milton employs such analogues to represent the figures of evil and tyranny in his society, the reader is invited to decode the political meanings embedded in narrative representation. The typological structures intrinsic to the construction of a narrative that functions through analogy not only point to England as God's New Israel and invoke Old Testament history as a mirror through which contemporary English culture can view itself and learn valuable lessons, but also facilitate the workings of a rhetoric that continues to demonize difference and Otherness.[59]

Samson's tragic experience presents in vivid terms Milton's particular understanding of fornication, a metaphor that he uses throughout his poems and prose works to signify the sin of idolatry. The two are inseparable in Milton's writings. Fornication subverts the divinely ordained hierarchical rule of the universe by enthroning the obsessive ego in the place once occupied by the supreme figure of authority—God. Intrinsic to the sin of fornication is the impulse to aspire to godhead, to replace the patriarchal figure of authority. The most powerful figure ever to attempt this assault on God's throne is Satan, who only succeeded in usurping the throne of deity by entering into and occupying the narrative domain of parody. Eve, cajoled by Satan to reenact his sin of fornication (thus particularly understood) and eventually doing so, is followed by Adam. Except that Adam's fornication differs from Eve's in one significant respect: Adam wants to replace God with Eve whereas Eve wants to displace God with herself, to occupy the place of deity by possessing the knowledge of good and evil. The desire to usurp patriarchal authority by replacing it with a feminine one can only fail for Milton, because the supreme authority of a patriarchal deity is indelibly inscribed in the Protestant milieu to which he is uncompromisingly indebted. Ironically, the desire to replace patriarchal authority with a feminine one is fulfilled for Adam and Eve when that authority manifests itself in the symbolic form of Dalila's harlot-lap. In describing the moment of awakening after the love-making scene that follows the fall, *Paradise Lost* alludes to Samson's awaking confused and shorn of his strength, the stronghold of the symbolic phallus now usurped by and contained in the bower whose emblem is the lower half of the female body. This bower of the female body (Dalila's "Harlot-lap" [*PL* 9.1060]) into which man had fallen signifies God's fair earth perverted into an order of nature governed by lust, sin, and death. The related term here is Augustine's *perversio,* a literal and figurative "turning aside" from the divine.

Augustine had already read fornication as a metaphor for idolatry, an idea directly communicated in God's express command to the nation of Israel in the early days of its consolidation not to intermingle with the peoples of other pagan tribes. Absolute separation between Israel as God's holy nation and the pagan Other is divinely mandated. Paul Stevens calls this process of exclusion "Leviticus thinking," a discursive frame of mind that legitimates communal and national identity by positing a foreign culture as sexually impure, a moral transgression that must be punished by God's holy community.[60] This kind of thinking, Stevens elaborates, "is the tendency of universalizing Christianity to articulate its own sense of transcendent exceptionalism by re-embodying the exclusive, community-building rhetoric of Israel, especially as it is formulated in the Law."[61] The definition of fornication as idolatry, elaborated succinctly in Milton's *Tetrachordon,* translates itself in *Paradise Lost* into the metaphor of the displaced marital relation.[62] The status of the marital relation appears to provide an index of man's moral relationship with God. It is no mere narrative accident that Milton's depiction of the original fall coincides with, is indeed inseparable from, the disintegration of the marital relationship between Adam and Eve.

Milton specifically locates this prototype of the domestic upheaval in man's first disobedience when he surrounds his epic redaction of the fall with allusions to the story of Solomon's relationship with his many wives and their pagan gods, as well as to that of Samson's seduction by the treacherous Dalila. The story of Solomon is particularly relevant to Milton's epic redaction of the fall because it tells of the downfall of Israel's wisest king who committed idolatry when he turned away from God to his seven hundred wives and three hundred concubines, with their pagan gods. 1 Kings 11:1 and 2 tell us that "king Solomon loved many strange women, together with the daughter of Pharaoh, women of the Moabites, Ammonites, Edomites, Zidonians, and Hittites; Of the nations concerning which the LORD said unto the children of Israel, Ye shall not go in to them, neither shall they come in unto you: for surely they will turn away your heart after their gods: Solomon clave unto these in love." Three of Milton's four references made to Solomon in *Paradise Lost* point to his idolatry and susceptibility to women. The "wisest heart / Of *Solomon*" was led astray by Moloch who built "His Temple right against the Temple of God" (*PL* 1.400–2). Turning away and being led astray carry the meanings communicated by Augustine's definition of original sin as *aversio*. 1 Kings 11:7 tells us that, beguiled by his wives, Solomon built "an high place for Chemosh, the abomination of Moab, in the hill that is before Jerusalem, and for Molech, the abomination of the children of Ammon." The idolatry of the king is reiterated shortly thereafter when Milton's roll call of false deities shows Solomon also led astray by "*Astoreth*, whom the *Phœnicians* call'd / *Astarte*" (*PL* 1.438–39). Astoreth's temple stood in Sion

> on th' offensive Mountain, built
> By that uxorious King, whose heart though large,
> Beguil'd by fair Idolatresses, fell
> To idols foul.
>
> (*PL* 1.443–46)

The third reference to Solomon is found in a passage where that part of the garden tended by the solitary Eve is described as the garden "where the Sapient King / Held dalliance with his fair *Egyptian* Spouse" (*PL* 9.442–43). The fair Egyptian spouse refers to Pharaoh's daughter whom Solomon took to wife in 1 Kings 11:1. Milton's allusion to Solomon and his bride situates itself in a description of the beautiful garden where Satan finds Eve alone: in this garden, Adam the "Sapient King" had enjoyed many pleasant moments with his queen. This allusion appears in a context where mythological gardens like that of Adonis are disparaged as fictions and where the hell from which Satan comes—a claustrophobic "populous" (*PL* 9.445) world described as a city (one recalls Pandemonium) "Where Houses thick and Sewers annoy the Air" (*PL* 9.446)—can only asphyxiate pastoral Eden and subvert all its idyllic symbology. Satan intrudes into this beautiful garden and dallies with Eve in a demonic parody of Solomon and his bride, intoxicating her reason (interestingly, with dreams of courts and queenship), and through her bringing about the theological fall.

The pathos contained in the identification of Adam with Solomon in this passage stems in part from its prolepsis of the fall. Eden's final moment before the temptation and fall is deliberately frozen in the scene of the perfect garden in which Adam had regularly played with Eve, like Solomon and his Egyptian bride.

The moment Adam eats the forbidden fruit to complete "the mortal sin / Original" (*PL* 9.1003–4), the joy with which he once dallied with Eve is transformed into intoxicating euphoria, the state of uncontrol and unreason:

> As with new Wine intoxicated both
> They swim in mirth, and fancy that they feel
> Divinity within them breeding wings
> Wherewith to scorn the Earth.
>
> (*PL* 9.1008–11)

Now filled with "Carnal desire inflaming" (*PL* 9.1013), Adam makes love to Eve in a passion that tellingly reveals his loss of innocence: Eve now exists as an object primarily to gratify Adam's lust. Thus in the fall, Adam and Eve become prototypical fornicators, the first man and woman guilty of the sin of idolatry that Solomon will repeat in history.

When Milton repeats "dalliance" and "Sapience" to describe the fallen condition of Adam and Eve, he persists in his allusions to Solomon's experience:

> in Lust they burn:
> Till *Adam* thus 'gan *Eve* to dalliance move.
> *Eve*, now I see thou are exact of taste,
> And elegant, of Sapience no small part,
> Since to each meaning savor we apply,
> And Palate call judicious; I the praise
> Yield thee.
>
> (*PL* 9.1015–21)

This repetition of terms is significant because it calls for a comparison to be made with the Solomon analogy introduced earlier, before the fall. The wisdom and sapience once equated with the exercise of reason are now lost when Adam appreciates them in terms of appetite, when "dalliance" has become inseparable from total irresponsibility. Once he has delivered his epic redaction of the fall, Milton no longer alludes to the Solomon who is "the Sapient King" of book 9, line 442, but to the Solomon who fell because he succumbed to strange women and their false gods. The Solomon whom Milton evokes before the fall in order to portray the joy and innocence of the garden that Satan plans to despoil is identified with the king celebrated for his splendor and wisdom in 1 Kings 1–10, just as the Solomon evoked to depict the state of Adam after the fall resembles the figure of the wayward king in 1 Kings 11. The wisdom of native innocence is lost when Adam's uxoriousness transforms Eve into his idol, and leads him to worship her god which is the tree of knowledge.

The sin of fornication in *Samson Agonistes* can be read, at least on one level, as the communal sin of a people. If Samson's fall represents one aspect of the English experience, it is the losing of a nation's birthright by falling in love with foreign women and their pagan gods. Any allegorical and associative connections made between Samson and England point to the nation's failure to fulfill its divine mission to inaugurate God's holy and Christian Commonwealth. Significantly, Milton's Samson castigates Israel for its irresponsibility: the failure of Israel's governors and the heads of her tribes to follow him is as crucial as his own failure.

Significantly, however, when Samson pulls down the temple of Dagon on God's enemies, he does so in an act that is deeply personal. This is because Milton, for reasons already discussed, wants to place greater emphasis on individual experience than on the communal. Samson's final iconoclastic act does not lead to any restoration of national identity. Northrop Frye makes the point that, according to the Bible, the Philistines became stronger than ever after the death of Samson, Dan's great champion, and Dan itself effectively ceased to be a tribe shortly after.[63] It is obvious that Milton's critique of England as a nation that had failed disastrously to carry out God's grand design for his Commonwealth is powerfully present in *Samson Agonistes*. This critique is delivered in Milton's consistent use of a rhetoric of exclusion that, throughout this book, I have identified as a characteristic feature of imperialist discourse. Milton recognizes that the most effective way of drawing attention to the sins of apostasy and neglect of God's plans for a people's national destiny is to highlight the wrath of God directed against the sins of fornication and idolatry. In so doing, he articulates his political convictions and ideology within a discourse that cannot be extricated from distinct imperialist tropes. The metaphorical relationship established between fornication and idolatry enables the poet-polemicist to demonize peoples and cultures different from his own. Underwriting this rhetoric is the conception of a holy nation set apart by God because of its purity. In the case of Milton, however, that conception is complicated by the failure of the English people to realize God's plans for the nation.

CONCLUSION

The antiimperial narratives in *Paradise Lost* and *Paradise Regained* point to Milton's disillusionment with England's failure to build a godly Commonwealth. They show up England deprived of a cultural mandate to expand its geographical and political boundaries to incorporate other lands and peoples. In addition, these narratives also form an intrinsic part of a discourse that performs a critique of royalist ideology. While Milton's *Paradise Lost* gives due recognition to the *Aeneid* as its great classical and epic precursor, its relationship to the Augustan text is an extremely uneasy one, not only because Milton needs to spiritualize a heroism removed from the secular activities of ocean travel, but also because he cannot accept the celebration of *imperium* that is Virgil's project. Revealing a continuing political engagement with the monarchy, Milton's critique of royalist ideology occupies singular space with the quietist impulse to be removed from such engagement. Hence *Paradise Lost* centers its vision of heroism on domestic life while *Paradise Regained* speaks about the importance of recognizing the primacy of the "inner light" given by the Puritans to the individual conscience. Interestingly, crystallizing an internalized space removed from historical and political contingencies generates the spirit of political activism not only because the "inner light" constitutes the privileged position from which war is waged against apostasy, but also because the absolute supremacy of the Puritan God endorses and legitimates Christian warfare. The transcendent position of Milton's Puritan God makes itself felt in a political rhetoric that sets up eternal contestation between soldiers of the Truth and the children of apostasy. This theological and political rhetoric cannot be separated from the discourse employed by colonialists to justify taking over land belonging to people who are uncivilized, pagan, or do not have souls (a debate the Catholic Church once engaged in).

When Milton first began his pamphleteering career in the 1640s, his primary aim was to spread Puritanism, which he saw as having a political dimension on this earth. With the inauguration of the Commonwealth shortly after, this aim certainly appeared to have enjoyed divine sanction. Believing in this mandate given by God, Milton found himself easily writing in support of Cromwell's plan to colonize Ireland. To Milton, the Cromwellian project brings spiritual consideration and political action into conjunction. After the collapse of the Commonwealth, however, Milton's aim to spread Puritanism to the world was replaced by a new stress on a strange otherworldliness, described by critics as quietism or the impulse to retreat from the political arena. In this phase of Milton's life, defined by the traumatic experience of defeat, the colonization of the Other that is an aspect of the desire to bring Reformation to the world, no longer proved a viable project. Even though the language of what I have called theological imperialism is still present in Milton's major poems, it is no longer a language applied either to the missionizing mandate or to a project like the colonization of Ireland. It now exists not only to engage the enemies of Truth present in destructive numbers in England itself, but also to recuperate that starting point in his early pamphleteering career when, for Milton, Puritanism was a viable faith. Now England's enemy is itself: the people who make up the nation; it is not the Indians in the Americas or the Irish in Ireland. In *Paradise Lost, Paradise Regained,* and *Samson Agonistes,* the biblical rhetoric of exclusivism is turned inward to scrutinize English society and politics itself. Milton's message is clear: if at one time, God gave to the English nation the mandate to venture forth, proselytize, and convert the heathen world, he now withdraws that mandate because England is mired in the worship of foreign gods. And if there is anything to learn from Old Testament history, such a state of apostasy inevitably awakes the wrath of God. From that history also, Milton recognizes that the evils of apostasy have on different occasions impelled God to send his chosen people into bondage and slavery. In the specific example of England, the English people themselves are solely responsible for the state of their enslavement to the tyranny of monarchy. Their condition does not make them bearers of the Truth, but enemies of God who need to be opposed and vanquished.

Notes

Introduction

1. To establish a relationship between the interest in cartography, navigation, and England's entry into the world mercantile scene in the sixteenth and seventeenth centuries, see Boies Penrose, *Travel and Discovery in the Renaissance* (Cambridge: Harvard University Press, 1952); R. V. Tooley, *Maps and Map-Makers* (London: B. T. Batsford, 1949); E. G. R. Taylor, *Tudor-Geography: 1485–1583* (London: Methuen & Co., 1930) and *The Haven-Finding Art: A History of Navigation from Odysseus to Captain Cook* (London: Hollis and Carter, 1956); David W. Waters, *The Art of Navigation in England in Elizabethan and Early Stuart Times*, 3 parts (Basildon: Trustees of the National Maritime Museum, 1978).

2. Richard Hakluyt, "The Epistle Dedicatorie in the First Edition, 1589," in *The Principal Navigations, Voyages, Traffiques & Discoveries of the English Nation*, 12 vols. (Glasgow: James MacLehose and Sons, Publishers to the University, 1903–5), 1: xvii–xviii. All subsequent references of the text are to this edition.

3. Richard Helgerson, *Forms of Nationhood: The Elizabethan Writing of England* (Chicago: University of Chicago Press, 1992), 151–91; David Quint, *Epic and Empire: Politics and Generic Form from Virgil to Milton* (Princeton: Princeton University Press, 1993). Quint also provides an interesting discussion of the relationship between the writing of epic poetry and class prejudice. Linked to the ethos of aristocratic hauteur and ethics of martial heroism, the epic poem typically casts merchandising and trading activities in a negative light. Different epic poems like the *Odyssey*, the *Liberata*, and *Lusíadas* address the often ambivalent signification of merchant adventuring in relation to the epic narrative of martial heroics: see 248–67.

4. Kim F. Hall, *Things of Darkness: Economies of Race and Gender in Early Modern England* (Ithaca: Cornell University Press, 1995), 44.

5. Hall, *Things of Darkness*, 46.

6. William Shakespeare, *The Merchant of Venice*, ed. John Russell Brown (1955; reprint, London: Methuen, 1984). Reference is to act, scene, and lines.

7. Thomas Moisan, "'Which is the Merchant Here? And which the Jew?': Subversion and Recuperation in *The Merchant of Venice*," in *Shakespeare Reproduced: The Text in History and Ideology*, ed. Jean E. Howard and Marion F. O'Connor (New York: Methuen, 1987), 195.

8. Ben Jonson, George Chapman, and John Marston, *Eastward Ho!*, ed. C. G. Petter (London: Ernest Benn, 1973). References are to act, scene, and lines; all subsequent references of the text are to this edition.

9. Carole Shammas, "English Commercial Development and American Colonization, 1560–1620," in *The Westward Enterprise: English Activities in Ireland, the Atlantic, and America: 1480–1650*, ed. K. R. Andrews, N. P. Canny, and P. E. H. Hair (Detroit: Wayne State University Press, 1979), 174.

10. Shammas, "English Commercial Development," 173.

11. Kenneth R. Andrews provides an assessment of Drakes's voyages in relation to the Elizabethan movement of maritime expansion in *Drake's Voyages: A*

Re-Assessment of Their Place in Elizabethan Maritime Expansion (London: Weidenfeld and Nicolson, 1967).

12. Edmund Spenser, *A View of the Present State of Ireland,* ed. W. L. Renwick (Oxford: Clarendon Press, 1970). All subsequent references of the text are to this edition, and will be designated as *View.*

13. Paul Brown, "'This Thing of Darkness I Acknowledge Mine': *The Tempest* and the Discourse of Colonialism," in *Political Shakespeare: New Essays in Cultural Materialism,* ed. Jonathan Dollimore and Alan Sinfield (Manchester: Manchester University Press, 1985), 48–71.

14. See Stephen Greenblatt, *Shakespearean Negotiations: The Circulation of Social Energy in Renaissance England* (Berkeley and Los Angeles: University of California Press, 1988), 129–63.

15. For a study of how *The Tempest* inscribes a discourse of colonialism that seeks to contain the threat of "masterlessness" and "savagism," see Brown, "This Thing of Darkness," 48–71. "Masterlessness," Brown summarizes, "analyses wandering or unfixed and unsupervised elements located in the internal margins of civil society," while "[s]avagism probes and categorises alien cultures on the external margins of expanding civil power": see 50. Brown argues that the masterless man was not a class or figure found in the discourse of the New World, but in the discourse of Ireland. The masterless barbarity of the footloose Irish embodied a distinct threat to civil order and society; this barbarity, expanded to forge a picture of uncivil Ireland, provides a powerful pretext for the British intent to suppress Ireland: see 56. See also Curt Breight, "'Treason Doth Never Prosper': *The Tempest* and the Discourse of Treason," *Shakespeare Quarterly* 41 (1990): 1–28.

16. For an excellent study of Shakespeare's use of the geographical coordinates given in Virgil's *The Aeneid* and of allusions made to contemporary voyagings to the New World, see Jan Kott, *The Bottom Translation: Marlowe and Shakespeare and the Carnival Tradition,* trans. Daniela Miedzyrzecka and Lillian Vallee (Evanston, Illinois: Northwestern University Press, 1987), 69–106.

17. William Shakespeare, *The Tempest,* ed. Frank Kermode (1954; reprint, London: Methuen, 1984). References are to act, scene, and lines; all subsequent references of the text are to this edition.

18. Stephen Greenblatt, *Marvelous Possessions: The Wonder of the New World* (Chicago: University of Chicago Press, 1991).

19. J. Martin Evans, *Milton's Imperial Epic: "Paradise Lost" and the Discourse of Colonialism* (Ithaca: Cornell University Press, 1996).

20. Jeffery Knapp, *An Empire Nowhere: England, America, and Literature from "Utopia" to "The Tempest"* (Berkeley and Los Angeles: University of California Press, 1992).

21. Knapp, *An Empire Nowhere,* 4.

22. Knapp, *An Empire Nowhere,* 4.

23. Helgerson, *Forms of Nationhood,* 8.

24. Andrew Hadfield, *Literature, Politics and National Identity: Reformation to Renaissance* (Cambridge: Cambridge University Press, 1993).

25. Brendan Bradshaw, Andrew Hadfield, and Willy Maley, ed. *Representing Ireland: Literature and the Origins of Conflict, 1534–1660* (Cambridge: Cambridge University Press, 1993).

CHAPTER 1. "TO SEEKE NEW WORLDS"

1. Richard S. Dunn, *Sugar and Slaves: The Rise of the Planter Class in the English West Indies, 1624–1713* (Chapel Hill: University of North Carolina Press, 1972), 10.

2. Dunn, *Sugar and Slaves*, 10–11. For an account of how, in the post-Armada years, the ships armed and put to sea by private adventurers enormously outnumbered those of the royal navy, see R. B. Wernham, *After the Armada: Elizabethan England and the Struggle for Western Europe* (1984; reprint, Oxford: Clarendon Press, 1986).

3. Sir Walter Ralegh, *Ocean to Cynthia*, in *The Poems of Sir Walter Ralegh*, ed. Agnes M. C. Latham (London: Constable & Co., 1929). All subsequent references of the poem are to this edition.

4. Steven W. May, *Sir Walter Ralegh* (Boston: G. K. Hall & Co., 1989), 79–103.

5. Sir Walter Ralegh, "The Discoverie of the large, rich, and beautifull Empire of Guiana, with a relation of the great and golden citie of Manoa (which the Spaniards call El Dorado) and the provinces of Emeria, Aromaia, Amapaia, and other countries, with their rivers adjoyning," in *The Principal Navigations*, 10:341. All subsequent references of the text are to this edition, and will be designated as *DG*.

6. David Norbrook, *Poetry and Politics in the English Renaissance* (London: Routledge and Kegan Paul, 1984), cited on 117.

7. Laurence Keymis, "A Relation of the Second Voyage to Guiana, Performed and Written in the Yeere 1596," in *The Principal Navigations*, 10:441. All subsequent references of the text are to this edition.

8. Keymis, "A Relation of the Second Voyage to Guiana," 10:487–88.

9. Sir Philip Sidney, *A Defence of Poetry*, ed. J. A. Van Dorsten (Oxford: Oxford University Press, 1966), 29.

10. Tzvetan Todorov, *The Conquest of America: The Question of the Other*, trans. Richard Howard (New York: Harper & Row, 1982), 99.

11. Mary B. Campbell, *The Witness and the Other World: Exotic European Travel Writing, 400–1600* (Ithaca: Cornell University Press, 1988), 240.

12. Keymis, "A Relation of the Second Voyage to Guiana," 10:470–71.

13. Peter N. Carroll and David W. Noble, *The Free and the Unfree: A New History of the United States* (Middlesex: Penguin Books, 1977), 42.

14. Richard Slotkin, *Regeneration Through Violence: The Mythology of the American Frontier, 1600–1860* (Middleton, Connecticut: Wesleyan University Press, 1973).

15. *The Proceedings of the English Colony in Virginia*, in *The Complete Works of Captain John Smith (1580–1631)*, ed. Philip L. Barbour, 3 vols. (Chapel Hill: University of North Carolina Press, 1986), 1:247. All subsequent references of the text are to this edition.

16. Patricia Parker, *Literary Fat Ladies: Rhetoric, Gender, Property* (London: Methuen, 1987), 126–54.

17. Parker, *Literary Fat Ladies*, 138–46.

18. Louis A. Montrose, "The Work of Gender in the Discourse of Discoverie," *Representations* 33 (1991): 34.

19. Kenneth J. E. Graham, *The Performance of Conviction: Plainness and Rhetoric in the Early English Renaissance* (Ithaca: Cornell University Press, 1994).

20. Campbell, *The Witness and the Other World*, 238.

21. Mary C. Fuller, "Ralegh's Fugitive Gold: Reference and Deferral in *The Discoverie of Guiana*," *Representations* 33 (1991): 55.

22. For a discussion of how Ralegh and other English poets handle the association of the search for gold with the greed of imperial Spain, see Knapp, *An Empire Nowhere*, 175–204.

23. Campbell, *The Witness and the Other World*, 247.

24. Montrose, "The Work of Gender," 25.

25. Montrose, "The Work of Gender," 25.

26. Montrose, "The Work of Gender," 14.

27. Stephen Greenblatt, *Sir Walter Ralegh: The Renaissance Man and His Roles* (New Haven: Yale University Press, 1973), 78–79.

28. Edmund Spenser, "Colin Clouts Come Home Againe," in *Spenser: Poetical Works*, ed. J. C. Smith and E. De Selincourt (1912; reprint, London: Oxford University Press, 1966). All subsequent references of the text are to this edition.

29. I am indebted to Stephen Greenblatt's summary of the salient features of the events that transpired in Ralegh's second voyage to Guiana in *Sir Walter Ralegh*, 99–126.

30. Greenblatt, *Sir Walter Ralegh*, 155–70.

31. Edward Edwards, ed. *The Life of Sir Walter Ralegh*, 2 vols. (London: Macmillan & Co., 1868), 2:369.

32. Edwards, *The Life of Sir Walter Ralegh*, 2:369.

33. Edwards, *The Life of Sir Walter Ralegh*, 2:369.

34. Edwards, *The Life of Sir Walter Ralegh*, 2:369.

35. Richard Wilson, *Will Power: Essays on Shakespearean Authority* (New York: Harvester Wheatsheaf, 1993), 119–20.

36. Wilson, *Will Power*, 122–23.

37. Wilson, *Will Power*, 118.

38. Jonathan Goldberg, *James I and the Politics of Literature: Jonson, Shakespeare, Donne, and Their Contemporaries* (Stanford: Stanford University Press, 1989). For a study in Elizabeth and James's contrasting use of symbols to define their particular royal identities, see especially 1–54.

39. Fuller, "Ralegh's Fugitive Gold," 42.

40. Fuller, "Ralegh's Fugitive Gold," cited on 42.

41. Fuller, "Ralegh's Fugitive Gold," 43.

42. Fuller, "Ralegh's Fugitive Gold," 44.

43. Fuller, "Ralegh's Fugitive Gold," 44.

44. Keymis, "A Relation of the Second Voyage to Guiana," 442.

45. Keymis, "A Relation of the Second Voyage to Guiana," 443.

46. George Chapman, "De Guiana, Carmen Epicum,' in *The Poems of George Chapman*, ed. Phyllis Brooks Bartlett (New York: Russell & Russell, 1962), 353–57.

47. Knapp, *An Empire Nowhere*, 193.

48. Knapp, *An Empire Nowhere*, 194.

49. Knapp, *An Empire Nowhere*, 197.

50. Montrose, "The Work of Gender," 17.

Chapter 2. "Let Us Possess One World"

1. Helgerson, *Forms of Nationhood*, 107–47.

2. Michael C. Schoenfeldt, *Prayer and Power: George Herbert and Renaissance Courtship* (Chicago: University of Chicago Press, 1991), 175.

3. Arthur F. Marotti, *John Donne, Coterie Poet* (Madison: University of Wisconsin Press, 1986), 50.

4. Marotti, *John Donne*, 50.

5. Marotti, *John Donne*, 49.

6. Achsah Guibbory, "'Oh, let mee not serve so': The Politics of Love in

Donne's *Elegies*," in *Critical Essays on John Donne* (New York: G. K. Hall & Co., 1994), 17–36.

7. Samuel Purchas, "Virginias Verger: Or a Discourse shewing the benefits which may grow to this Kingdome from American English Plantations, and especially those of Virginia and Summer Ilands," in *Hakluytus Posthumus or Purchas His Pilgrimes: Contayning a History of the World in Sea Voyages and Lande Travells by Englishmen and Others* (Glasgow: James MacLehose and Sons, Publishers to the University, 1905–7), 19: 242. All subsequent references of the text are to this edition, and will be designated as *VV.*

8. John Donne, *The Complete English Poems*, ed. A. J. Smith (1971; reprint, Middlesex: Penguin Books, 1983). All subsequent references of Donne's poetry are to this edition.

9. Cited in Campbell, *The Witness and the Other World*, 178.

10. Cited in Leslie A. Fiedler, *The Return of the Vanishing American* (1968; reprint, London: Paladin, 1972), 64.

11. Fiedler, *The Return of the Vanishing American*, 70.

12. Ann Kibbey, *The Interpretation of Material Shapes in Puritanism: A Study of Rhetoric, Prejudice, and Violence* (Cambridge: Cambridge University Press, 1986).

13. Greenblatt, *Renaissance Self-Fashioning*, 157–92.

14. The only copy of Christopher Brooke's "A Poem on the Late Massacre in Virginia," owned by A. S. W. Rosenbach, is held at the New York Public Library. The parts of Brooke's poem emphasizing that Indians are not God's creatures, and should therefore be extirpated, can be found in Stanley Johnson, "John Donne and the Virginia Company," *ELH* 14 (1947), 133 and W. Moelwyn Merchant, "Donne's Sermon to the Virginia Company, 13 November 1622," in *John Donne: Essays in Celebration*, ed. A. J. Smith (London: Methuen & Co., 1972), 442.

15. For critical commentaries on Caliban's hybrid nature, see Bernard W. Sheehan, *Savagism and Civility: Indians and Englishmen in Colonial Virginia* (Cambridge: Cambridge University Press, 1980), 84–88. It is important to note that even though much of the discourse of European perceptions of the New World in the sixteenth century was shaped by an often naive and incomplete understanding of the societies and cultures of the American natives, there existed a more sophisticated discourse. As John Hale informs us, missionary ethnographers in the sixteenth century already realized that underneath an apparently "natural way" of life could be found complex religious beliefs, laws, and codes of behavior: see *The Civilization of Europe in the Renaissance* (London: Fontana Press, 1994), 49–50. Obviously this anthropological understanding did not necessarily lead to an embracing of cultural relativism, as in Montaigne. More often than not, the recognition that New World societies possessed their own organizational structures became subordinated to the interests of missionizing activities and colonial acquisition of land. For studies of the etymologies of Caliban's name and its place in the cultural history of colonialism, see Peter Hulme, *Colonial Encounters: Europe and the Native Caribbean, 1492–1797* (New York: Methuen, 1986), 45–134; Alden T. and Virginia Mason Vaughan, *Shakespeare's Caliban: A Cultural History* (Cambridge: Cambridge University Press, 1991), 23–55; Eric Cheyfitz, *The Poetics of Imperialism: Translation and Colonization from "The Tempest" to "Tarzan"* (Oxford: Oxford University Press, 1991), 59–82.

16. James I, *A Counter-Blaste to Tobacco* (London: The Rodale Press, 1954).

17. John Donne, "A Sermon Preached to the Honourable Company of the Virginian Plantation," in *The Sermons of John Donne*, ed. Evelyn M. Simpson and

George R. Potter, 10 vols. (Berkeley and Los Angeles: University of California Press, 1953–62), 4:264–82; the citation is from 265. All subsequent references of Donne's sermons are to this edition unless otherwise stated.

18. Donne, "A Sermon Preached to the Honourable Company," 4:265–66.

19. Richard Hakluyt, *A Discourse of Western Planting*, in *The Voyages of the English Nation to America Before the Year 1600*, ed. Edmund Goldsmid, 4 vols. (Edinburgh: E. & G. Goldsmid, 1889–90), 2:175–76.

20. Donne, "A Sermon Preached to the Honourable Company," 4:269.

21. For an account of Donne's involvement in these expeditions, see John Carey, *John Donne: Life, Mind and Art* (London: Faber & Faber, 1981), especially 64–68. Carey relates this involvement to Donne's deep ambition for preferment.

22. John Donne, *Essays in Divinity*, ed. Evelyn M. Simpson (Oxford: Clarendon Press, 1952), 20.

23. John Donne, "The Second of my Prebend Sermons Upon My Five Psalmes. Preached at S. Pauls, January 29.1625," in *John Donne's Sermons on the Psalms and Gospels*, ed. Evelyn M. Simpson (Berkeley and Los Angeles: University of California Press, 1963), 112.

24. Donne, "A Sermon Preached to the Honourable Company," 4:280–81.

25. Fulke Greville, *A Dedication to Sir Philip Sidney*, in *The Prose Works of Fulke Greville, Lord Brooke*, ed. John Gouws (Oxford: Clarendon Press, 1986), 51. All subsequent references of the text are to this edition.

26. Anthony Pagden, *Lords of All the World: Ideologies of Empire in Spain, Britain and France, c. 1500-c.1800* (New Haven: Yale University Press, 1995), 76.

27. Pagden, *Lords of All the World*, 76.

28. Pagden, *Lords of All the World*, 77.

29. Donne, "A Sermon Preached to the Honourable Company," 4:274.

30. William Shakespeare, *King Henry V*, ed. T. W. Craik (London: Routledge, 1995). All subsequent references of the text are to this edition; references are to act, scene, and lines.

31. Smith, *The Proceedings of the English Colony in Virginia*, 1:269.

32. Smith, *The Proceedings of the English Colony in Virginia*, 1:259–65.

33. James I, *A Counter-Blaste to Tobacco*, 12–13.

34. Goldberg, *James I and the Politics of Literature*, 219.

35. Hulme, *Colonial Encounters*, 158.

36. Robert Gray, *A Good Speed to Virginia*, in *Illustrations of Early English Popular Literature*, ed. J. Payne Collier, 2 vols. (1863; reprint, New York: Benjamin Blom: 1966), 2:23. All subsequent references of the text are to this edition. I have also modernized the use of the long "s" to facilitate reading of Gray's text.

37. Gray, *A Good Speed to Virginia*, 2:23.

38. Gray, *A Good Speed to Virginia*, 2:23.

39. In *Things of Darkness*, Kim Hall offers a reading of the Song of Solomon as the "*Ur*-text for European renditions of blackness": see 107. Not only does this Old Testament book of the Bible furnish "an earlier model for a rhetoric of praise that dismembers women in poetic display," it also becomes "a key part of the 'typology of colonialism,' which came of age during these years of exploration": see 108. For Solomon "is both an exemplar of the sage colonial ruler and an example of the dangers of erotic entanglements with foreign women": see 108.

40. Kibbey, *The Interpretation of Material Shapes*, 87–88.

41. Hall, *Things of Darkness*, 56.

42. Hall, *Things of Darkness*, 57.

43. Cheyfitz, *The Poetics of Imperialism*, 57.

44. Cheyfitz, *The Poetics of Imperialism*, 41–82.

45. John Locke, *Second Treatise of Government*, ed. C. B. Macpherson (Indianapolis: Hackett Publishing Co., 1980), 24–25. All subsequent references of the text are to this edition.

46. Locke, *Second Treatise of Government*, 24.

47. Pagden, *Lords of All the World*, 77–78.

48. Pagden, *Lords of All the World*, cited on 77.

49. Pagden, *Lords of All the World*, cited on 35.

50. John Parker, "Religion and the Virginia Colony, 1609–10," in *The Westward Enterprise*, ed. Andrews, 269.

51. William Symonds, *Virginia. A Sermon preached at White-Chappel, in the presence of many, honourable and worshipfull, the adventurers and planters for Virginia. 25. April. 1609. Published for the benefit and use of the colony, planted, and to bee planted there, and for the advancement of their Christian purpose* (London, 1609).

52. William Crashaw, *A Sermon preached in London before the right honourable the Lord Lawarre, Lord Governour and Captaine Generall of Virginea . . . at the said Lord Generall his leave taking of England . . . and departure for Virginea, Febr. 21, 1609* (London, 1610).

53. William Bradford, *Of Plymouth Plantation: 1620–1647*, ed. Samuel Eliot Morison (New York: Alfred A. Knopf, 1970). All subsequent references of the text are to this edition.

54. Bradford, *Of Plymouth Plantation*, 114.

55. Kibbey, *The Interpretation of Material Shapes in Puritanism*, 58 and 102.

56. Andrew Marvell, "Bermudas," in *The Poems and Letters of Andrew Marvell*, ed. H. M. Margoliouth, 2 vols. (Oxford: Clarendon Press, 1971), 1 : 17–18.

57. Michael Drayton, "To the Virginian Voyage," in *The Later Renaissance in England: Nondramatic Verse and Prose, 1600–1660*, ed. Herschel Baker (Boston: Houghton Mifflin Company, 1975).

58. Sacvan Bercovitch outlines differences in perceptions of the land of the New World separating the Puritan colonists from those who settled in the American South. The Puritans understood that the New World belonged to them by divine decree, equating colonization with the progress of the saints, while the colonists of the American South never saw the land as belonging to them by reason of predestination and divine fiat. The myth of the American South was ultimately tied up with the dream of Utopia, seeking to improve imperfect human institutions; the source for this utopianism can be traced to Spanish views of the New World. Unlike the Puritans whose relationship with the old England was marked by antagonism and the spirit of separatism, the Southerner brought Europe into America. See *The Puritan Origins of the American Self* (New Haven: Yale University Press, 1975), 136–48.

59. For a detailed and excellent account of the place of violence in American mythology, and its role in the construction of American social and cultural identity, see Slotkin, *Regeneration Though Violence*.

Chapter 3. "More Faire Than Black"

1. Philip L. Barbour, *Pocahontas and Her World* (Boston: Houghton Mifflin Co., 1969), 98–111.

2. Barbour, *Pocahontas and Her World*, 112–27.

3. Barbour, *Pocahontas and Her World*, 128–37.

4. John Rolfe, "Letter of John Rolfe, 1614," in Lyon Gardiner Tyler, ed. *Narratives of Early Virginia: 1606–1625* (1946; reprint, New York: Barnes & Noble, 1966), 240. All subsequent references of the text are to this edition.

5. Rolfe, "Letter of John Rolfe," 242.

6. Rolfe, "Letter of John Rolfe," 243.

7. Hulme, *Colonial Encounters*, 147.

8. Hulme, *Colonial Encounters*, 137–73.

9. William Shakespeare, *Othello*, ed. M. R. Ridley (1958; reprint, London: Methuen, 1984). All subsequent references of the text are to this edition; references are to act, scene, and lines.

10. Eldred Jones, *Othello's Countrymen: The African in English Renaissance Drama* (Oxford: Oxford University Press, 1965), 22. For an important study of the English writing of Africa and cultural significations of blackness in early modern England, see Hall, *Things of Darkness*.

11. Hall, *Things of Darkness*, 7.

12. William Shakespeare, *Titus Andronicus*, ed. J. C. Maxwell (1953; reprint, London: Methuen, 1984). All subsequent references of the text are to this edition; references are to act, scene, and lines.

13. Jonathan Dollimore, *Sexual Dissidence: Augustine to Wilde, Freud to Foucault* (Oxford: Clarendon Press, 1991), 156.

14. Hale, *Civilization of Europe*, 41–42. For an excellent summary of the "double-think" that the Europeans brought to understanding the nature of the Moslem infidel, see 38–50. John Hale finds that unlike Africa, Asia offered much more of a challenge to the Europeans because its radically different culture compels them to reconsider the nature of European-ness.

15. For an interesting reading of the relationship between gerontological anxieties and the cultivation of anxiety as a means of exercising control over the threat posed by the unruly will, see Stephen Greenblatt, *Learning to Curse: Essays in Early Modern Culture* (New York: Routledge, 1990), 80–98.

16. According to Lawrence Stone, children in early modern England encounter an inherent problem and dilemma when they desire to be dutiful. This dilemma can be traced to the expressions of a Puritan moral theology that caused children to experience "an impossible conflict of role models. They had to try to reconcile the often incompatible demands for obedience to parental wishes on the one hand and expectations of affection in marriage on the other." See *The Family, Sex and Marriage in England, 1500–1800* (New York: Harper & Row, 1977), 137. See also 151–59, 178–91, and 195–302.

17. Patricia Parker, "Fantasies of 'Race' and 'Gender': Africa, *Othello* and Bringing to Light," in *Women, "Race," and Writing in the Early Modern Period*, ed. Margo Hendricks and Patricia Parker (New York: Routledge, 1994), 84–100.

18. Stephen Greenblatt, *Renaissance Self-Fashioning: From More to Shakespeare* (Chicago: University of Chicago Press, 1980), 242. Greenblatt's reading of the colonial motif in *Othello* points to an important aspect of the tragedy that has not been explored fully by previous readers of the text. Referring to the treachery of Spanish colonial activities in an outlying island in the Lucayas, Greenblatt argues that Othello and Iago's interaction and relationship can be interpreted in colonial terms, where Iago who possesses an amazing capacity for "empathy" is able to exercise unhindered power over the Moor. The colonial analogy analyzed by Greenblatt can benefit from a further consideration of the society that made possible the creation and production of *Othello*. Shakespeare's powerful depiction

of Othello and Iago's encounter as a dominantly colonial one owes much to literary materials available in late sixteenth- and early seventeenth-century England. In addition to such materials, there also exists an entire cultural response to the phenomenon of blackness, one shaped in part by economic considerations and Queen Elizabeth's own perception of Africans living in England.

19. Greenblatt, *Renaissance Self-Fashioning*, 245.

20. This useful phrase is employed by Parker in "Fantasies of 'Race' and 'Gender': Africa, *Othello,* and Bringing to Light."

21. Karen Newman, "'And Wash the Ethiop White': Femininity and the Monstrous in *Othello,*" in *Shakespeare Reproduced,* 141–62.

22. Thomas Rymer, "A Short View of Tragedy," in *Critical Essays of the Seventeenth Century,* ed. J. E. Spingarn, 3 vols. (Oxford: Clarendon Press, 1908–9), 2:222–23.

23. Samuel Taylor Coleridge, *Lectures and Notes on Shakespeare* (London: G. Bell and Sons, 1914), 386.

24. See Jones, *Othello's Countrymen,* 8–9. Jones tells us that Eden refers to the peoples of North and West Africa as Moors, while he refers to the peoples of Guinea as black Moors, Ethiopians, or Negroes: see 10. There is awareness in the latter half of the sixteenth century in England concerning the difference between the Moor and the blackamoor.

25. Germán Arciníegas, *Caribbean: Sea of the New World* (New York: Alfred A. Knopf, 1946), 132–34.

26. K. R. Andrews, "The English in the Caribbean, 1560–1620," in *The Westward Enterprise,* 109.

27. John Hawkins, "The Third Troublesome Voyage Made with the Jesus of Lubeck, the Minion, and Foure Other Ships, to the Parts of Guinea, and the West Indies, in the Yeeres 1567 and 1568," in Hakluyt, *The Principal Navigations,* 10:64–74.

28. Hawkins, "The Third Troublesome Voyage," 10:66–67.

29. For a history of the black presence in sixteenth- and seventeenth-century England, read Peter Fryer, *Staying Power: The History of Black People in Britain* (London: Pluto Press, 1984), chapters 1–3.

30. Michel de Montaigne, *Essays,* trans. J. M. Cohen (Middlesex: Penguin Books, 1958), 109. All subsequent references of the text are to this edition.

31. Montaigne, *Essays,* 108.

32. Hale, *The Civilization of Europe,* 41.

33. See Fryer, *Staying Power,* 10–11. This response of Elizabeth I to the subject of "Negars and Blackamoors" has also been commented upon by different critics, including Karen Newman in "And Wash the Ethiop White," 147–48; Ania Loomba in *Gender, Race, Renaissance Drama,* 43; Dollimore in *Sexual Dissidence,* 148–65; and Hall in *Things of Darkness,* 13–14 and 175–76.

34. G. B. Harrison, *A Second Elizabethan Journal: Being a Record of those Things Most Talked of During the Years 1595–1598* (London: Routledge & Kegan Paul, 1931), 109.

35. Harrison, *A Second Elizabethan Journal,* 111.

36. Cited in Fryer, *Staying Power,* 12.

37. Critical commentaries on George Best's *Discourse* are offered by Karen Newman in "And Wash the Ethiop White," 145–49; Lynda Boose in "'The Getting of a Lawful Race': Racial Discourse in Early Modern England and the Unrepresentable Black Woman," in *Women, "Race," and Writing,* 43–48; and Hall in *Things of Darkness,* 11–12 and 259–60.

38. George Best, *Discourse,* in *The Principal Navigations,* 7:261–62.

39. Best, *Discourse,* 7:263–64.

40. Best, *Discourse,* 7:264.

41. Luis Vaz de Camões, *The Lusiads,* trans. William C. Atkinson (London: Penguin Books, 1952), 126–27.

42. Hulme, *Colonial Encounters,* 161.

43. Boose, "The Getting of a Lawful Race," 35–54.

44. Boose, "The Getting of a Lawful race," 46.

45. Benedict Anderson, *Imagined Communities: Reflections on the Origin and Spread of Nationalism* (London: Verso, 1991), 149.

46. Anderson, *Imagined Communities,* 146.

47. Anderson, *Imagined Communities,* 148.

48. Boose, "The Getting of a Lawful Race," 38.

49. Hall, *Things of Darkness,* 123–28.

50. John Williams, *Lord Bishop of Lincolne, Great Britains Salomon: A Sermon Preached at the Magnificent Funerall, of the Most High and Mighty King James* (London: John Bill, 1625), 3.

51. John Donne, "Sermon Number 14," in *The Sermons of John Donne,* 6:286.

52. Goldberg, *James I and the Politics of Literature,* 215.

53. Hall, *Things of Darkness,* 128.

54. C. H. Herford and Percy and Evelyn Simpson, ed. *Ben Jonson,* 11 vols. (Oxford: Clarendon Press, 1925–52), 7:169–80. All subsequent references of the text are to this edition.

55. David Riggs offers a reading of the gender politics embedded in *The Masque of Blackness* in *Ben Jonson: A Life* (Cambridge: Harvard University Press, 1989), 118–24 and 147–48; the gesture made in the direction of affirming a kind of symbolic female autonomy in *The Masque of Blackness* finds its place in the backdrop of Jacobean court life in which Anne bitterly resented the clique of Scottish favorites who had taken over her place in the king's affections: see 123. Anne, Riggs tells us, will not hesitate to enjoy a laugh at her husband's expense: see 124. Compared to *Blackness, The Masque of Beauty* is even more pronounced in its celebration of a Platonized female sexuality. For a reading of the political significations of *The Masque of Blackness* and its sequel, *The Masque of Beauty,* enacted three years later, see also Boose, "The Getting of a Lawful Race," 49–53, and Hall, *Things of Darkness,* 128–41.

56. Kim Hall places less emphasis on the gendered and symbolic contestation implicit in the two masques because, for her, "Although Anne was the impetus for the performance of the masques, the actual power to do the impossible, to 'wash the Ethiope white,' is credited to Britain's chief poet and sun, James. . . . [T]he force behind the masque becomes the royal James, who watches a spectacle brought about by his kingly powers": see *Things of Darkness,* 135.

57. Boose, "The Getting of a Lawful Race," 53.

58. Hall, *Things of Darkness,* 133.

59. Newman, "And Wash the Ethiop White," 154.

60. For a study of the English colonists who chose, in the seventeenth century, to settle in the Caribbean islands instead of the mainland, see Dunn, *Sugar and Slaves.* Dunn reminds us that these English colonists who settled in St. Christopher (1624), Barbados (1627), Nevis (1628), Montserrat and Antigua (1630s), and Jamaica (1655) were members of the same migration as the first Chesapeake and New England colonists.

61. Maureen Quilligan, "Freedom, Service, and the Trade in Slaves: the Prob-

lem of Labor in *Paradise Lost*," in *Subject and Object in Renaissance Culture*, ed. Margreta de Grazia, Maureen Quilligan, and Peter Stallybrass (Cambridge: Cambridge University Press, 1996), 213–34; the citation is from 221.

62. Quilligan, "Freedom, Service, and the Trade in Slaves," 218–19.

63. Newman, "And Wash the Ethiop White," 153–55.

64. Dunn, *Sugar and Slaves*, 224.

CHAPTER 4. FIGURING JUSTICE

1. Edmund Spenser, *The Faerie Queene*, ed. Thomas P. Roche, Jr. (1978; reprint, London: Penguin Books, 1987). All subsequent references of the text are to this edition; reference is to book, canto, and lines.

2. See Knapp's compelling and important meditations on the subject in *An Empire Nowhere*, especially 62–133.

3. For a sympathetic view of Grey's massacre of the troops who had surrendered at Smerwick, see Renwick's commentary in his edition of Spenser's *View*, 185–87.

4. Readers have responded to the unfinished state of *The Faerie Queene* in different ways. Balachandra Rajan argues that as an "unfinished" poem, *The Faerie Queene*'s resistance to closure is a signature of its particular ontological identity. Rajan's mystification of the poem by giving it a life of its own is not totally convincing, but his summary and reading of editorial features and decisions in the 1590, 1596, and 1609 versions of the poem provide useful information on the history of its publication and development. See *The Form of the Unfinished: English Poetics from Spenser to Pound* (Princeton: Princeton University Press, 1985), 44–84. Patricia Parker relates the poem's incomplete state to the digressive mode of Spenserian allegory in *Inescapable Romance: Studies in the Poetics of a Mode* (Princeton: Princeton University Press, 1979), 54–113. Making use of poststructuralist notions of deferral, Parker argues that this mode constitutes a form of the medieval and Renaissance concept of *dilatatio*. Spenser achieves *dilation* in his romance narrative through repetition and doubling, where fragments of one episode proliferate into others.

5. Quoted by Renwick on 213.

6. We are led to wonder whether a similar disappointment is registered in the Mercilla/Duessa episode, when Spenser appears to associate Elizabeth's mercy with the virtue of a bygone age. Spenser's suggestion that mercy is displaced at the present time compromises encomium in this episode. For a detailed analysis of this disruption of encomiastic praise, see Thomas H. Cain, *Praise in "The Faerie Queene"* (Lincoln: University of Nebraska Press, 1978), 144–45. Cain's *Praise* provides a useful study of Spenser's ambiguous celebration of Elizabeth in *The Faerie Queene*.

7. For an incisive reading of the politics of Spenser's allegory in book 5 of *The Faerie Queene*, see David Norbrook, *Poetry and Politics in the English Renaissance* (London: Routledge and Kegan Paul, 1984), 109–313. In his study, Norbrook also addresses, in much more balanced fashion, the interests of recent feminist, poststructuralist, and new historicist criticism—gender politics, textual ambiguities, English imperialism.

8. See Roche's note for 5.10.8–10 in *The Faerie Queene*, 1206. See also Richard F. Hardin, *Civil Idolatry: Desacralizing and Monarchy in Spenser, Shakespeare, and Milton* (London: Associated University Presses, 1992), 111–16. Hardin describes

accurately much of the political significance of the Geryoneo allegory, identifying allusions made to the Inquisition, the Mass, and Catholic veneration of relics.

9. See Roche's note for 5.10.13 in *The Faerie Queene*, 1206.

10. Fulke Greville, *A Dedication to Sir Philip Sidney*, in *The Prose Works of Fulke Greville, Lord Brooke*, ed. John Gouws (Oxford: Clarendon Press, 1986). All subsequent references of the text are to this edition.

11. Greville, *A Dedication*, 16.

12. Greville, *A Dedication*, 16.

13. Greville, *A Dedication*, 26.

14. Greville, *A Dedication*, 54.

15. Martin Luther, "An Appeal to the Ruling Class of German Nationality as to the Amelioration of the State of Christendom," in *Martin Luther: Selections from His Writings*, ed. John Dillenberger (New York: Anchor Books, 1961), 403–85.

16. Greville, *A Dedication*, 33.

17. Greville, *A Dedication*, 28–29.

18. Maureen Quilligan, "Sidney and His Queen," in *The Historical Renaissance: New Essays on Tudor and Stuart Literature and Culture*, ed. Heather Dubrow and Richard Strier (Chicago: University of Chicago Press, 1988), 181.

19. Greville, *A Dedication*, 59–60.

20. James Nohrnberg, *The Analogy of "The Faerie Queene"* (Princeton: Princeton University Press, 1976), 362.

21. Nohrnberg, *Analogy*, 403–5.

22. Nohrnberg, *Analogy*, 379: note 183.

23. Richard A. McCabe, "The Fate of Irena: Spenser and Political Violence," in *Spenser and Ireland: An Interdisciplinary Perspective*, ed. Patricia Coughlan and introd. Nicholas Canny (Cork: Cork University Press, 1989), 109–25; the citation is from 113.

24. Ludovico Ariosto, *Orlando Furioso*, trans. Guido Waldman (1974; reprint, Oxford: Oxford University Press, 1983), 310–13. All subsequent references of the text are to this edition.

25. Ludovico Ariosto, *Orlando Furioso*, trans. Barbara Reynolds (1973; reprint, London: Penguin Books, 1975), see Introduction, especially 11–14.

26. Ariosto, *Orlando Furioso*, 155.

27. Ariosto, *Orlando Furioso*, 156.

28. Ariosto, *Orlando Furioso*, 156.

29. Ariosto, *Orlando Furioso*, 156.

30. If pastoral is employed here by Spenser to undermine rhetorically the dark world of court politics, it is complicated elsewhere, as in *The Shepheardes Calender*, to compromise the queen's symbolic identity as Eliza. See Knapp, *An Empire Nowhere*, especially 62–133.

31. Jacques Ellul, *The Technological Society*, trans. John Wilkinson and introd. Robert K. Merton (New York: Vintage Books, 1964), see especially 57–58.

32. Ellul, *The Technological Society*, vii.

33. Other reasons have been offered to explain the censorship of Spenser's *View*. Jonathan Goldberg argues that Spenser's Machiavellian analysis of Ireland revealed the darker side of a political and cultural discourse that had defined itself through the language of eternity and the myths of chivalry. See Goldberg, *James I and the Politics of Literature*, 9. Clark Hulse suggests that Spenser's perception that the Anglo-Irish posed a major obstacle to his vision of Irish colonization, aimed fundamentally at subjection and not reconciliation, was in direct conflict with Elizabeth's own view. The queen herself had counted on the Anglo-

NOTES TO CHAPTER 4

Irish to reconcile the cultures of England and Ireland. See Clark Hulse, "Spenser, Bacon, and the Myth of Power," in *The Historical Renaissance*, 329–30.

34. Louis Adrian Montrose, "The Elizabethan Subject and the Spenserian Text," in *Literary Theory/Renaissance Texts*, ed. Patricia Parker and David Quint (Baltimore: Johns Hopkins University Press, 1986), 303–40.

35. Maureen Quilligan, *Milton's Spenser: The Politics of Reading* (Ithaca: Cornell University Press, 1983), 68.

36. Francis Bacon, *The Essays*, ed. John Pitcher (London: Penguin Books, 1985): see "Of Judicature," 225.

37. M. E. Rickey and T. B. Stroup, ed. *Certaine Sermons or Homilies Appointed to be Read in Churches in the Time of Queene Elizabeth I (1547–1571)* (Gainesville: Scholars' Facsimiles and Reprints, 1968), 69–70.

38. Annabel Patterson, *Reading Between the Lines* (Madison: University of Wisconsin Press, 1993), cited on 112.

39. Spenser, *Poetical Works*, 602.

40. See Hardin's discussion of the Spenserian polity in *Civil Idolatry*, 93–101.

41. Jonathan Goldberg puts it this way: "James's complaint to Elizabeth is extraordinary because the poet's words have become the mediating terms in the struggle for power between the two monarchs—James continually wanting assurances that his mother's treason did not bar his way to the English throne, Elizabeth recalcitrantly withholding her wishes for a successor." See *James I and the Politics of Literature*, 2. Goldberg discusses at some length James's response to the Mercilla-Duessa episode and Spenser's representation of power in book 5 and *A View* in 1–17.

42. Cited in Nicholas Canny, "The Ideology of English Colonization: From Ireland to America," *William and Mary Quarterly* 30 (1973): 582.

43. For a study of the relationship between ritual dismemberment as theater and the hermeneutics of censorship, see Annabel Patterson, *Censorship and Interpretation: The Conditions of Writing and Reading in Early Modern England* (Madison: University of Wisconsin Press, 1984), esp. 52–127. For an interesting and persuasive reading of censorship and the mechanisms of control in the reign of James I, see Philip J. Finkelpearl, "'The Comedians' Liberty': Censorship of the Jacobean Stage Reconsidered," in *Renaissance Historicism: Selections From "English Literary Renaissance"*, ed. Arthur F. Kinney and Dan S. Collins (Amherst: University of Massachusetts Press, 1987), 191–206. Finkelpearl argues that, at least during the Jacobean period, the existing mechanism of censorship to control dissident expression was much less coherent and efficient than commonly accounted for. Literary writers especially never found themselves subjected to the brutal punishment of mutilation that has been meted out for the crime of "libel," the legal term used to describe the crime of speaking too freely about persons or state affairs. Finkelpearl proposes that some reasons explaining why literary writers rarely found themselves subjected to spectacles of torture include James I's ability to forgive and forget, a court that did not possess a coherent and monolithic ideology, the lack of seriousness with which those in power responded to words or actions on the stage, and a powerful noble's ability to blunt the powers of the Master of the Revels.

44. Breight, "Treason doth Never Prosper," 4.

45. For a discussion of the use of force and fraud in the Machiavellian prince's exercise of justice and law, see Jane Aptekar, *Icons of Justice: Iconography and Thematic Imagery in Book V of "The Faerie Queene"* (New York: Columbia University Press, 1969), 108–24. Aptekar also provides an interesting account of how the

emblem of the crocodile in book 5 highlights justice as an ambivalent principle in 87–107.

46. John Milton, "The Tenure of Kings and Magistrates," in *Complete Prose Works of John Milton*, ed. Don Wolfe et al, 8 vols. (New Haven: Yale University Press, 1953–82), 3:202. All subsequent references to Milton's prose works are to this edition, and will be designated as *Yale*. Reference is to volume and page.

47. This position is succinctly articulated by Greenblatt in *Renaissance Self-Fashioning*, 157–92.

48. For a study of the thematics of property, marriage, and lineage in Spenser's writings, see Louis A. Montrose, "Spenser's Domestic Domain: Poetry, Property, and the Early Modern Subject," in *Subject and Object in Renaissance Culture*, 83–130. Montrose's essay also offers an interesting reading of Spenser's understanding of "home" in the light of his social identity as a colonist and also of his inscription in the dominant patronage mode of literary production.

49. Niccolò Machiavelli, *The Prince*, trans. Peter Bondanella and Mark Musa (Oxford: Oxford University Press, 1984), 21.

50. Machiavelli, *The Prince*, 86.

51. Niccolò Machiavelli, *The Discourses*, trans. Leslie J. Walker and ed. Bernard Crick (London: Penguin, 1970), 175–77.

52. Sir Philip Sidney, *The Prose Works of Sir Philip Sidney*, ed. Albert Feuillerat, 4 vols. (Cambridge: Cambridge University Press, 1968), 3:46–50; the citations are from 49–50.

53. For an account of how Spenser's representation of Ireland in his writings, and particularly in *A View*, is marked by tensions in thought, attitude, and perspective, see Patricia Coughlan, "'Some Secret Scourge which shall by her come unto England': Ireland and Incivility in Spenser," in *Spenser and Ireland*, 46–74.

54. For a study of political violence as moral imperative and its relation to Protestant discourse in Spenser's *View*, see McCabe, "The fate of Irena," 109–25.

55. Karl S. Bottigheimer, "Kingdom and Colony: Ireland in the Westward Enterprise, 1536–1660," in *The Westward Enterprise*, ed. Andrews, 45–64; read especially 49–52.

56. Joel B. Altman, "'Vile Participation': The Amplification of Violence in the Theater of *Henry V*," *Shakespeare Quarterly* 42 (1991): 1–32.

57. Altman, "Vile Participation," cited on 10.

58. Too often, readers of the *View* find Spenser's endorsement of England's use of the sword to subdue the Irish consistent and uncompromising throughout the text. In a recent study, for example, Andrew Hadfield argues that "'The royal power of the prince' is what makes the metaphor of the sword possible; it stands as the master trope, free from the contingent nature of other analogies and representations. The 'sword' must reassert its right to rule Ireland and clear the ground for the legal reform that cannot take place without its effective sanction." See Andrew Hadfield, "Spenser, Ireland, and Sixteenth-Century Political Theory," *The Modern Language Review* 89 (1994): 1–18; my citation of Hadfield is from 5. The view expressed above misses out on important fissures in Spenser's text, fissures that draw our attention not only to the difficulties encountered in articulating a coherent colonialist program, but also to the presence of an extratextual court politics with which the *View* must engage.

59. Interestingly, Spenser understood well before Foucault that *discipline* can be enacted by the state through different social institutions. In *Discipline and Punish*, Michel Foucault writes about how the architectures of the camp, hospital, and school have served to facilitate surveillance and exercise control in the inter-

ests of the state. According to Foucault, *discipline* is "the specific technique of a power that regards individuals both as objects and as instruments of its exercise." See *Discipline and Punish: The Birth of the Prison*, trans. Alan Sheridan (New York: Random House, 1977), 170. Foucault also argues that control over detail generates real power: "A meticulous observation of detail, and at the same time a political awareness of these small things, for the control and use of men, emerge through the classical age bearing with them a whole set of techniques, a whole corpus of methods and knowledge, descriptions, plans and data": see 141. Institutions like schools and hospitals make possible the description, anatomy, documentation, and hence control and domination of the individual.

60. Machiavelli, *The Discourses*, 381–82.

61. See Note 6 above.

62. Roger Lockyer, *Tudor and Stuart Britain: 1471–1714* (New York: St. Martin's Press, 1964), 160.

63. It must be remembered that even though policies concerning the colonization of Ireland were far from crystallized in Elizabethan England, actual administration of the land took on a harshness and even brutality seldom encountered before Elizabeth's reign. Actions taken to suppress the rebellious Irish enabled the English to forge a distinct ideology of colonization, one that shaped English colonial activities in the New World at that time. See Canny, "The Ideology of English Colonization," 575–98.

64. See Renwick's commentary in his edition of Spenser's *View*, 181.

65. Lockyer, *Tudor and Stuart Britain*, 160.

66. Christopher Hibbert, *The Virgin Queene: Elizabeth I, Genius of the Golden Age* (New York: Addison-Wesley Publishing Co., 1991), 238.

67. Translations of the French letters written by Elizabeth are found in Elizabeth I, *The Letters of Queen Elizabeth*, ed. G. B. Harrison (London: Cassell & Co., 1935), 280–83.

68. [John Price?], "Walwins Wiles," in *The Leveller Tracts: 1647–1653*, ed. William Haller and Godfrey Davies (Gloucester, Massachusetts: Peter Smith, 1964), 288–89.

69. [Price?], "Walwins Wiles," 310.

70. William Walwyn, *The Compassionate Samaritan*, in *The later Renaissance in England*, 596–99. All subsequent references of the text are to this edition.

71. Walwyn, *The Compassionate Samaritan*, 597.

72. Walwyn, *The Compassionate Samaritan*, 597.

73. Michael Wilding, "Marvell's 'An Horatian Ode Upon Cromwell's Return From Ireland', The Levellers, and the Junta," *The Modern Language Review* 82 (1987): 1–14. For an interesting portrait of Marvell as a poet of radical ambiguity and instability, read Rajan, *The Form of the Unfinished*, 24–43.

74. See Willy Maley, "How Milton and Some Contemporaries Read Spenser's *View*," in *Representing Ireland: Literature and the Origins of Conflict, 1534–1660*, ed. Brendan Bradshaw, Andrew Hadfield, and Willy Maley (Cambridge: Cambridge University Press, 1993), 191–208. I wish to thank Dr. Maley for kindly sending me a copy of this essay.

75. Roger Lockyer, *Tudor and Stuart Britain*, 410–11.

CHAPTER 5. "SPACE MAY PRODUCE NEW WORLDS"

1. J. Martin Evans, *Milton's Imperial Epic: "Paradise Lost" and the Discourse of Colonialism* (Ithaca: Cornell University Press, 1996).

2. John Milton, *Paradise Lost*, in *The Complete Poems and Major Prose*, ed. Merritt Y. Hughes (Indianapolis: Bobbs Merrill, 1957). All subsequent references of Milton's poems are to this edition. Milton's major poems are abbreviated as follows: *PL—Paradise Lost, PR—Paradise Regained,* and *SA—Samson Agonistes.*

3. Evans, *Milton's Imperial Epic*, 142.

4. Evans, *Milton's Imperial Epic*, 147.

5. Evans, *Milton's Imperial Epic*, 11.

6. Evans, *Milton's Imperial Epic*, 10–11.

7. The text of *A Declaration* is taken from *The Works of John Milton*, ed. Frank Allan Patterson et al, 20 vols. (New York: Columbia University Press, 1931–38), 13:509–63.

8. Evans, *Milton's Imperial Epic*, 6.

9. Milton, *The Works of John Milton*, 13:517.

10. For an account of Las Casas's debt to Augustine's "Christian political realism" and parallels with Luther's reforming energies, see John D. Cox, *Shakespeare and the Dramaturgy of Power* (Princeton: Princeton University Press, 1989), 3–21. Las Casas, Cox argues, was unable to bring the implications and effects of his radical proposals—like liberating the Indians—into the workings of the Old World. He saw no inconsistency, for instance, when he proposed in 1516 to provide for every Spanish colonist to own black slaves.

11. Hakluyt, *Voyages of the English Nation*, 2:263.

12. Milton, *The Works of John Milton*, 13:527.

13. Milton, *The Works of John Milton*, 13:531.

14. Milton, *The Works of John Milton*, 13:555.

15. Milton, *The Works of John Milton*, 13:555.

16. Thomas N. Corns, "Milton's *Observations Upon the Articles of Peace:* Ireland Under English Eyes," in *Politics, Poetics, and Hermeneutics in Milton's Prose*, ed. David Loewenstein and James Grantham Turner (Cambridge: Cambridge University Press, 1990), 123.

17. Corns, "Milton's *Observations*," 123.

18. See *Yale* 3.303, note 9.

19. See Maley, "How Milton and Some Contemporaries Read Spenser's *View*," 191–208.

20. Quilligan, "Freedom, Service, and the Trade in Slaves," 222.

21. For a reading of Milton's representation of India as "site of infernality," see Balachandra Rajan, "Banyan Trees and Fig Leaves: Some Thoughts on Milton's India," in *Of Poetry and Politics: New Essays on Milton and His World*, ed. P. G. Stanwood (Binghamton, New York: Medieval and Renaissance Texts and Studies, 1995), 213–28.

22. For a reading of Camões's conflicted subjectivity as he attempts to subordinate Portugal's mercantile expansionism to the creation of an ideal image of the nation's heroic and nonmercantile self in the *Lusíadas*, see Helgerson, *Forms of Nationhood*, 151–91.

23. Camões, *The Lusiads*, 169.

24. Camões, *The Lusiads*, 192.

25. Quint, *Epic and Empire*, 253–67. Quint also provides an interesting discussion of the relationship existing between the writing of epic poetry and class prejudice. Linked to the ethos of aristocratic hauteur and ethics of martial heroism, the epic poem typically casts merchandising and trading activities in a negative light. Different epic poems like the *Odyssey*, the *Liberata*, and the *Lusíadas*

address the often ambivalent signification of merchant adventuring in relation to the epic narrative of martial heroics: see 248–67.

26. Christopher Hill, *The Century of Revolution: 1603–1714* (New York: W. W. Norton & Co., 1961), 145–61.

27. Christopher Hill, *Milton and the English Revolution* (New York: The Viking Press, 1977), 341–53.

28. See also Hill, *Milton and the English Revolution*, 354–412.

29. Arthur Barker, "Calm Regained through Passion Spent: The Conclusions of the Miltonic Effort," in *The Prison and the Pinnacle*, ed. Balachandra Rajan (Toronto: University of Toronto Press, 1973), 3–48; the citation is from 8. For further readings of the relationship between quietism and political activism expressed in Milton's writings, see also John R. Knott, Jr., "'Suffering for Truths sake': Milton and Martyrdom," *Politics, Poetics, and Hermeneutics in Milton's Prose*, 153–70; Joan S. Bennett, *Reviving Liberty: Radical Christian Humanism in Milton's Great Poems* (Cambridge: Harvard University Press, 1989); and David Quint, "David's Census: Milton's Politics and *Paradise Regained*," *Re-membering Milton: Essays of the Texts and Traditions*, ed. Mary Nyquist and Margaret W. Ferguson (New York: Methuen, 1988), 128–47.

30. For a study of plainness as rhetoric in different domains—political, epistemological, psychological, and theological—see Graham, *The Performance of Conviction*. Graham's study also offers a cogent analysis of the place of plainness in Reformation thought and poetics.

31. Lawrence Lipking, "The Genius of the Shore: Lycidas, Adamastor, and the Poetics of Nationalism," *PMLA* 111 (1996): 205–221; the citation is from 205.

32. Hill, *Milton and the English Revolution*, 341–53.

33. Michael Fixler, *Milton and the Kingdoms of God* (London: Faber and Faber, 1964), 265–66.

34. Quint, *Epic and Empire*, 3–10.

35. Barbara Kiefer Lewalski, *"Paradise Lost" and the Rhetoric of Literary Forms* (Princeton: Princeton University Press, 1985), 58–59.

36. For another discussion that arrives at similar conclusions, see Quint, *Epic and Empire*, 248–67. In this chapter, "Tasso, Milton, and the Boat of Romance," Quint also offers a useful reading on the significations of boats and the journey motif in relation to Renaissance experience of mercantile ventures and voyages of discovery.

37. Paul Yachnin, "'Courtiers of Beauteous Freedom': *Antony and Cleopatra* in Its Time," *Renaissance and Reformation* 26 (1991): 9–10. I wish to thank Professor Yachnin for sending me a copy of his essay.

38. Stevie Davies, *Images of Kingship in "Paradise Lost": Milton's Politics and Christian Liberty* (Columbia: University of Missouri Press, 1983), especially 111–12.

39. Philip R. Hardie, *Virgil's "Aeneid": "Cosmos" and "Imperium"* (Oxford: Clarendon Press, 1986), 241–92.

40. Hardie, *Virgil's "Aeneid"*, 353.

41. Northrop Frye, *The Great Code: The Bible and Literature* (Toronto: Academic Press Canada, 1982), 80–81.

42. Francis Bacon, *The Advancement of Learning*, ed. G. W. Kitchin (London: J. M. Dent & Sons, 1973), 9. All subsequent references of the text are to this edition.

43. Bacon, *Advancement*, 48.

44. Francis Bacon, *The Essays*, ed. John Pitcher (London: Penguin Books, 1985), 149. All subsequent references of the text are to this edition.

45. Bacon, *Essays*, 153.
46. Bacon, *Essays*, 153.
47. Bacon, *Essays*, 151.
48. Bacon, *Essays*, 151.
49. David S. Shields, *Oracles of Empire: Poetry, Politics, and Commerce in British America, 1690–1750* (Chicago: University of Chicago Press, 1990), 15.
50. For Milton's attitudes toward the subject of war, see James A. Freeman, *Milton and the Martial Muse: "Paradise Lost" and European Traditions of War* (Princeton: Princeton University Press, 1980).
51. Bacon, *Essays*, 150.
52. Machiavelli, *The Discourses*, 281–88.
53. See Bacon's "Of Simulation and Dissimulation" in *Essays*, 76–78.
54. For a reading of Samson's highly ambivalent status in seventeenth-century England, see Joseph Wittreich, *Interpreting "Samson Agonistes"* (Princeton: Princeton University Press, 1986).
55. See Christopher Hill, *The Experience of Defeat: Milton and Some Contemporaries* (New York: Viking Penguin, 1984), 70–71; N. H. Keeble, *The Literary Culture of Nonconformity in Later Seventeenth-Century England* (Athens: University of Georgia Press, 1987); and Gerald R. Cragg, *Puritanism in the Period of the Great Persecution: 1660–1688* (Cambridge: Cambridge University Press, 1957), especially 66–87.
56. Hill, *The Experience of Defeat*, 71–72. If some regicides clung to their millenarian hopes, other former millenarians gave them up. See also *The Collected Essays*, 2:233–34.
57. Hill, *The Experience of Defeat*, 72–74.
58. Jonas Barish, *The Antitheatrical Prejudice* (Berkeley and Los Angeles: University of California Press, 1981), 166.
59. For studies of the place of figures and typology in Milton's poetry and in Protestant poetics, see Hugh MacCallum, "Milton and Sacred History: Books XI and XII of *Paradise Lost*," *Essays in English Literature from the Renaissance to the Victorian Age*, eds. Millar MacLure and F. W. Watt (Toronto: University of Toronto Press, 1964), 149–68; Barbara Kiefer Lewalski, *Protestant Poetics and the Seventeenth-Century Religious Lyric* (Princeton: Princeton University Press, 1979), 72–144; and Ira Clark, *Christ Revealed: The History of the Neotypological Lyric in the English Renaissance*, University of Florida Monographs, Humanities no. 51 (Gainesville: University Press of Florida, 1982).
60. Paul Stevens, "'Leviticus Thinking' and the Rhetoric of Early Modern Colonialism," *Criticism* 35 (1993): 441–61. I wish to thank Professor Stevens for sending me a copy of this article.
61. Stevens, "Leviticus Thinking," 458. For a consideration of the contribution of Wisdom literature toward the construction of a colonial rhetoric, see also Paul Stevens, "Spenser and Milton on Ireland: Civility, Exclusion, and the Politics of Wisdom," *Ariel* 26 (1995): 151–67.
62. In *Tetrachordon*, Milton writes that "fornication" carries a meaning similar to that of "idolatry": there he interprets "fornication" as disobedience, distrust, and mental disaffection. Milton's definition resembles Augustine's in the *Confessions*, where "fornication" is seen as sexual on one level: "Clouds of muddy carnal concupiscence,' "the bubbling impulses of puberty," "lust's darkness," "precipitous rocks of desire," "a whirlpool of vice." See St. Augustine, *Confessions*, trans. Henry Chadwick (Oxford: Oxford University Press, 1992), 24. But for Augustine, "fornication" is also used as a metaphor for the soul's turning away

from God: "So the soul fornicates" (Ps. 72:27) when it is turned away from you and seeks outside you the pure and clear intentions which are not to be found except by returning to you": see 32. Like Augustine, Milton transforms "fornication" into a generic labeling for the dislocated relationship between man and God. He appears to have constructed this metaphor based on an elaborate account of "The Folly and Evil Effects of Idolatry" (ch. 14:1–31) in *The Wisdom of Solomon*, and specifically on its twelfth verse: "For the devising of idols is the beginning of fornication, and the invention of them the corruption of life": W. O. E. Oesterley, ed., *The Wisdom of Solomon* (New York: Macmillan, 1918), 71.

63. Northrop Frye, *Spiritus Mundi: Essays on Literature, Myth, and Society* (Bloomington: Indiana University Press, 1976), 222–23.

Works Cited

Altman, Joel B. "'Vile Participation': The Amplification of Violence in the Theater of *Henry V*." *Shakespeare Quarterly* 42 (1991):1–32.

Anderson, Benedict. *Imagined Communities: Reflections on the Origin and Spread of Nationalism.* London: Verso, 1991.

Andrews, Kenneth R. *Drake's Voyages: A Re-Assessment of Their Place in Elizabethan Maritime Expansion.* London: Weidenfeld and Nicolson, 1967.

———. "The English in the Caribbean, 1560–1620." In *The Westward Enterprise: English Activities in Ireland, the Atlantic, and America 1480–1650.* Edited by K. R. Andrews, N. P. Canny, and P. E. H. Hair, 103–23. Detroit: Wayne State University Press, 1979.

Aptekar, Jane. *Icons of Justice: Iconography and Thematic Imagery in Book V of "The Faerie Queene".* New York: Columbia University Press, 1969.

Arciniegas, Germán. *Caribbean: Sea of the New World.* New York: Alfred A. Knopf, 1946.

Ariosto, Ludovico. *Orlando Furioso.* Translated by Barbara Reynolds. 1973. Reprint. London: Penguin Books, 1975.

———. *Orlando Furioso.* Translated by Guido Waldman. 1974. Reprint. Oxford: Oxford University Press, 1983.

Bacon, Francis. *The Advancement of Learning.* Edited by G. W. Kitchin. London: J. M. Dent & Sons, 1973.

———. *The Essays.* Edited by John Pitcher. London: Penguin Books, 1985.

Barbour, Philip L. *Pocahontas and Her World.* Boston: Houghton Mifflin Co., 1969.

Barish, Jonas. *The Antitheatrical Prejudice.* Berkeley and Los Angeles: University of California Press, 1981.

Barker, Arthur. "Calm Regained through Passion Spent: The Conclusions of the Miltonic Effort." In *The Prison and the Pinnacle.* Edited by Balachandra Rajan, 3–48. Toronto: University of Toronto Press, 1973.

Bennett, Joan S. *Reviving Liberty: Radical Christian Humanism in Milton's Great Poems.* Cambridge: Harvard University Press, 1989.

Bercovitch, Sacvan. *The Puritan Origins of the American Self.* New Haven: Yale University Press, 1975.

Best, George. *Discourse.* Vol. 7 of *The Principal Navigations, Voyages, Traffiques & Discoveries of the English Nation.* Compiled by Richard Hakluyt. 12 vols. Glasgow: James MacLehose and Sons, Publishers to the University, 1903–5.

Boose, Lynda E. "'The Getting of a Lawful Race': Racial Discourse in Early Modern England and the Unrepresentable Black Woman." In *Women, 'Race,'*

261

and Writing in the Early Modern Period. Edited by Margo Hendricks and Patricia Parker, 35–54. London: Routledge, 1994.

Bottigheimer, Karl S. "Kingdom and Colony: Ireland in the Westward Enterprise, 1536–1660." In *The Westward Enterprise: English Activities in Ireland, the Atlantic, and America 1480–1650.* Edited by K. R. Andrews, N. P. Canny, and P. E. H. Hair, 45–64. Detroit: Wayne State University Press, 1979.

Bradford, William. *Of Plymouth Plantation: 1620–1647.* Edited by Samuel Eliot Morison. New York: Alfred A. Knopf, 1970.

Breight, Curt. "'Treason Doth Never Prosper': *The Tempest* and the Discourse of Treason." *Shakespeare Quarterly* 41 (1990): 1–28.

Brown, Paul. "'This Thing of Darkness I Acknowledge Mine': *The Tempest* and the Discourse of Colonialism." In *Political Shakespeare: New Essays in Cultural Materialism.* Edited by Jonathan Dollimore and Alan Sinfield, 48–71. Manchester: Manchester University Press, 1985.

Cain, Thomas H. *Praise in "The Faerie Queene".* Lincoln: University of Nebraska Press, 1978.

Camões, Luis Vaz de. *The Lusiads.* Translated by William C. Atkinson. London: Penguin Books, 1952.

Campbell, Mary B. *The Witness and the Other World: Exotic European Travel Writing, 400–1600.* Ithaca: Cornell University Press, 1988.

Canny, Nicholas. "The Ideology of English Colonization: From Ireland to America." *William and Mary Quarterly* 30 (1973): 575–98.

Carey, John. *John Donne: Life, Mind and Art.* London: Faber & Faber, 1981.

Carroll, Peter N., and David W. Noble. *The Free and the Unfree: A New History of the United States.* Middlesex: Penguin Books, 1977.

Cartelli, Thomas. "Prospero in Africa: *The Tempest* as Colonialist Text and Pre-text." In *Shakespeare Reproduced: The Text in History and Ideology.* Edited by Jean E. Howard and Marion F. O'Connor, 99–115. New York: Methuen, 1987.

Cheyfitz, Eric. *The Poetics of Imperialism: Translation and Colonization from "The Tempest" to "Tarzan".* Oxford: Oxford University Press, 1991.

Clark, Ira. *Christ Revealed: The History of the Neotypological Lyric in the English Renaissance.* University of Florida Monographs, Humanities No. 51. Gainesville: University Press of Florida, 1982.

Coleridge, Samuel Taylor. *Lectures and Notes on Shakespeare.* London: G. Bell & Sons, 1914.

Corns, Thomas N. "Milton's *Observations Upon the Articles of Peace:* Ireland Under English Eyes." In *Politics, Poetics, and Hermeneutics in Milton's Prose.* Edited by David Loewenstein and James Grantham Turner, 123–34. Cambridge: Cambridge University Press, 1990.

Coughlan, Patricia. "'Some Secret Scourge which shall by her come unto England': Ireland and Incivility in Spenser." In *Spenser and Ireland: An Interdisciplinary Perspective.* Edited by Patricia Coughlan and Introduced by Nicholas Canny, 46–74. Cork: Cork University Press, 1989.

Cox, John D. *Shakespeare and the Dramaturgy of Power.* Princeton: Princeton University Press, 1989.

Cragg, Gerald R. *Puritanism in the Period of the Great Persecution: 1660–1688.* Cambridge: Cambridge University Press, 1957.

Crashaw, William. *A Sermon preached in London before the right honorable the Lord*

Lawarre, Lord Governour and Captaine Generall of Virginea . . . at the said Lord Generall his leave taking of England . . . and departure for Virginea, Febr. 21, 1609. London, 1610.

Davies, Stevie. *Images of Kingship in "Paradise Lost": Milton's Politics and Christian Liberty.* Columbia: University of Missouri Press, 1983.

Dollimore, Jonathan. *Sexual Dissidence: Augustine to Wilde, Freud to Foucault.* Oxford: Clarendon Press, 1991.

Donne, John. *The Complete English Poems.* Edited by A. J. Smith. 1971. Reprint. Middlesex: Penguin Books, 1983.

———. *Essays in Divinity.* Edited by Evelyn M. Simpson. Oxford: Clarendon Press, 1952.

———. "A Sermon Preached to the Honourable Company of the Virginian Plantation." Vol. 4 of *The Sermons of John Donne.* Edited by Evelyn M. Simpson and George R. Potter. 10 vols. Berkeley and Los Angeles: University of California Press, 1953–62.

———. "Sermon Number 14." Vol. 6 of *The Sermons of John Donne.* Edited by Evelyn M. Simpson and George R. Potter. 10 vols. Berkeley and Los Angeles: University of California Press, 1953–62.

———. "The Second of my Prebend Sermons Upon My Five Psalmes. Preached at S. Pauls, January 29. 1625." In *John Donne's Sermons on the Psalms and Gospels.* Edited by Evelyn M. Simpson. Berkeley and Los Angeles: University of California Press, 1963.

Drayton, Michael. "To the Virginian Voyage." In *The Later Renaissance in England: Nondramatic Verse and Prose, 1600–1660.* Edited by Herschel Baker. Boston: Houghton Mifflin Company, 1975.

Dunn, Richard S. *Sugar and Slaves: The Rise of the Planter Class in the English West Indies, 1624–1713.* Chapel Hill: University of North Carolina Press, 1972.

Elizabeth I. *The Letters of Queen Elizabeth.* Edited by G. B. Harrison. London: Cassell & Co., 1935.

Ellul, Jacques. *The Technological Society.* Translated by John Wilkinson and Introduced by Robert K. Merton. New York: Vintage Books, 1964.

Evans, Martin J. *Milton's Imperial Epic: "Paradise Lost" and the Discourse of Colonialism.* Ithaca: Cornell University Press, 1996.

Fiedler, Leslie A. *The Return of the Vanishing American.* 1968. Reprint. London: Paladin, 1972.

Finkelpearl, Philip J. "'The Comedians' Liberty': Censorship of the Jacobean Stage Reconsidered." In *Renaissance Historicism: Selections From "English Literary Renaissance".* Edited by Arthur F. Kinney and Dan S. Collins, 191–206. Amherst: University of Massachussetts Press, 1987.

Fixler, Michael. *Milton and the Kingdoms of God.* London: Faber and Faber, 1964.

Foucault, Michel. *Discipline and Punish: The Birth of the Prison.* Translated by Alan Sheridan. New York: Random House, 1977.

Freeman, James A. *Milton and the Martial Muse: "Paradise Lost" and European Traditions of War.* Princeton: Princeton University Press, 1980.

Frye, Northrop. *Spiritus Mundi: Essays on Literature, Myth, and Society.* Bloomington: Indiana University Press, 1976.

———. *The Great Code: The Bible and Literature.* Toronto: Academic Press Canada, 1981.

Fryer, Peter. *Staying Power: The History of Black People in Britain.* London: Pluto Press, 1984.

Fuller, Mary C. "Ralegh's Fugitive Gold: Reference and Deferral in *The Discoverie of Guiana.*" *Representations* 33 (1991): 42–64.

Goldberg, Jonathan. *James I and the Politics of Literature: Jonson, Shakespeare, Donne, and Their Contemporaries.* Stanford: Stanford University Press, 1989.

Graham, Kenneth J. E. *The Performance of Conviction: Plainness and Rhetoric in the Early English Renaissance.* Ithaca: Cornell University Press, 1994.

Gray, Robert. *A Good Speed to Virginia.* Vol. 2 of *Illustrations of Early English Popular Literature.* Edited by J. Payne Collier. 2 vols. 1863. Reprint. New York: Benjamin Blom, 1966.

Greenblatt, Stephen. *Sir Walter Ralegh: The Renaissance Man and His Roles.* New Haven: Yale University Press, 1973.

———. *Renaissance Self-Fashioning: From More to Shakespeare.* Chicago: University of Chicago Press, 1980.

———. *Shakespearean Negotiations: The Circulation of Social Energy in Renaissance England.* Berkeley and Los Angeles: University of California Press, 1988.

———. *Learning to Curse: Essays in Early Modern Culture.* New York: Routledge, 1990.

———. *Marvelous Possessions: The Wonder of the New World.* Chicago: University of Chicago Press, 1991.

Greville, Fulke. *A Dedication to Sir Philip Sidney.* In *The Prose Works of Fulke Greville, Lord Brooke.* Edited by John Gouws. Oxford: Clarendon Press, 1986.

Guibbory, Achsah. "'Oh, let mee not serve so': The Politics of Love in Donne's *Elegies.*" In *Critical Essays on John Donne.* Edited by Arthur F. Marotti, 17–36. New York: G. K. Hall & Co., 1994.

Hadfield, Andrew. "Spenser, Ireland, and Sixteenth-Century Political Theory." *The Modern Language Review* 89 (1994): 1–18.

Hakluyt, Richard. *A Discourse of Western Planting.* Vol. 2 of *The Voyages of the English Nation to America Before the Year 1600.* Edited by Edmund Goldsmid. 4 vols. Edinburgh: E. & G. Goldsmid, 1889–90.

———. *The Principal Navigations, Voyages, Traffiques & Discoveries of the English Nation.* 12 vols. Glasgow: James MacLehose and Sons, Publishers to the University, 1903–5.

Hale, John. *The Civilization of Europe in the Renaissance.* London: Fontana Press, 1994.

Hall, Kim F. *Things of Darkness: Economies of Race and Gender in Early Modern England.* Ithaca: Cornell University Press, 1995.

Halpern, Richard. "The Lyric in the Field of Information: Autopoiesis and History in Donne's *Songs and Sonnets.*" In *Critical Essays on John Donne.* Edited by Arthur F. Marotti, 49–76. New York: G. K. Hall & Co., 1994.

Hardie, Philip R. *Virgil's "Aeneid": "Cosmos" and "Imperium".* Oxford: Clarendon Press, 1986.

Hardin, Richard F. *Civil Idolatry: Desacralizing and Monarchy in Spenser, Shakespeare, and Milton.* London: Associated University Presses, 1992.

Harrison, G. B. *A Second Elizabethan Journal: Being a Record of those Things Most Talked of During the Years 1595–1598.* London: Routledge & Kegan Paul, 1931.

Hawkins, John. "The Third Troublesome Voyage Made with the Jesus of Lubeck, the Minion, and Foure Other Ships, to the Parts of Guinea, and the West Indies, in the Yeeres 1567 and 1568." Vol. 10 of *The Principal Navigations, Voyages, Traffiques & Discoveries of the English Nation*. Compiled by Richard Hakluyt. 12 vols. Glasgow: James MacLehose and Sons, Publishers to the University, 1903–5.

Helgerson, Richard. *Forms of Nationhood: The Elizabethan Writing of England*. Chicago: University of Chicago Press, 1992.

Hibbert, Christopher. *The Virgin Queene: Elizabeth I, Genius of the Golden Age*. New York: Addison-Wesley Publishing Co., 1991.

Hill, Christopher. *The Cer ury of Revolution: 1603–1714*. New York: W. W. Norton & Co., 1961.

———. *Milton and the English Revolution*. New York: The Viking Press, 1977.

———. *The Experience of Defeat: Milton and Some Contemporaries*. New York: Viking Penguin, 1984.

———. *The Collected Essays of Christopher Hill*. 3 vols. Amherst: University of Massachusetts Press, 1985.

Hulme, Peter. *Colonial Encounters: Europe and the Native Caribbean, 1492–1797*. New York: Methuen, 1986.

Hulse, Clark, "Spenser, Bacon, and the Myth of Power." In *The Historical Renaissance: New Essays on Tudor and Stuart Literature and Culture*. Edited by Heather Dubrow and Richard Strier, 315–46. Chicago: University of Chicago Press, 1988.

Johnson, Stanley. "John Donne and the Virginia Company." *ELH* 14 (1947): 127–38.

James I. *A Counter-Blaste to Tobacco*. London: The Rodale Press, 1954.

Jones, Eldred. *Othello's Countrymen: The African in English Renaissance Drama*. London: Oxford University Press, 1965.

Jonson, Ben. *Ben Jonson*. Edited by C. H. Herford, and Percy and Evelyn Simpson. 11 vols. Oxford: Clarendon Press, 1925–52.

Jonson, Ben. *Three Comedies*. Edited by Michael Jamieson. London: Penguin Books, 1966.

———, Chapman, George, and Marston, John. *Eastward Ho!*. Edited by C. G. Petter. London: Ernest Benn, 1973.

Keymis, Laurence. "A Relation of the Second Voyage to Guiana, Performed and Written in the Yeere 1596." Vol. 10 of *The Principal Navigations, Voyages, Traffiques & Discoveries of the English Nation*. Compiled by Richard Hakluyt. 12 vols. Glasgow: James MacLehose and Sons, Publishers to the University, 1903–5.

Keeble, N. H. *The Literary Culture of Nonconformity in Later Seventeenth-Century England*. Athens: University of Georgia Press, 1987.

Kibbey, Ann. *The Interpretation of Material Shapes in Puritanism: A Study of Rhetoric, Prejudice, and Violence*. Cambridge: Cambridge University Press, 1986.

Knapp, Jeffrey. *An Empire Nowhere: England, America, and Literature from "Utopia" to "The Tempest"*. Berkeley and Los Angeles: University of California Press, 1992.

Knott, Jr., John R. "'Suffering for Truths Sake': Milton and Martyrdom." In *Politics, Poetics, and Hermeneutics in Milton's Prose*. Edited by David Loewenstein and James Grantham Turner, 153–70. Cambridge: Cambridge University Press, 1990.

Kott, Jan. *The Bottom Translation: Marlowe and Shakespeare and the Carnival Tradition.* Translated by Daniela Miedzyrzecka and Lillian Vallee. Evanston, Illinois: Northwestern University Press, 1987.

Lewalski, Barbara Kiefer. *Protestant Poetics and the Seventeenth-Century Religious Lyric.* Princeton: Princeton University Press, 1979.

———. *"Paradise Lost" and the Rhetoric of Literary Forms.* Princeton: Princeton University Press, 1985.

Lipking, Lawrence. "The Genius of the Shore: Lycidas, Adamastor, and the Poetics of Nationalism." *PMLA* 111 (1996): 205–221.

Locke, John. *Second Treatise of Government.* Edited by C. B. Macpherson. Indianapolis: Hackett Publishing Co., 1980.

Lockyer, Roger. *Tudor and Stuart Britain: 1471–1714.* New York: St. Martin's Press, 1964.

Loomba, Ania. *Gender, Race, Renaissance Drama.* Manchester: Manchester University Press, 1989.

Luther, Martin. "An Appeal to the Ruling Class of German Nationality as to the Amelioration of the State of Christendom." In *Martin Luther: Selections from His Writings.* Edited by John Dillenberger. New York: Anchor Books, 1961.

MacCallum, Hugh. "Milton and Sacred History: Books XI and XII of *Paradise Lost.*" In *Essays in English Literature from the Renaissance to the Victorian Age.* Edited by Millar MacLure and F. W. Watt, 149–68. Toronto: University of Toronto Press, 1964.

Machiavelli, Niccolò. *The Discourses.* Translated by Leslie J. Walker and Edited by Bernard Crick. London: Penguin, 1970.

———. *The Prince.* Translated by Peter Bondanella and Mark Musa. Oxford: Oxford University Press, 1984.

Maley, Willy. "How Milton and Some Contemporaries Read Spenser's *View.*" In *Representing Ireland: Literature and the Origins of Conflict 1534–1660.* Edited by Brendan Bradshaw, Andrew Hadfield, and Willy Maley, 191–208. Cambridge: Cambridge University Press, 1993.

Marotti, Arthur F. *John Donne, Coterie Poet.* Madison: University of Wisconsin Press, 1986.

Marvell, Andrew. "Bermudas." Vol. 1 of *The Poems and Letters of Andrew Marvell.* Edited by H. M. Margoliouth. 2 vols. Oxford: Clarendon Press, 1971.

McCabe, Richard A. "The Fate of Irena: Spenser and Political Violence." In *Spenser and Ireland: An Interdisciplinary Perspective.* Edited by Patricia Coughlan and Introduced by Nicholas Canny. Cork: Cork University Press, 1989.

Merchant, W. Moelwyn. "Donne's Sermon to the Virginia Company, 13 November 1622." In *John Donne: Essays in Celebration.* Edited by A. J. Smith, 433–52. London: Methuen & Co., 1972.

Milton, John. *The Complete Poems and Major Prose.* Edited by Merritt Y. Hughes. Indianapolis: Bobbs Merrill, 1957.

———. *A Declaration of His Highness, by the Advice of His Council; Setting Forth, on the Behalf of This Commonwealth, the Justice of Their Cause Against Spain.* Vol. 13 of *The Works of John Milton.* Edited by Frank Allan et al. 20 vols. New York: Columbia University Press, 1931–38.

------. *Complete Prose Works of John Milton*. Edited by Don Wolfe et al. 8 vols. New Haven: Yale University Press, 1953–82.

Moisan, Thomas. "'Which is the Merchant Here? And which the Jew?': Subversion and Recuperation in *The Merchant of Venice*." In *Shakespeare Reproduced: The Text in History and Ideology*. Edited by Jean E. Howard and Marion F. O'Connor, 188–206. New York: Methuen, 1987.

Montaigne, Michel de. *Essays*. Translated by J. M. Cohen. Middlesex: Penguin Books, 1958.

Montrose, Louis A. "The Elizabethan Subject and the Spenserian Text." In *Literary Theory/Renaissance Texts*. Edited by Patricia Parker and David Quint, 303–40. Baltimore: Johns Hopkins University Press, 1986.

------. "The Work of Gender in the Discourse of Discoverie." *Representations* 33 (1991): 1–41.

------. "Spenser's Domestic Domain: Poetry, Property, and the Early Modern Subject." In *Subject and Object in Renaissance Culture*. Edited by Margreta de Grazia, Maureen Quilligan, and Peter Stallybrass, 83–130. Cambridge: Cambridge University Press, 1996.

Newman, Karen. "'And Wash the Ethiop White': Femininity and the Monstrous in *Othello*." In *Shakespeare Reproduced: The Text in History and Ideology*. Edited by Jean E. Howard and Marion F. O'Connor, 141–62. New York: Methuen, 1987.

Nixon, Rob. "Caribbean and African Appropriations of *The Tempest*." *Critical Inquiry* 13 (1987): 557–78.

Nohrnberg, James. *The Analogy of "The Faerie Queene"*. Princeton: Princeton University Press, 1976.

Norbrook, David. *Poetry and Politics in the English Renaissance*. London: Routledge and Kegan Paul, 1984.

Oesterley, W. O. E., ed. *The Wisdom of Solomon*. New York: Macmillan, 1918.

Pagden, Anthony. *Lords of All the World: Ideologies of Empire in Spain, Britain and France, c. 1500–c.1800*. New Haven: Yale University Press, 1995.

Parker, John. "Religion and the Virginia Colony, 1609–10." In *The Westward Enterprise: English Activities in Ireland, the Atlantic, and America 1480–1650*. Edited by K. R. Andrews, N. P. Canny, and P. E. H. Hair, 245–70. Detroit: Wayne State University Press, 1979.

Parker, Patricia. *Inescapable Romance: Studies in the Poetics of a Mode*. Princeton: Princeton University Press, 1979.

------. *Literary Fat Ladies: Rhetoric, Gender, Property*. London: Methuen, 1987.

------. "Fantasies of 'Race' and 'Gender': Africa, *Othello* and Bringing to Light." In *Women, 'Race,' and Writing in the Early Modern Period*. Edited by Margo Hendricks and Patricia Parker, 84–100. New York: Routledge, 1994.

Patterson, Annabel. *Censorship and Interpretation: The Conditions of Writing and Reading in Early Modern England*. Madison: University of Wisconsin Press, 1984.

------. *Reading Between the Lines*. Madison: University of Wisconsin Press, 1993.

Penrose, Boies. *Travel and Discovery in the Renaissance*. Cambridge: Harvard University Press, 1952.

[Price, John?] "Walwins Wiles." In *The Leveller Tracts: 1647–1653*. Edited by William Haller and Godfrey Davies. Gloucester, Massachusetts: Peter Smith, 1964.

Purchas, Samuel. "Virginias Verger: Or a Discourse shewing the benefits which may grow to this Kingdome from American English Plantations, and especially those of Virginia and Summer Ilands." Vol. 19 of *Hakluytus Posthumus or Purchas His Pilgrimes: Contayning a History of the World in Sea Voyages and Lande Travells by Englishmen and Others*. 20 vols. Glasgow: James MacLehose and Sons, Publishers to the University, 1905–7.

Quilligan, Maureen. *Milton's Spenser: The Politics of Reading*. Ithaca: Cornell University Press, 1983.

————. "Sidney and His Queen." *The Historical Renaissance: New Essays on Tudor and Stuart Literature and Culture*. Edited by Heather Dubrow and Richard Strier, 171–96. Chicago: University of Chicago Press, 1988.

————. "Freedom, Service, and the Trade in Slaves: the Problem of Labor in *Paradise Lost*." In *Subject and Object in Renaissance Culture*. Edited by Margreta de Grazia, Maureen Quilligan, and Peter Stallybrass, 213–34. Cambridge: Cambridge University Press, 1996.

Quint, David. *Epic and Empire: Politics and Generic Form from Virgil to Milton*. Princeton: Princeton University Press, 1993.

————. "David's Census: Milton's Politics and *Paradise Regained*." *Re-membering Milton: Essays of the Texts and Traditions*. Edited by Mary Nyquist and Margaret W. Ferguson, 128–47. New York: Methuen & Co., 1988.

Rajan, Balachandra. *The Form of the Unfinished: English Poetics from Spenser to Pound*. Princeton: Princeton University Press, 1985.

————. "Banyan Trees and Fig Leaves: Some Thoughts on Milton's India." In *Of Poetry and Politics: New Essays on Milton and His World*. Edited by P. G. Stanwood, 213–28. Binghamton, New York: Medieval and Renaissance Texts and Studies, 1995.

Ralegh, Sir Walter. "The Discoverie of the large, rich, and beautifull Empire of Guiana, with a relation of the great and golden citie of Manoa (which the Spaniards call El Dorado) and the provinces of Emeria, Aromaia, Amapaia, and other countries, with their rivers adjoyning." Vol. 10 of *The Principal Navigations, Voyages, Traffiques & Discoveries of the English Nation*. Compiled by Richard Hakluyt. 12 vols. Glasgow: James MacLehose and Sons, Publishers to the University, 1903–5.

————. *The Poems of Sir Walter Ralegh*. Edited by Agnes M. C. Latham. London: Constable & Co., 1929.

Rickey, M. E., and Stroup, T. B., ed. *Certaine Sermons or Homilies Appointed to be Read in Churches in the Time of Queene Elizabeth I (1547–1571)*. Gainesville: Scholars Facsimiles and Reprints, 1968.

Riggs, David. *Ben Jonson: A Life*. Cambridge: Harvard University Press, 1989.

Rolfe, John. "Letter of John Rolfe, 1614." In *Narratives of Early Virginia: 1606–1625*. 1946. Reprint. New York: Barnes & Noble, 1966.

Rymer, Thomas. "A Short View of Tragedy." Vol. 2 of *Critical Essays of the Seventeenth Century*. Edited J. E. Spingarn. 3 vols. Oxford: Clarendon Press, 1908–9.

St. Augustine. *Confessions*. Translated by Henry Chadwick. Oxford: Oxford University Press, 1992.

Schoenfeldt, Michael C. *Prayer and Power: George Herbert and Renaissance Courtship*. Chicago: University of Chicago Press, 1991.

Shakespeare, William. *Titus Andronicus*. Edited by J. C. Maxwell. 1953. Reprint. London: Methuen, 1984.

————. *The Tempest.* Edited by Frank Kermode. 1954. Reprint. London: 1984.

————. *The Merchant of Venice.* Edited by John Russell Brown. 1955. Reprint. London: Methuen, 1984.

————. *Othello.* Edited by M. R. Ridley. 1958. Reprint. London: Methuen, 1984.

————.*King Henry V.* Edited by T. W. Craik. London: Routledge, 1995.

Shammas, Carole. "English Commercial Development and American Colonization, 1560–1620." In *The Westward Enterprise: English Activities in Ireland, the Atlantic, and America 1480–1650.* Edited by K. R. Andrews, N. P. Canny, and P. E. H. Hair, 151–74. Detroit: Wayne State University Press, 1979.

Sheehan, Bernard W. *Savagism and Civility: Indians and Englishmen in Colonial Virginia.* Cambridge: Cambridge University Press, 1980.

Shields, David S. *Oracles of Empire: Poetry, Politics, and Commerce in British America, 1690–1750.* Chicago: University of Chicago Press, 1990.

Sidney, Sir Philip. *A Defence of Poetry.* Edited by J. A. Van Dorsten. Oxford: Oxford University Press, 1966.

————. "A Discourse on Irish Affairs." Vol. 3 of *The Prose Works of Sir Philip Sidney.* Edited by Albert Feuillerat. 4 vols. Cambridge: Cambridge University Press, 1968.

Slotkin, Richard. *Regeneration Through Violence: The Mythology of the American Frontier, 1600–1860.* Middleton, Connecticut: Wesleyan University Press, 1973.

Spenser, Edmund. *Spenser: Poetical Works.* Edited by J. C. Smith and E. De Selincourt. 1912. Reprint. London: Oxford University Press, 1966.

————. *A View of the Present State of Ireland.* Edited by W. L. Renwick. Oxford: Clarendon Press, 1970.

————. *The Faerie Queene.* Edited by Thomas P. Roche Jr., 1978. Reprint. London: Penguin Books, 1987.

Stevens, Paul. "'Leviticus Thinking' and the Rhetoric of Early Modern Colonialism." *Criticism* 35 (1993): 441–61.

————. "Spenser and Milton on Ireland: Civility, Exclusion, and the Politics of Wisdom." *Ariel* 26 (1995): 151–67.

Stone, Lawrence. *The Family, Sex and Marriage in England, 1500–1800.* New York: Harper & Row, 1977.

Symonds, William. *Virginia. A Sermon preached at White-Chappel, in the presence of many, honourable and worshipfull, the adventurers and planters for Virginia. 25. April, 1609. Published for the benefit and use of the colony, planted, and to bee planted there, and for the advancement of their Christian purpose.* London, 1609.

Taylor, E. G. R. *Tudor-Geography: 1485–1583.* London: Methuen & Co., 1930.

————. *The Haven-Finding Art: A History of Navigation from Odysseus to Captain Cook.* London: Hollis and Carter, 1956.

The Proceedings of the English Colony in Virginia. Vol. 1 of *The Complete Works of Captain John Smith (1580–1631).* Edited by Philip L. Barbour. 3 vols. Chapel Hill: University of North Carolina Press, 1986.

Todorov, Tzvetan. *The Conquest of America: The Question of the Other.* Translated by Richard Howard. New York: Harper & Row, 1982.

Tooley, R. V. *Maps and Map-Makers.* London: B. T. Batsford, 1949.

Turner, James Grantham. *One Flesh: Paradisal Marriage and Sexual Relations in the Age of Milton.* Oxford: Clarendon Press, 1987.

Vaughan, Alden T. and Virginia Mason. *Shakespeare's Caliban: A Cultural History.* Cambridge: Cambridge University Press, 1991.

Walwyn, William. *The Compassionate Samaritan.* In *The Later Renaissance in England: Nondramatic Verse and Prose, 1600–1660.* Edited by Herschel Baker. Boston: Houghton Mifflin Co., 1975.

Waters, David W. *The Art of Navigation in England in Elizabethan and Early Stuart Times.* 3 parts. Basildon: Trustees of the National Maritime Museum, 1978.

Wernham, R. B. *After the Armada: Elizabethan England and the Struggle for Western Europe.* 1984. Reprint. Oxford: Clarendon Press, 1986.

Wilding, Michael. "Marvell's 'An Horatian Ode Upon Cromwell's Return From Ireland,' The Levellers, and the Junta." *The Modern Language Review* 82 (1987): 1–14.

Williams, John. *Lord Bishop of Lincolne, Great Britains Salomon: A Sermon Preached at the Magnificent Funerall, of the Most High and Mighty King James.* London: John Bill, 1625.

Wittreich, Joseph. *Interpreting "Samson Agonistes".* Princeton: Princeton University Press, 1986.

Yachnin, Paul. "'Courtiers of Beauteous Freedom': *Antony and Cleopatra* in Its Time." *Renaissance and Reformation* 26 (1991): 1–20.

Index